THE REVOLUTION IN DEVELOPMENT ECONOMICS

FOREWORD BY VÁCLAV KLAUS

THE REVOLUTION IN DEVELOPMENT ECONOMICS

EDITED BY JAMES A. DORN,
STEVE H. HANKE, AND ALAN A. WALTERS

Washington, D.C.

Library of Congress Cataloging-in-Publication Data

The revolution in development economics / edited by James A. Dorn, Steve H. Hanke, and Alan A. Walters; foreword by Václav Klaus.
p. cm.
Includes bibliographical references and index.
ISBN 1-882577-55-8. — ISBN 1-882577-56-6
1. Development economics. 2. Economic development. 3. Free trade. 4. Central planning. I. Dorn, James A. II. Hanke, Steve H. III. Walters, A. A. (Alan Arthur), 1926– .
HD75.R48 1998
338.9—dc21 97-53294
CIP

Printed in the United States of America.

CATO INSTITUTE
1000 Massachusetts Ave., N.W.
Washington, D.C. 20001

To Peter Bauer

Peter Bauer

Contents

FOREWORD
The Rise of Market Liberalism

Václav Klaus

Human history and our own experience prove that social and economic progress spring both from the individual's efforts to do something positive and from his freedom to follow his own objectives and interests. They prove as well that human society is not an unorganized chaos of accidentally and unsystematically interacting individuals. We know that human society is based on a discipline and logic of existing social institutions.

Where those institutions emerge from the spontaneous activities of free individuals, they guarantee freedom and progress. Where they emerge from the power of government, they bring oppression rather than freedom, corruption rather than the rule of law, and decay rather than efficiency and equity. This general rule is valid for the whole world, for developed and developing countries, for arctic cold and equatorial heat, for mountains and lowlands, for all of us.

The free market is undoubtedly the most striking example of an institution of spontaneous order. It represents the precondition for freedom and prosperity. Social planning, on the other hand, though it proclaims devotion to the fulfillment of basic human values, actually undermines them. Communist regimes in Europe and their recent collapse give us the best evidence of that.

The citizens of former communist countries abandoned futile attempts to plan and started to change fundamentally their social, political, and economic systems—aiming at creating a free society, democracy, and a market economy. We are now witnessing an unprecedented transformation of those societies: a transformation of the formerly closed and undemocratic countries and their centrally

The author is former Prime Minister of the Czech Republic.

planned economies into open, free societies with democratic governments and a market system, into societies with restored respect for the individual after decades of collectivism, into societies with renewed belief in the market after many decades of planning.

This revolutionary process has short-term costs that cannot be avoided. We especially cannot avoid or diminish them by stretching the process over a longer period, because that could create a danger of relying on malfunctioning old institutions without giving new institutions enough space and room to replace them. It was therefore necessary to organize major systemic changes immediately after the political change in our country. The crucial measures were based on radical liberalization of prices and rapid, massive privatization of state enterprises.

We did not hesitate, and experience shows that we were right. We succeeded in giving citizens a vision of prosperity based on liberalism and the free market. Most of them, in contrast to most Western "development experts," understand that we must rely on our own abilities and efforts, and that no foreign consultants and no foreign aid, however unselfish, can do the job for us and instead of us.

There have been few Western thinkers who understood all that and who preached such ideas in developing countries in the period of interventionism, statism, and social engineering. Many of them are represented in this book. We owe them much.

EDITORS' PREFACE

The collapse of communism in Eastern Europe and the Soviet Union revealed dramatically the bankruptcy of state-led development policy. For most of the postwar era, but especially in the 1950s, 1960s, and 1970s, conventional wisdom in the field of development economics held that government intervention was necessary to lift Third World countries out of the so-called poverty trap. Prominent academics pointed to "market failure" but overlooked the danger of government failure.

Under the spell of formal models of perfect competition, many development "experts" neglected evident reality and lost sight of the role of property rights and market prices in the development process. Sound economic reasoning gave way to social engineering and overly simplified models emphasizing capital accumulation and foreign aid as key determinants of economic growth, without taking into account the institutional infrastructure necessary for efficient use of capital and the dynamic gains from trade. Even fewer experts realized the moral hazard problem that foreign aid presents or the public choice implications of official aid.

The failure of central planning and the broad recognition that foreign aid has done little to foster economic growth, and may have even retarded it, have created a revolution in development economics. Today, the role of development planning is diminishing while the market is ascending as a mechanism for creating long-run prosperity.

This book examines the shortcomings of conventional development theory and contrasts that theory with the new development economics that focuses on the role of institutions, incentives, and information in determining economic performance. The book is dedicated to Peter Bauer, whose long-held views on the futility of development planning and the detrimental effects of foreign aid have been vindicated by recent events. Many of the chapters reflect his early insights, and many of the authors continue his practice of using case studies to gain first-hand evidence of the forces that promote or retard economic growth.

For many years, Bauer was a pariah in the field of development economics. His dissent fell on deaf ears. Today, however, Bauer and other market liberals are no longer outcasts. Their ideas are on the cutting edge of a growing consensus. Indeed, there has been a revolution—even the World Bank is joining the march from plan to market and reexamining the role of the state. The bank's 1996 development report, *From Plan to Market,* contains none of the formal growth theory that development experts have come to love, and the thrust of the report falls squarely on the side of the market. The various economic freedom studies that have appeared in the last several years also attest to the strength of Bauer's vision, showing the positive link between economic freedom and economic growth.

Careful economic reasoning, attention to formal and informal institutional arrangements, and crisp writing have always characterized Bauer's work. We have tried to uphold those standards in selecting papers for this volume. The distinctive mark of many of them is their price-theoretic approach and reliance on comparative institutional analysis. Experience has taught that in the subdiscipline of development economics no simple model works. That is why the contributors to this volume take an interdisciplinary approach to understanding why some economies prosper and others remain impoverished.

The interplay of culture, ethics, politics, and economic development is complex and fascinating. The goal of this book is to shed light on that complexity so that nations can move more easily from poverty to wealth. In this way, the book also reflects Bauer's deep respect for the dignity, rationality, and capabilities of poor people around the world versus the patronizing undertones of the development experts who made up "the spurious consensus."

Several acknowledgments are in order. First and foremost, we wish to thank the Earhart Foundation for its generous support and especially David B. Kennedy for his encouragement from start to finish. Second, we thank all the authors for their contributions to the volume and acknowledge the assistance of Kurt Schuler in preparing the papers for publication. We also express our appreciation to Ed Crane and the Cato Institute for supporting this project and for sponsoring a conference in honor of Peter Bauer that generated many of the papers in this book. Finally, Jim Dorn gratefully acknowledges a grant from the Towson University Faculty Research Committee.

1. Introduction—Competing Visions of Development Policy

James A. Dorn

> Economic achievement depends primarily on people's abilities and attitudes and also on their social and political institutions. Differences in these determinants or factors largely explain differences in levels of economic achievement and rates of material progress.
>
> —P.T. Bauer
> *Dissent on Development*

Comprehensive Planning versus the Free Market

The love affair with comprehensive central planning ended with the collapse of communism in Eastern Europe in 1989 and with the demise of the Soviet Union two years later. But long before the 1989 liberal revolution, it was clear that state-led development policy was doomed to failure. Economists such as Ludwig von Mises, Friedrich Hayek, and Peter Bauer recognized the internal contradictions of trying to direct a complex economic system without the guidance of prices and profits and without well-defined private property rights protected by the rule of law.

Initial successes with Soviet-style central planning misled development experts into thinking that top-down systems of economic organization could correct for "market failures" and that input-output models could duplicate a competitive price system in allocating scarce resources. Conventional wisdom held that planners could better use existing information and achieve greater economic progress than could free individuals operating in a spontaneous market order.

James A. Dorn is Vice President for Academic Affairs at the Cato Institute and Professor of Economics at Towson University.

A few examples will suffice to illustrate the faith placed in central planning during the heyday of state-led development policy in the immediate postwar era. In 1957, Stanford University economist Paul A. Baran wrote, "The establishment of a socialist planned economy is an essential, indeed indispensable, condition for the attainment of economic and social progress in underdeveloped countries" (Baran 1957, p. 261). One year earlier, Gunnar Myrdal had written, "The special advisers to underdeveloped countries who have taken the time and trouble to acquaint themselves with the problem . . . all recommend central planning as the first condition of progress" (Myrdal 1956, p. 201).

The planning mentality encompassed social engineering: the goal was not merely to control the economy but to control people and remake society. Myrdal's main thesis was, as Bauer (1976, p. 188) pointed out, that "personal conduct and social attitudes are to be restructured in the interest, or at least the declared interest, of higher per capita incomes." The consensus of development experts was that "good advisers and technical experts would formulate good policies, which good governments would then implement for the good of society" (World Bank 1997, p. 1).[1]

The socialist mentality and the vision of state-led development were so ingrained that as late as 1985, after years of failure, Indian prime minister Rajiv Gandhi could write,

> While there is a problem of collecting, coordinating, sorting out and analysing the tremendous amount of information needed for developmental planning at the national level, the solution perhaps lies in improving the tools of collection and analysis of data and not in abandoning the planning effort itself.[2]

The socialist dream turned out to be a "fatal conceit" (Hayek 1988). Both logic and history have proven the architects of comprehensive planning to have been less visionary than market liberals who follow the path of Adam Smith and place the individual and liberty above

[1]On the widespread agreement of expert opinion in the field of development economics during the 1950s, 1960s, and 1970s, see Krauss (1997, chap. 6).

[2]This quote is from a letter the prime minister sent to Cato Institute President Ed Crane, after Gandhi had received a copy of Don Lavoie's (1985) book, *National Economic Planning: What Is Left?*

the state and coercion.[3] As Václav Klaus noted in the foreword, "Where . . . institutions emerge from the spontaneous activities of free individuals, they guarantee freedom and progress. Where they emerge from the power of government, they bring oppression rather than freedom, corruption rather than the rule of law, and decay rather than efficiency and equity." Even the World Bank (1997, pp. 1–2) now admits that the costs of state-led development policy far exceeded the benefits: "Governments embarked on fanciful schemes. Private investors, lacking confidence in public policies or in the steadfastness of leaders, held back. Powerful rulers acted arbitrarily. Corruption became endemic. Development faltered, and poverty endured."

The two competing visions of development policy—one that trusts the state, the other that trusts freedom—are the focus of this book. The fall of the Berlin Wall in 1989 marked the rise of market liberalism and the transition from plan to market. Policymakers were confronted with the problem of how to create a spontaneous market order out of the rubble of socialism. By necessity, the focus of development economics had to shift to questions about institutions and incentives, and about the role of government in the post-Cold War era.

Today the search for the determinants of economic growth centers not on physical capital and foreign aid but on human capital and market liberalization. It is also generally recognized that noneconomic factors must to be taken into account and that no general model of economic development is feasible. Thus, in determining whether a country will prosper or stagnate, one needs to consider the property rights regime, culture, and political factors.

The work of Peter Bauer has been instrumental in this shift of focus in the field of development economics. His pioneering work, in which he studied the Malayan rubber industry and West African trade, led him to question and eventually overturn many of the commonly held beliefs of development economics. He

- refuted the idea that poverty is self-perpetuating and showed that central planning and large-scale capital investment are not prerequisites for growth;

[3]For an early discussion of how comprehensive economic planning retards material advance, see Bauer (1976, pp. 84–86).

- demonstrated that foreign aid, restrictive immigration and population policies, and trade barriers typically hinder economic progress; and
- cautioned against the indiscriminate use of mathematical formalism, as found in simple economic growth models, and criticized the historical determinism inherent in stages-of-growth models.

He emphasized the fundamental role of basic economic principles—in conjunction with a knowledge of institutions, culture, and history—in understanding the development process.[4]

More recent work, including that done by scholars in the subdisciplines of institutional economics, growth theory, public choice, and constitutional economics, confirms Bauer's view that markets embedded in a regime of private property and limited government are more apt to generate freedom and prosperity than is a command-and-control system designed to satisfy planners' preferences and redistribute income.

Central planning destroys civil society along with economic vitality because, as Bauer (1976, p. 84) writes,

> It reinforces the authoritarian tradition of many underdeveloped societies, which inhibits the development of faculties and motivations congenial to material advance. By continuing and extending state control over the lives of the population central planning reinforces the subjection of the individual to authority. Such a development discourages self-reliance, personal provision for the future, sustained curiosity and an experimental turn of mind.

The market-liberal revolution has shattered the Soviet illusion, but the transition from plan to market will take time. Adoption of new institutions and new ways of thinking do not occur overnight. The essays in this book will help lay the basis for that revolution and further entrench the spirit of Bauer's work in the new development economics. Part I provides a detailed discussion of the dissent on development economics; part II examines the role of property rights

[4]For Bauer's critique of formal growth models and stages-of-growth theories, as well as his more realistic approach to development economics, see Bauer (1976, pp. 294–97).

in the development process; part III considers the failure of state-led development policy; and part IV discusses the relation between economic liberalism and economic growth.

Dissent on Development Economics

The idea that government intervention is "indispensable" for lifting underdeveloped countries out of poverty was "taken for granted" by most development experts when Bauer wrote his now famous essay "The Dissent on Development" in 1969 (Bauer 1976, p. 69). In chapter 2, he reiterates the themes of his earlier essay and emphasizes "the disregard of reality" that characterized much of the postwar literature on development economics. The bias of development experts against the free market and in favor of planning is obvious, as is their misuse of formal growth models and their neglect of social and political institutions. Bauer's forceful argument is that development economics actually regressed because many economists lost sight of basic economic principles and evident reality.

One widely accepted fallacy, notes Bauer, was the notion of a "vicious circle of poverty"—the idea that poor countries cannot generate sufficient savings and investment to lift themselves out of poverty. But as Bauer observes, the reality is that many individuals and countries have escaped the initial poverty that characterizes the human condition: individuals have achieved higher incomes by hard work, thrift, and prudence; and nations have become wealthy by allowing individuals the freedom to trade and pursue happiness under the rule of law. Bauer also criticizes mainstream development experts for accepting the notion that Third World impoverishment is the result of commercial contacts with the West. That belief ignores the principle of comparative advantage and the fact that voluntary exchange is mutually beneficial. As Bauer notes, the less-developed countries (LDCs) that have had the least amount of trade with the West have also experienced the lowest living standards.

The mathematization of economics has resulted in bypassing important noneconomic variables that are difficult to quantify, argues Bauer. That attempt has led to overlooking the relevance of history in determining how nations grow rich and passing over the time dimension in studying the process of development. Cultural factors, personal beliefs, and ambitions, as well as property rights, are all difficult to quantify, notes Bauer, but they play an important role in material advance. In trying to apply the methodology of the natural sciences to the study of society, economists have misunderstood the essential difference between those areas of inquiry. As a result, says Bauer, mainstream development economists have offered policy proposals that are unrelated to reality.

The disregard of reality is also evident in the call by international organizations and world opinion leaders for redistributions of wealth from developed countries to the Third World in the name of equality or "social justice." According to Bauer, that call ignores reality: wealth is dependent on productivity, and forced redistribution weakens incentives to produce and is inconsistent with the real spirit of charity. Relying on First World guilt to relieve Third World poverty is a recipe for disaster. As Bauer points out, that approach to development inevitably invites policies that will undermine the very institutions and human traits that have been instrumental in reducing world poverty and stimulating economic growth.

Finally, Bauer criticizes the "misuse of language" by development experts, especially their use of the term "Third World," a term that is more a political contrivance than a description of an existing homogeneous entity. The use of ordinary language to describe reality is a moral imperative for Bauer. Without clear use of language, he argues, the world could face a new barbarism—one that depreciates the moral traditions of the West and the discipline necessary for progress.

In chapter 3, the late Karl Brunner examines the role of the state in producing wealth. Like Bauer, he recognizes that it is a myth to think "that the state produces wealth" or "that little wealth will be created without the detailed and controlling intervention of the state." What is important for Brunner is to distinguish between a minimal or "protective" state and a redistributive state. In the first case, the power of government is narrowly limited and the role of government is to set the framework for freedom by enforcing laws that safeguard persons and property, so that the competitive market process can operate smoothly to create wealth. In the second case, the role of government is unlimited because the pursuit of "social justice" is open-ended—when plunder becomes legal, no one is safe. The policy implication of Brunner's analysis is that the closer government approaches the ideal of the minimal state, the more freedom and wealth there will be; but the closer it approaches the redistributive state, the more coercion and poverty there will be.

Deepak Lal describes the transformation that is taking place as formerly planned economies march toward the market. In chapter 4, he discusses the events leading up to the 1989 market-liberal revolution and how the intellectual climate has changed in the field of development economics in the postwar era. In this way, he expands on Bauer's pioneering work. Whereas economic planning and autarky characterized the mind set of development experts in the 1950s through the 1970s, today the consensus is in favor of globalization, privatization, and liberalization.

Like Bauer, Lal rejects the notion of a general theory of development: there are too many noneconomic variables that matter, and such complexity cannot be captured in simple growth models. Character and culture need to be taken account of as do other determinants of development, especially the political system. Lal distinguishes between government as a "civil association" based on the consent of the governed and government as an "enterprise association" based on the coercive power of the state. "A good government," writes Lal, "is one that promotes 'opulence' through a policy of preserving 'natural liberty' by establishing laws of justice which guarantee free exchange and peaceful competition, leaving the improvement of morality to institutions outside the government." When government moves from being the servant of the people to being the master, both the market order and civil society suffer.

The present danger, warns Lal, is that, as underdeveloped countries are moving away from the plan and toward the market, there will be a temptation "to create Western-style welfare states." He views that temptation with alarm because "every turn toward making the state an enterprise association saps the lower-level 'vigorous virtues' of productivity, thrift, and self-reliance that classical liberals see as underpinning the market and 'opulence.' " If corruption and rent-seeking behavior are to be stemmed, he argues, government needs to be limited, economic life needs to be insulated from politics, and good works need to be left to the private voluntary sector. For Lal what is important is to preserve "the classical-liberal vision of the state as a civil association." All cultures can find meaning in that vision because it promises freedom rather than tyranny and generates prosperity rather than poverty.

The final chapter in part I deals with the question of whether population growth is detrimental to economic growth. Bauer (1995,

p. 3) dealt with that question by emphasizing that what is important is not the number of people but their character and conduct, and that the decision about the number of children a family should have is a private matter, not one for state officials to determine through coercion.[5] He criticized the flaws in national income accounting, wherein "the birth of a calf represents an increase in living standards but the birth of a child represents a fall"—because per capita income declines when a child is born (Bauer 1976, p. 63). From close observation, Bauer (1976, p. 126) concluded that "neither acceleration of population growth nor population pressure is a significant independent cause of the poverty of the underdeveloped world." On the basis of his analysis, he could not justify foreign aid in the event of higher population growth. Bauer (1976, p. 125) argued that "routine foreign aid (as distinct from emergency measures) is irrelevant to starvation in the underdeveloped world and may indeed aggravate it."

Julian Simon shares Bauer's conclusions and, in chapter 5, provides further evidence that population growth is not "a drag on economic development." Like Bauer, he contends that too much attention has been paid to population growth as a determinant of development and far too little attention to economic and political institutions. In particular, where the institutional infrastructure for a free private market system exists, as it has in Hong Kong, population density and population growth are not detrimental to economic progress. Thus, spending on foreign aid to reduce population growth in LDCs is misguided and, where coercive practices are used, wrong. Instead of devoting so much time and energy to reducing population growth, people ought to be "fighting tyranny and working for economic freedom," writes Simon. Recent studies showing the positive influence of economic freedom on economic growth and political freedom lend credence to Simon's argument.

Institutional Choice and Economic Development

In 1957, Bauer and Basil S. Yamey, who collaborated with Bauer for many years, wrote a path-breaking book entitled *The Economics of Under-Developed Countries.* That book dispelled many of the myths of conventional development economics and called for a study of

[5]See also Bauer and Yamey (1981).

comparative institutions to see which ones would be most conducive to economic growth. Many of the themes that Bauer later developed can be found in the 1957 volume. Bauer and Yamey criticized the excessive attention given to the role of capital accumulation in the development process and the neglect of prevailing social and political institutions. One major insight was that "it is often nearer the truth to say that capital is created in the process of development than that development is a function of capital accumulation" (Bauer and Yamey 1957, p. 127).

Instead of taking the institutional framework—which includes the system of property rights and informal codes of conduct—as given, Bauer and Yamey recognized the need to include those noneconomic variables as important determinants of development. Their early work is well supported by more recent studies of the impact of legal and institutional factors on economic growth. Robert Barro, for example, has shown that the rule of law, which he uses as a proxy for a system of private property rights and limited government, has a positive influence on living standards. As he writes, "greater maintenance of the rule of law is favorable to growth" (Barro 1997, p. 28). And, nearly a decade before Barro, Gerald Scully (1988, p. 661) found:

> The choice of the institutional framework has profound consequences on the efficiency and growth of economies. Politically open societies, which bind themselves to the rule of law, to private property, and to the market allocation of resources, grow at three times (2.73 to 0.91 percent annually) the rate and are two and one-half times as efficient as societies in which these freedoms are circumscribed or proscribed.[6]

By neglecting the role of market-supporting institutions, many development experts erred in their predictions about the future course of LDCs. Perhaps the most glaring forecasting error was made by Robert Montgomery Martin, the British colonial treasurer in Hong Kong, who, in 1844, predicted, "There does not appear the slightest probability that, under any circumstances, Hong Kong will ever become a place of trade" (Sanger 1997, p. 1). The idea that a country lacking natural resources is destined to poverty has been disproved by the phenomenal success of Hong Kong. What matters

[6]For an elaboration, see Scully (1992).

most is not physical resources but the hard infrastructure of a market-liberal system in which private property, broadly construed, and freedom of contract are protected by law. That is the message that Bauer and Yamey emphasized over 40 years ago, and that is the message of the contributors to part II of this book.

In chapter 6, Nobel laureate economist Douglass North contends that economic performance is shaped by both institutions and ideology. Institutions affect transactions costs, which affect production and exchange. Clearly defined private property rights lower transactions costs and widen markets: more can be produced and consumed in an economy that safeguards persons and property from the abusive power of government or coercive entities. Informal rules also matter but change slowly, and both formal and informal rules are affected by people's subjective views or ideology, argues North. Thus, like Bauer, North emphasizes the time dimension of any transition from one property rights regime to another.

Instead of using the conventional norm of perfect competition to judge market efficiency, North views competition as a learning process.[7] He introduces the idea of "adaptive efficiency" and judges markets by how well they adapt to change, which will depend on rules that "encourage trials and eliminate errors." What matters for North is not the number of firms but whether entry is open, markets are contestable, and contracts are enforced—so that individuals can learn from their mistakes. Underdeveloped countries need not strive for perfect competition, an unattainable ideal, but rather should help create the institutional framework for real competition by opening markets and abiding by the rule of law.

Alan Rufus Waters was one of the first development economists to recognize the significance of property rights in the development process. In chapter 7, he reiterates his message that although culture plays a significant role in determining economic performance, it is not as important as the effective ownership structure. For private ownership to be effective, however, individuals must have exclusive use of their property, be able to freely buy and sell property, be allowed to partition their bundle of ownership rights, and have certainty of ownership. The role of government is to enforce those rights, so that individuals are held responsible for their actions.

[7]Compare Hayek's notion of "competition as a discovery procedure" (Hayek 1978).

Private owners will then have a strong incentive to add value to scarce resources by employing them in profitable uses to satisfy consumers' preferences.

Like North, Waters notes that if an economic system is to be successful in creating wealth, people must be allowed to fail and to learn from their mistakes. By allowing failure, the market generates success. The flexibility that free markets permit is the hallmark of a healthy and prosperous economic system, according to Waters. That is why "effective private property rights are essential to long-run economic growth." If LDCs want to achieve the prosperity of the West, argues Waters, they need to begin by privatizing state-owned enterprises and establishing a transparent legal system that protects property as a basic human right.

In chapter 8, Charles Rowley provides a public-choice perspective on economic development. Conventional development economics treated government as an organic whole and assumed policymakers had better information and higher motives than did market participants. Rowley shows why that view was naive and explains how an understanding of public choice theory and constitutional economics can provide valuable lessons.

One of the key lessons is that without constraints on the power of government, democracy will degenerate into a rent-seeking society that ultimately impoverishes people. Many LDCs have politicized economic life to such a degree that corruption has become rampant. Rowley focuses on Sub-Saharan Africa to show why countries with abundant natural resources have failed to prosper because of lack of stable political institutions that protect individual rights to life, liberty, and property. Once the rent-seeking process starts in LDCs, or in developed countries, it is very difficult to stop. To do so, notes Rowley, requires constitutional change; and the best place to start, in his opinion, would be with an appreciation of the principles of freedom that underpin the U.S. Constitution.

Steve Hanke and Barney Dowdle use the experience of Native Americans to shed light on the nexus between institutional choice and economic development. In chapter 9, they liken reservations to LDCs and show that the lack of saleable shares in timberlands has resulted in an inefficient use of those lands by Native Americans. They calculate that privatization of communal property would greatly enhance the value of Indian lands and increase the well-being of Native Americans.

In chapter 10, Wayne Brough and Mwangi Kimenyi apply property rights theory to help understand the plight of the Sahel. They point out that at one time the Sahel was at the center of trade routes and there was a move toward privatization. Although droughts occurred, market activity and informal rules helped to limit their adverse effects. The arrival of French colonial governments, postcolonial bureaucrats, and foreign aid, however, prevented progress toward establishing private property rights in the Sahel and tended to upset the delicate balance between man and nature. Without well-defined property rights, overgrazing and wasteful use of water have exacerbated the desertification process and worsened the age-old problem of famine. Brough and Kimenyi conclude that "poor policymaking and indiscriminate Western aid have laid to waste what could have been a prosperous region."

Emily Chamlee-Wright illustrates why Bauer was right to focus on indigenous institutions rather than on outside aid or large-scale capital projects as determinants of material advance. In chapter 11, she undertakes an intensive study of the role of women as small traders and investors in Ghana, West Africa—and shows how economic controls, the failure of municipal authorities to privatize market stalls, and underdeveloped credit institutions have limited the advance of market activity.

Formal Western-style credit institutions have done little to alleviate the situation. Mutual assistance organizations and other indigenous credit institutions have helped fill the gap. However, as Chamlee-Wright notes, the surest way to limit corruption and disruption of market activity and generate new investment funds would be to get government bureaucrats out of the market. She urges development experts to recognize the importance of tailoring Western institutions to the local culture and to abandon the one-policy-fits-all mentality. Allowing indigenous market institutions to evolve would spur development in West Africa and elsewhere.

The Failure of State-Led Development Policy

Although comprehensive economic planning was the rage among development experts in the immediate postwar era, state-led development strategy experienced diminishing returns as time moved on. The more the state grew, the less efficient markets became, until it was obvious that the only way to improve long-run economic performance was to dismantle the plan and move toward the market (see World Bank 1996). Many studies are now appearing that attest to the failure of development planning (e.g., Osterfeld 1992, Boettke 1994, Roberts and Araujo 1997). Once again, Bauer was among the first to clearly see that the real plight of underdeveloped countries is not market failure but government failure—that is, the failure of government to protect property rights, enforce contracts, and leave markets alone.

Bauer criticized mainstream development economists for having too much trust in government and not enough in the market. He recognized early on that expanding the power of government in a vain attempt to improve existing markets and achieve a more efficient use of resources risks giving up an attainable outcome for an unattainable ideal and, in the process, actually reduces economic performance. The focus on market failure, in effect, diverted attention from the danger of government failure. As Bauer (1984, p. 30) noted,

> The literature of market failure has been used largely as a collection of sticks with which to beat the market system. The critics who propose replacing the market system by political decisions rarely address themselves to such crucial matters as the concentration of economic power in political hands, the implications of restriction of choice, the objectives of politicians and administrators, and the quality and extent of knowledge in a society and of its methods of transmission.

The politicization of economic life, the loss of freedom, and the damage done to civil society under comprehensive economic planning are now well-known. That is why attention is finally shifting from the model of state-led development to the nature of institutions and the role of government in fostering the spontaneous market process. As the World Bank (1997, p. 1) pointed out in its 1997 development report, "State-led intervention emphasized market failures and accorded the state a central role in correcting them. But the institutional assumptions implicit in this world view were, as we all realize today, too simplistic." The papers in part III explain why.

In chapter 12, Doug Bandow argues that development experts in the West, including those who advise multilateral lending organizations, share responsibility for perpetuating poverty in the Third World. For much of the postwar era, those experts were the major proponents of state-led development. Conventional wisdom held that Third World economies were not responsive to market prices, that import-substitution polices were superior to export-led growth, that forced industrialization (at the expense of agriculture) would lead to higher per capita income, and that official aid was necessary to break the "vicious circle of poverty." None of those doctrines held up in reality. Now that the World Bank, the International Monetary Fund, and other major players in the development process have turned toward the market, it is worth remembering their "misbegotten economic legacy" to underdeveloped countries (see Bandow and Vásquez 1994).

Paul Craig Roberts provides further evidence of the failure of state-led development policy by taking a close look at how Western aid and advice misdirected the LDCs in Latin America. In chapter 13, he blames international development institutions for the spread of planning and government intervention in Latin America. Like Bandow, he reminds us that we should not forget the damage development experts inflicted on LDCs by their antimarket mentality. "Latin America's failures were a monument to misguided economic ideas."

Chile's free-market revolution in the 1970s set an example for the rest of Latin America, and in the 1980s Mexico, Argentina, and others began to change course. Today many Latin American countries have adopted market-liberal policies—not because the World Bank or IMF demanded such policies but because those policies are in the best interest of the Latin American people. In Roberts's view, "the development banks should be privatized or closed." The United States could initiate that process by unilaterally pulling out of the World Bank, the IMF, and the Inter-American Development Bank. Private capital and market-led development could then drive the development process and minimize the problem of "moral hazard."[8]

In chapter 14, Peter Bauer makes the case that Western aid is neither necessary nor sufficient for economic reform in Eastern

[8]When debtor nations know that the risk of default is shared with taxpayers in the creditor countries, they have an incentive to borrow more and use the money less wisely than if they alone were liable for loss. Likewise, investors have an incentive to be less cautious in their investments with the knowledge that their losses will be cut in the event of a financial crisis. Thus, the problem of moral hazard is inherent whenever multilateral development banks enter the picture.

Europe. History shows that external subsidies politicize economic life and delay real reform.[9] In making the transition from plan to market in former communist countries, it is essential to recognize that free markets require internal institutional change, not external aid. Thus, Bauer advocates that instead of making people in the East dependent on government aid, Western governments should open their markets to the East and liberalize trade relations.

Another example of state-led development policy is the use of agricultural marketing boards in LDCs to "stabilize" prices and promote industrialization. In chapter 15, Alan Walters examines the use of moving average smoothing in British West Africa and shows that what passes in theory as price stabilization is in reality price controls that often exploit poor farmers. In his view, the use of MAS failed to promote adjustment to world market prices and merely provided "a veil of legitimacy and intellectual respectability for exploitation and inefficiency."

In chapter 16, John Powelson criticizes postwar development planners for forcing the agricultural sector in LDCs to subsidize industrial development through import-substitution policies and marketing boards. Farmers were caught in a squeeze: they had to buy their inputs from the state at high prices and had to sell their outputs to state marketing boards at artificially low prices. Urban industry benefited but only at the expense of the peasants. Land reform was instituted, but the peasants continued to be exploited because they were still dependent on government, argues Powelson. Land was given to the peasants by the "grace" of the rulers; effective private property rights were never instituted. As a condition of acquiring land, peasants in many cases had to "agree" to sell to the state and to buy their supplies from the state, and often farmers were forced into "cooperatives." In the 1980s things began to change, but political power remains concentrated in a few hands in many LDCs. The challenge, says Powelson, is to institute political reform

[9]Foreign aid has been a dismal failure because economic liberty, not economic aid, is the key ingredient in fostering material advance. Bauer has made that point repeatedly and recent studies support his long-held views. For example, Bryan Johnson and Thomas Sheehy (1996, p. 2) found that "of the 34 long-term recipients of U.S. foreign aid ranked by the *Index* as lacking economic freedom, 26 are no better off than they were over three decades ago."

that limits the power of government and establishes effective private property rights so that peasants are no longer serfs of the state.

Economic Liberalization, Trade, and Growth

The worldwide market-liberal revolution that began in 1989 rests on the idea that freedom is not only a right but a value; people value freedom because it allows them to be left alone of pursue happiness. State planning and control have failed to deliver on the promise of long-run prosperity because economic life is too complex (and personal happiness too subjective) to be left to government bureaucrats.

One of the key lessons of the 20th century is that economic freedom is the real engine of economic growth and that, when economic freedom is lost, an economy may grow for a time, but stagnation will inevitably follow. The globalization of trade, the information revolution, and the liberalization of economic life have created tremendous wealth and have made market-led development the wave of the future. But when Bauer first began writing, that wave was a mere ripple on an ocean of government-led development.

In chapter 17, Bauer criticizes conventional development economists for neglecting the role of traders in the transition from a subsistence to an exchange economy. Internal trade, in particular, is an important source of growth for LDCs, as Bauer found in his study of West African trade. The emergence of a merchant class—a class of small traders and shopkeepers—helps "to create commercial institutions and practices and to raise the level of human capital," writes Bauer. The result is an increase both in economic efficiency and in economic growth. Thus, there are both "static and dynamic" gains from *internal* trading activities.[10]

[10]By focusing on the static efficiency gains from specialization and trade, mainstream development theorists overlooked the dynamic gains from trade liberalization. (For a discussion of those gains, see Yeager and Tuerck 1966, pp. 62–67.) The "new growth theory," developed by Paul Romer and others (see Holmes, Johnson, and Kirkpatrick 1997, pp. 4–6), does consider the dynamic gains from trade, but the formal models really only rediscover what Adam Smith and his contemporaries already understood—namely, that external trade increases the spread of knowledge and technology, makes domestic firms more competitive, and increases investment. Unfortunately, postwar development experts were more influenced by Marx and Keynes than by Smith and his heirs.

Although Bauer focuses on internal trade, he also notes the dynamic gains from *external* trade: "Contacts through traders and trade are prime agents in the spread of new ideas, modes of behavior, and methods of production." In his view, trade, not aid, is an important determinant of development. Those technocrats who argue that LDCs cannot grow without outside help and that poverty is self-perpetuating neglect the fact that "to have money is the result of economic achievement, not its precondition." And, as Bauer emphasizes, that achievement is based on individual effort, free trade, and the ability of governments to limit their reach and abide by the rule of law.

Bryan Johnson and Thomas Sheehy explain the methodology used to construct their Index of Economic Freedom. In chapter 18, they use the Index to explore the relation between economic freedom and economic development. They rank over 100 countries on a scale of 1 to 5, with 1 being the highest degree of economic freedom. Drawing on the most recent data, they find that "countries with the most economic freedom enjoy the most economic prosperity." That result is broadly consistent with several other studies of economic freedom.[11] They also find, as Bauer observed, that economic liberalization tends to bring about political liberalization—as has been the case in South Korea and Taiwan. Finally, they point to the futility of foreign aid as a tool for escaping poverty.

In chapter 19, the late Karl Brunner shows that behind the competing visions of development policy there are competing notions of justice. In the market-led approach to development, justice means that individual rights to trade and own property are protected by government and there is equality under the law. The free-market process is just because it is a *voluntary* process based on free choice—the gains from free trade are mutual: both parties benefit. Thus, the focus is on just rules of conduct, not on equal outcomes (see Hayek 1960, 1976).

In state-led development, on the other hand, the notion of justice is based on distributive shares—that is, on end states or outcomes—rather than on rules and conduct. But, if individuals have a "right" to some pre-specified income share, no one's property is safe and

[11]For a survey of the various freedom indices and their relation to economic performance, see Hanke and Walters (1997).

rights become the dictate of government rather than the legitimate possessions of individuals. Moreover, as Hayek (1976) stated, the concept of "social justice" is a vague policy guide because there is no way to objectively measure social welfare.

Brunner compares the protective state, which is consistent with the market-process view of justice, with the redistributive state, which emerges when true justice is turned on its head under the end-state or outcome concept of justice. He concludes that "the quest for social justice" politicizes life, reduces freedom, and hampers the spontaneous market process (cf. Bauer 1981, chap. 1), thereby weakening the incentive to create wealth and slowing economic growth. Redistribution from rich to poor countries will not, in Brunner's opinion, solve the problem of poverty; indeed, it will worsen it. "The dream of an egalitarian society," writes Brunner, "will never be realized, and attempts to impose it produce only poverty, stagnation, and oppression."

In the final chapter, Alvin Rabushka investigates the often neglected relation between taxation and economic development. The usual medicine prescribed by IMF austerity programs is to hike taxes, but that policy does nothing to reduce institutional barriers to development—and high tax rates and low tax thresholds, as Rabushka shows, retard economic growth. He therefore criticizes mainstream development experts for neglecting the effect of taxation on incentives and performance in LDCs, and he lays out principles for an "ideal tax system" for developing countries. Such a system should be simple and raise enough revenue for legitimate government functions; rates should be low and thresholds high so as not to interfere with incentives to work, save, and invest.

Several important findings emerge from Rabushka's study: (1) "rates of taxation are more important than overall tax burdens in affecting growth in LDCs"; (2) "countries with high [tax] thresholds turned in consistently higher growth than those with low thresholds"; (3) "once economic growth exceeds 3 percent, political and civil rights scores significantly improve"; and (4) "high growth may not be a sufficient condition of individual liberties, but it appears to be a necessary condition for the gradual emergence of political and civil rights." More recent studies support his findings, as well as his general conclusion that "a humanist view of the developing world dictates the application of low-tax-rate, growth-oriented economic policies."

Conclusion

The freedom of people to choose and of prices to move are essential for civil society and human progress. Under central planning, the dream of equality became the nightmare of unlimited political power concentrated in the hands of the ruling elite. Economic freedom cannot be divorced from overall freedom; when private property rights are eroded, civil liberties suffer. The fact that economic freedom and economic growth go hand in hand is not sufficient to protect the future of freedom. China has achieved high rates of economic growth for nearly two decades by moving toward a free-market economy, but that nation is still dominated by one-party rule and enjoys little personal freedom. To create an open society, it is necessary to limit the power of government. What China needs is a new constitution—a "constitution of liberty"—that constrains government and protects human rights, including the right to private property.[12]

The danger is that as economic liberalization leads to political liberalization, as it has in Chile and some East Asian countries, weak democracies—without sound constitutional checks on governmental power—will become rent-seeking societies (see Lal 1997). That danger becomes even more apparent when one considers the rapid growth of the redistributive state over the postwar era in the United States and Europe.

The contributors to this book offer a vivid portrait of the determinants of economic growth and the importance of taking an interdisciplinary approach to the study of economic development. No general model can capture the complexities of the development process. As Bauer (1976, p. 41) wrote,

> There is no general rule to ensure that all countries or regions should reach the same level of economic attainment or the same rate of progress at any given time or over any given period. Economic achievement and progress depend largely on human aptitudes and attitudes, on social and political institutions and arrangements which derive from these, on historical experience, and to a lesser extent on external contacts, market opportunities and on natural resources. And if these factors favourable to material progress are present, persons, groups and even societies will not stagnate, so that

[12]On the nature of a "constitution of liberty," see Hayek (1960).

> it is the absence of the favourable determinants, and not poverty, which is the causal factor in prolonged stagnation.

Knowledge of the price system, economic theory combined with an understanding of the role of institutions in shaping incentives and behavior, and evidence from case studies will help pave the way for future growth and prosperity—provided the political impulse to win votes by redistributing income and engaging in social engineering can be constrained. Although central planning is dead, politicians in both the East and the West still distrust the market; the notion of a "spontaneous market order" is a threat to them. The challenge is for those people who understand the market process and its supporting institutions to effectively convey their ideas to the larger public, so that state-led development policy does not give way to market socialism rather than market liberalism.

References

Bandow, Doug, and Vásquez, Ian, eds. *Perpetuating Poverty: The World Bank, the IMF, and the Developing World.* Washington, D.C.: Cato Institute, 1994.

Baran, Paul A. *The Political Economy of Growth.* New York: Monthly Review Press, 1957.

Barro, Robert J. *Determinants of Economic Growth.* Cambridge, Mass.: MIT Press, 1997.

Bauer, Peter T. *Dissent on Development.* Revised ed. Cambridge, Mass.: Harvard University Press, 1976.

Bauer, Peter T. *Equality, the Third World, and Economic Delusion.* Cambridge, Mass.: Harvard University Press, 1981.

Bauer, Peter T. *Reality and Rhetoric: Studies in the Economics of Development.* Cambridge, Mass.: Harvard University Press, 1984.

Bauer, Peter T. "Population Growth: Disaster or Blessing?" Cato Institute Distinguished Lecturer Series cosponsored with the Institute for Political Economy. Washington, D.C.: Cato Institute, 1995.

Bauer, Peter T., and Yamey, Basil S. *The Economics of Under-Developed Countries.* Chicago: University of Chicago Press, 1957.

Bauer, Peter T., and Yamey, Basil S. "The Population Explosion: Myths and Realities." In Bauer (1981, chap. 3).

Boettke, Peter J. *The Collapse of Development Planning.* New York: New York University Press, 1994.

Gandhi, Rajiv. Letter to Edward H. Crane, 26 November 1985.

Hanke, Steve H., and Walters, Stephen J.K. "Economic Freedom, Prosperity, and Equality: A Survey." *Cato Journal* 17 (2) 1997.

Hayek, Friedrich A. *The Constitution of Liberty.* Chicago: University of Chicago Press, 1960.

Hayek, Friedrich A. *Law, Legislation and Liberty*. Vol. 2: *The Mirage of Social Justice*. Chicago: University of Chicago Press, 1976.

Hayek, Friedrich A. "Competition as a Discovery Procedure." In Hayek, *New Studies in Philosophy, Politics, Economics and the History of Ideas*, pp. 179–90. Chicago: University of Chicago Press, 1978.

Hayek, Friedrich A. *The Fatal Conceit: The Errors of Socialism*. London: Routledge & Kegan Paul, 1988.

Holmes, Kim R.; Johnson, Bryan, T.; and Kirkpatrick, Melanie, eds. *1997 Index of Economic Freedom*. Washington, D.C., and New York: Heritage Foundation and Dow Jones & Co, Inc., 1997.

Johnson, Bryan T., and Sheehy, Thomas P. *1996 Index of Economic Freedom*. Washington, D.C.: Heritage Foundation, 1996.

Krauss, Melvyn. *How Nations Grow Rich*. New York: Oxford University Press, 1997.

Lal, Deepak. "From Planning to Regulation: Toward a New Dirigisme?" *Cato Journal* 17 (2) 1997.

Lavoie, Don. *National Economic Planning: What Is Left?* Cambridge, Mass.: Ballinger, 1985.

Myrdal, Gunnar. *An International Economy: Problems and Prospects*. New York: Harper, 1956.

Osterfeld, David. *Prosperity versus Planning: How Government Stifles Economic Growth*. New York: Oxford University Press, 1992.

Roberts, Paul Craig, and Araujo, Karen LaFollette. *The Capitalist Revolution in Latin America*. New York: Oxford University Press, 1997.

Sanger, David E. "There Is (Was?) No Place Like Hong Kong." *New York Times*, 29 June 1997.

Scully, Gerald W. "The Institutional Framework and Economic Development." *Journal of Political Economy* 96 (1988): 652–62.

Scully, Gerald W. *Constitutional Environments and Economic Growth*. Princeton, N.J.: Princeton University Press, 1992.

World Bank. *World Development Report 1996: From Plan to Market*. New York: Oxford University Press for the World Bank, 1996.

World Bank. *World Development Report 1997: The State in a Changing World*. New York: Oxford University Press for the World Bank, 1997.

Yeager, Leland B., and Tuerck, David G. *Trade Policy and the Price System*. Scranton, Pa.: International Textbook Co., 1966.

Part I

Dissent on Development Economics

2. The Disregard of Reality

Peter Bauer

High Hopes and Emerging Doubts

According to Hegel, the Owl of Minerva spreads its wings only at dusk. The later stages of one's career should be propitious for discerning tendencies and forces at work in society. Earlier preoccupations with specific studies can be helpful for subsequent reflection on wider issues but meanwhile absorb time and attention.

Like many of my contemporaries, fellow undergraduates and young academics alike, in my early days I expected much from economics, both in public policy and in intellectual interest. The great advances in the subject and the high intelligence of my academic colleagues seemed to confirm these hopes. Nevertheless, from about the early 1950s increasing claims for economics by its practitioners ran parallel with my own increasing doubts and reservations.

I came to realize for instance that the economists systematically exaggerate the impact of their ideas. In an oft-quoted passage in *The General Theory,* Keynes insisted that in the long run the world is governed by little else than the ideas of economists and political philosophers. If this were true, the world would have enjoyed the benefits of free trade for at least 100 years. Apart from being obviously unsustainable, Keynes' opinion is also naively parochial in attributing exclusive influence to the ideas of economists and political philosophers. He neglects the impact of the founders and leaders of religious movements, including the Buddha, Christ, Mohammed, and of military commanders such as Alexander the Great, Julius Caesar and Napoleon.

Peter Bauer is Emeritus Professor of Economics at the London School of Economics and Political Science and a Fellow of the British Academy. This chapter is reprinted, with some revisions, from his article in the Spring/Summer 1987 *Cato Journal* (Bauer 1987).

The ideas of economists do affect the wider scene; like other ideas they have consequences. As Milton Friedman has reminded us, economists can suggest possible options to politicians. But we must not delude ourselves by overstating our influence, whether in the short period or over the longer run.

Well before my retirement I came to be increasingly perplexed by what was going on in economics. I observed, in particular, a widespread disregard of evident reality, in which I include neglect of basic propositions of the subject. Impressive advances coexisted with alarming retrogression.

Unexpected Transgressions

It was in the 1950s that I first noticed the disregard of reality in economics. It was notable in two contexts: the dollar problem, and the vicious circle of poverty.

For well over a decade in the 1940s and 1950s economists wrote about an indefinitely persistent and inescapable worldwide shortage of dollars. Some of these contributions and predictions were ostensibly sophisticated. In fact, they systematically ignored the rate of exchange, that is, the price of the dollar, as well as major determinants of this price such as interest rates and financial policy. This neglect of basics soon met the fate it deserved. In the later 1950s the shortage of dollars vanished and, indeed, was replaced by a glut. Many leading economists, and not just some amateurs and novices, had overlooked that supply of and demand for dollars depend on price.[1] This particular discussion subsided with the end of the dollar shortage. But its method of approach soon resurfaced in the idea, which is still with us, that poor countries face inescapable balance of payments difficulties.

The theory of the indefinite dollar shortage was not an example of tentative steps in the construction of exciting, and potentially fruitful, theorems or analytical instruments. Nor did the ostensibly elaborate analyses hinge on novel assumptions about expectations or dynamic processes. Rather, the episode was nothing but a serious transgression.

I now come to the vicious circle of poverty. According to this notion, stagnation and poverty are necessarily self-perpetuating:

[1]Or more precisely, quantities supplied and demanded.

poor people generally and poor countries or societies in particular are trapped in their poverty, and cannot generate sufficient savings to escape from the trap. This notion became a cornerstone of mainstream development economics. It was the signature tune of the advocates of foreign aid throughout the 1950s. It is still often invoked. Yet it is in obvious conflict with simple reality. Throughout history innumerable individuals, families, groups, societies, and countries—both in the West and the Third World—have moved from poverty to prosperity without external donations. All developed countries began as underdeveloped. If the notion of the vicious circle were valid, mankind would still be in the Stone Age at best.

These episodes also alerted me to the role of intellectual and political fashion in much of economics. Prominent, distinguished practitioners seem often to find it difficult to resist the vagaries and winds of fashion, even when these are ephemeral or blow them off course.

I have recently reread part of the literature of these two subjects with a mixture of incredulity, embarrassment and amusement. It looked as if the queen of the social sciences was being dethroned by her entourage.

The two examples I have taken represent unequivocal examples of intellectual retrogression made possible by the disregard of reality. In the interwar years the role of the rate of exchange in the supply of and demand for currencies was routinely recognized. And before World War II, no one would have suggested that poor societies or countries were doomed to stagnation. Historians, anthropologists, administrators, and economists then discussed in detail the impact and implications of rapid changes in less developed countries (LDCs).

Alongside these instances of evident retrogression there took place major advances in economics, including advances in international trade theory and the theory of foreign exchanges, both closely related to the lapses.

There were dissenters from the most widely articulated opinion. This was particularly so in the case of the dollar problem, but applied also to the vicious circle. Some of the dissenters had high academic credentials, yet their views did not have much impact in academic circles and did not reach a wider public. This was because on the contemporary scene, also in academe, a voice is rarely effective without an echo. Dissenters find this difficult to secure unless their dissent is modish. The exponents of the dollar problem and the vicious circle of poverty, especially the latter, were supported and encouraged by articulate groups in the academies and the media. Dissent was crowded out.

These two episodes first prepared me to question received opinion, even when endorsed by the great and the good. Since the 1950s there has been an overdose of examples where reality is simply ignored or brushed aside.

Let me take a further example. Since World War II, many academics (as well as clerics, public figures, politicians and spokesmen of the official international organizations) have argued that commercial contacts between the West and LDCs inflict economic damage on the peoples of the Third World. Sometimes it is said that Third World poverty is the result of Western neglect; but more often it is claimed that poverty results from Western oppression, exploitation, and manipulation of international trade. These widely canvassed opinions are not confined to Marxist-Leninists. (One should really say Leninists, since Marx was at times lyrical about the achievements of capitalism in transforming backward societies.) Yet as is abundantly evident throughout the Third World the poorest and most backward societies and areas are those which have fewest commercial contacts with the West, and the most advanced are those with the most extensive and diversified contacts, including contacts with those bogeymen, the Western multinationals. Throughout the Third World the level of economic attainment declines as one moves away from regions with most Western contacts to the aborigines and pygmies at the other end of the spectrum.

Those interested in the survival of ideas may like to know that the notions of the vicious circle of poverty and of the malign economic effects of commercial contacts with the West are alive and well.

Advances in Economics

Over the period in which I have been active in academic economics I have seen remarkable advances and also, as I have just noted, lapses which amount to blatant retrogression.

Advances in knowledge are what is expected from an academic discipline, especially when it has enjoyed a large expansion of resources and of opportunities. Even a necessarily incomplete list of significant advances must include various contributions to price theory, including the recognition of transaction costs; to the role and nature of the firm, including the economics of vertical integration; to the concept and implications of social cost; to the theory of international trade and the theory of the foreign exchanges; to the analysis of the diffusion and use of knowledge; to the economics of property rights; and to the economics of political and bureaucratic processes. Some of these advances have been helpful far outside economics and have been useful to historians, anthropologists, political scientists, and demographers.

Such advances go a long way to support the sanguine expectations of my early days. So do the intellectual capacity and technical competence of so many practitioners. My academic colleagues in recent years have been no less bright and competent than were most of my teachers a generation ago. If I am now perplexed, it is because I have encountered a plethora of instances of retrogression stemming from the disregard of reality.

The retrogressions are of a quite different order from what went on in economics in the past. The writings of 19th-century and early 20th-century economists were often unsophisticated, even naive. But they were not in such evident conflict with reality as is so much of the more recent literature.

The Emperor Inverted

Mathematization of the subject has perhaps been the most conspicuous thread running through economics since I first entered it. In the 1930s one could read the journals without much knowledge of mathematics, with the exception only of *Econometrica* and the *Review of Economic Studies.* Today one is regarded as unqualified without some knowledge of mathematics, and especially of its language. As economics deals very largely with functional relationships and dynamic processes, some understanding of mathematics is undoubtedly valuable in many contexts ranging from the proper understanding of the concept of elasticity to the appreciation of feedback effects. And it is often convenient to express in mathematical form, inferences and conclusions derived from reasoning and empirical evidence. The appropriate procedure is, however, to reason to mathematics, rather than from mathematics. But as highly qualified practitioners have argued, mathematical methods and formulations have run riot in economics without proper appreciation of their limitations. The major limitations have been pointed out by outstanding scholars with technical mathematical credentials, including Marshall, Pigou, Keynes, Leontief, Stigler, and their observations have often been pointed, specific, and pertinent. Those of Norbert Wiener, one of the great figures of modern mathematics, were particularly vigorous. In one of my books I have referred at some length to his *God and Golem, Inc.*, published posthumously in 1964.[2] Yet these critical observations have made little impact. Reading the journals one gets the impression that economics has become little more than a branch of applied mathematics and one that can be successfully pursued with little reference to real life phenomena.

Another conspicuous development in economics since I first studied the subject has been the use of econometric methods. Much useful work has been done with these methods. But far better qualified people than myself have demonstrated their frequent abuse, and the misapplication or misinterpretation of their results.

Here I want to draw attention only to some of the ways in which mathematical economics and the use of econometrics have contributed to the disregard or neglect of evident reality. Their use has led to unwarranted concentration in economics on variables tractable to formal analysis. As a corollary, it has led to the neglect of influences which, even when highly pertinent, are not amenable to such treatment. Similarly, it has encouraged confusion between the significant, on the one hand, and the quantifiable (often only spuriously quantifiable) on the other. It has contributed to the neglect of background conditions and historical processes where they are indispensable for understanding. For instance, differences in income and wealth, both domestic and international, cannot be considered helpfully without attention to their antecedents and background.

Belief in the well-nigh universal applicability of testing by econometric methods has led to inappropriate claims for these methods. It has also smothered other forms of reasoning and inference. What has become of the traditional method of direct observation, reflection, tracing of connections, reaching tentative conclusions and referring these back to observation and to established propositions of the discipline, or to findings of cognate disciplines? Such procedures

[2]See Bauer (1981, pp. 263–64), citing Wiener (1964).

are no less informative than quantitative analysis. For instance, with the traditional approaches the economist was much more likely to be aware of the gap between theoretical concepts and the available information.

The acceptance of quantitative methods as the most respectable procedure has permitted the burgeoning of incompetent or inappropriate econometric studies, including those based on seriously flawed data. Conversely, studies based on direct observation or detailed examination of slices of history are apt to be dismissed as anecdotal, unscholarly or unscientific, even if they are informative. All too often their findings are dismissed as no more than casual empiricism or expressions of opinion. Moreover, in what passes for high-level discourse, insistence on the obvious can be made to sound trivial and therefore not worth saying. In short, preoccupation with mathematical and quantitative methods has brought with it a regrettable atrophy of close observation and simple reflection.

I have just asked the rhetorical question of what has happened in economics to the traditional sequence of observation, reflection, inference, tentative conclusion and reference to established propositions, and to findings of other fields of study. Being rhetorical, the question can be answered readily. This type of reasoning and its vocabulary have contracted greatly throughout the subject and have virtually disappeared in large parts of it. And the traditional method has retreated not because it has been proved less informative than the methods that have replaced it. It has retreated because it has been castigated as being less rigorous than its more modish successors, largely because it less resembles the procedures of the natural sciences, especially those of physics.

I think that in the course of this shift of approach pertinent differences between the study of nature, especially physics, and economics have not been sufficiently recognized. Some differences may be only of degree, others are sufficiently pronounced to be more nearly differences in kind.

Natural scientists seek to establish uniformities about phenomena and relationships which are substantially invariant. Some of the phenomena and relationships studied by economists are also largely invariant. Others are not so constant, or at any rate their constant components are embedded in so many others that it is often difficult to discern the presence and extent of uniformities. Again, concepts and distinctions widely used by economists—or even regarded as basic—are imprecise, arbitrary, and shifting, and their real life equivalents difficult to pin down: primary, secondary, and tertiary activity, or manufacturing and service activity; voluntary and involuntary unemployment; developed and underdeveloped countries; final and intermediate goods (a distinction that is critical for the definition of income); and many others. This extensive fuzziness of concepts and categories in economics limits informative use of mathematical methods: in mathematics the concepts and relationships, although completely abstract, are more precise and consistent.

For these various reasons, the methods for discerning uniformities, and their extent and limitations, differ considerably between the natural sciences, on the one hand—especially those like physics and chemistry that have been most successfully mathematicized—and social study, including economics on the other hand.[3] Some parts of economics, most obviously development economics, deal with events and sequences the informative study of which needs to incorporate practices from historical scholarship, such as reliance on primary sources, close observation, sustained reflection, the tracing of connections, and others.

These remarks on the differences between the study of nature and the study of society are not intended in the least to endorse the view that in economics, or social study generally, objective reasoning is impossible, which is another matter altogether. As I have written on this issue in a number of publications, I shall not develop it here and simply say that objective reasoning is quite as possible in economics as in the natural sciences.[4]

Mathematical methods often provide an effective facade or screen which covers or conceals empty formalism. They can camouflage disregard of basic propositions or simple evidence in models purporting to serve as basis for policy. Statistics, technical jargon, and sophisticated econometric techniques can also serve as a protective screen. But the use of mathematics is particularly effective because of the language barrier it provides. What we see is an inversion of

[3]There is a large literature on this controversial subject. Apart from Wiener's short essay already mentioned, I have found particularly helpful the observations of Sir Peter Medawar (Nobel laureate biologist) in *The Art of the Soluble* (1967).

[4]See, for example, Bauer (1972, chap. 15; 1984, chap. 9).

the familiar Hans Andersen story of the Emperor's New Clothes. Here there *are* new clothes, and at times they are *haute couture*. But all too often there is no Emperor within.

The achievements of mathematical economics and of econometric techniques have been secured at a great price. This price is not reflected adequately in the direct resource costs. In the book to which I have referred, Wiener insisted that the adoption of mathematical formulation and econometric methods involves misconceived imitation of the natural sciences; and also that it has enabled economists to remove both themselves and their public from the perception of reality.

The Wider Scene

It is not surprising that indifference to reality is not confined to economics, but is extensive on the wider scene also. This divorce from reality is particularly baffling in view of well-nigh universal literacy in the West and the advances in the transmission of information. It is baffling also in view of the profound advances in science and technology. These latter subjects depend on reasoning which, although necessarily abstract, cannot fly in the face of reality.

Disregard of reality encompasses the refusal to accept the plain evidence of one's senses, neglect of simple connected reasoning, and the inability to recognize simple inconsistencies. What is behind all this?

Attempts to explain people's opinions always involve conjecture. Arguments can be assessed conclusively on the basis of logic or evidence. But why people accept or canvass them cannot be determined so confidently. In certain contexts some dominant influences are discernible. Many influences themselves represent a disregard of reality and also promote it; as in so many social situations, the process and the outcome are intertwined, even inseparable.

There are some who argue that there is nothing perplexing about conduct and opinions in evident conflict with reality, since they reflect no more than the promotion of self-interest. In this scheme of things apparently paradoxical and anomalous ideas and modes of conduct emerge from the operation of special interest groups or coalitions, including politicians, public servants, academics, and sections of the electorate. This factor can be significant.

Yet the operation of special interest groups cannot account for some conspicuous anomalies. Thus it can explain neither the hostility to the West in major international organizations nor the supine conduct of the West in them. Some of these organizations existed in embryonic form before World War II: the League of Nations in Geneva and the International Institute of Agriculture in Rome were precursors of today's UN and FAO. But their stances differed radically from what goes on there now. Moreover, the West supports lavishly and treats with deference African rulers who consistently vilify it. Such a stance by the West would have been unthinkable in the 1930s. These rulers have no votes in the West, nor do they advertise much in the media.

Amputation of the Time Perspective

Confusion between advancement of knowledge and promotion of policy undoubtedly contributes to indifference to reality. This influence is certainly important in economics. That this is so is suggested by the profusion of transgressions against reality in those parts of the subject close to policy, such as development economics, the economics of Soviet-type planning, labor economics, the economics of poverty, and the economics of market failure. Some practitioners acknowledge the pursuit of political objectives; they also urge that in any event in social study objective reasoning is impossible. I may mention an experience of mine. On several occasions when my lectures criticized the notion of the vicious circle of poverty, members of the audience said that, whatever the validity of my criticisms, the notion was invaluable in the advocacy of foreign aid.

Much contemporary discourse is also afflicted by ignorance of the past and neglect of the time dimension in cultural and social phenomena. Sir Ernst Gombrich has termed this phenomenon the amputation of the time dimension from our culture. It has vitiated discourse in much of contemporary economics including, for example, mainstream development economics and the discussion of domestic and international income differences. In these and other parts of economics we cannot understand the situation we observe unless we know how it has arisen. For instance, the low income compared with the West in many LDCs with substantial exports of cash crops has often been adduced to support the contention that external contacts and the production of cash crops are not effective for economic progress, or indeed inhibit it. In fact, many cash-crop exporting countries have progressed very rapidly over the last century or less. But how can we expect societies which in the late 19th century were still extremely backward, or even barbarous, to reach, within a few decades, the level of societies with many centuries, or even millennia, of economic development behind them? Another example is provided by changes in the distribution of income within a country. A higher degree of inequality may result say from a greater reduction in mortality among the poor (which would represent an improvement in their condition) or from the imposition of a regressive tax regime.

The factors behind the debilitating lack of the time perspective and neglect of evidently pertinent background include the speed of social and technical change and the multiplicity of messages reaching people, often about distant events. Very rapid and discontinuous social and technical change can unnerve and even unhinge people. There is only so much change that people can absorb as individuals, families, or societies. By disrupting sustained observation, these influences inhibit both connected thinking and the poise provided by background and time perspective.

Again, any inclination to equate the methods of natural science with those of the social sciences contributes to the downgrading or neglect of antecedents and processes. Whilst antecedents and processes are largely irrelevant in chemistry and physics, and wholly irrelevant in mathematics, they are critical for the understanding of social phenomena. The signal achievements of natural sciences and the pervasive results of their applications encourage habits of thought in social sciences based on misleading analogies between the two realms of study.

Whatever the factors behind them—and the list proposed here is both tentative and incomplete—lack of knowledge of the past and neglect of the time perspective are evident in much contemporary discourse. The resulting loss of collective memory has also opened the way for the manipulation and rewriting of history.

Collective Guilt

The widespread or at any rate widely articulated feeling of guilt in the West is a significant influence behind some of the novel and baffling manifestations of the contemporary disregard of reality or even its denial. It helps to explain such matters as the acceptance of unfounded notions about Western responsibility for Third World backwardness and of the allegedly damaging effects of commercial contacts between the West and LDCs; the spineless conduct of the West toward African despots with negligible external power and resources, and the readiness of the West to support them in spite of their hostility to the West and in the face sometimes of inhuman domestic policies; and also the readiness of the West to finance international organizations that serve as forums for the embarrassment and undermining of the West. The guilt feeling in the West is reflected, for example, in the readiness to give aid to Asian and African rulers without questioning their policies. Guild-ridden people hope to assuage their feelings simply by giving away money (especially taxpayers' money) without questioning the results: what matters is to give away money, not what results from the process.

Although some elements of guilt feeling are part of the Judaeo-Christian tradition, guilt today is novel. Materially, the West has never had it so good, nor ever felt so bad about it. One reason for this is probably the failure of material prosperity to bring about the contentment and happiness so widely expected from it. Guilt has contributed to the confusion between the merits of charity in helping the less fortunate and the notion that income differences as such are reprehensible results of oppression and exploitation. These differences are commonly referred to as inequalities or even as inequities. The confusion has been encouraged by an eagerness of churchmen to see themselves not as spiritual leaders but as social welfare workers or political activists.

Moreover, many influential opinion formers, including teachers, clerics, and people in the media, have come to dislike Western society, or even to hate it. They are apt both to harbor and to provoke feelings of guilt.

A major factor behind the emergence of contemporary collective guilt has been presumably the erosion of personal responsibility under the impact of social determinism. Participation in collective guilt has taken the place of individual responsibility. External forces are held responsible both for personal misconduct and personal misfortune. And if we are all guilty, then no individual is.

Guilt feeling in Western societies has promoted indifference to reality, a loss of poise and a loss of confidence. Loss of continuity and the amputation of the time perspective reinforce these effects of collective guilt. Kenneth Clark wrote that he was not sure what were all the necessary ingredients for civilization, but he was sure that confidence and continuity were indispensable. Both have been seriously eroded in recent decades.

Misuse of Language

In recent decades many thoughtful people have commented on the misuse of language, both in public discourse and in education. Disregard of reality promotes erosion of language, which promotes further disregard of reality. Language is to a culture or a society what money is to an economy; their erosion leads to a disintegration. Misuse of language covers the shifting interpretation of concepts such as socialism, equality, growth, monopoly, and many others. At times misuse of language is even acknowledged. If a country is officially designated as a democratic or as a people's republic, we know that it is one in which people have no say in the government. Another category of examples is the treatment of countries and other collectivities as if they were single decision-making entities, or entities within which all the people have identical interests, experiences, and conditions. The aggregation of two-thirds of mankind as the Third World is a conspicuous example.

The growth of specialization, including long periods of specialized training, inhibits the exercise of critical faculty outside a narrow range and engenders disregard of reality in much academic and public discourse. This disregard of reality is also facilitated by an understandable and rational reluctance of people to exercise their critical faculties in matters which affect them but about which they feel they can do little or nothing.

The vast expansion of information in recent decades may have been critical in the widespread atrophy of reflection. People, including academics, are expected to absorb so much information and technique that all too often they have little time, inclination, and capacity left for reflection and observation, even for simple assessment of the information reaching them.

The decline of traditional religious belief may also have contributed to a disregard of reality. This explanation could be appealing both to believers and to skeptics. Traditional religious belief provides a unified coherent world view, the erosion of which enfeebles connected thinking. Conversely, it can be argued that the decline of religious belief diffuses the credulity of mankind over wide and more diverse areas. The speed of the decline reinforces such effects.

In this section and its three predecessors I have suggested some of the forces and influences behind the contemporary disregard of reality. I must remind the reader, however, that such suggestions are necessarily somewhat speculative. This is especially true of reflections on the varied and complex forces behind the Zeitgeist.

Need to Restate the Obvious

What has happened to us in the West for us to be so ready to fly in the face of reality and to reject the evidence of our senses? What makes us lose our poise and self-respect? It is as if amidst unprecedented prosperity and scientific achievement, inexplicable malevolent forces had undermined our mental and moral faculties.

The extensive and baffling indifference to reality matters greatly. Among other results, it has undermined standards in parts of economics, in other social studies, and in wider areas of ostensibly serious discourse. It is reversion to barbarism. Ortega y Gasset wrote that the absence of standards is the essence of barbarism. It is because this condition prevails in parts of economics alongside its great achievements of recent decades that I am now so baffled by the present state of the subject.

The tendency to disregard simple realities has undermined the poise, self-assurance, and stance of the West in the international arena. It has also underpinned the uncritical acceptance of ideas and policies damaging to the West, and much more so to the peoples of the Third World. This is not surprising. Polities and societies bent on disregarding reality must be vulnerable to adversity, and also to threats from within and without.

Such concerns highlight the perceptiveness of two observations by authors widely separated in time and very different in general outlook. Their observations make a fitting conclusion to this essay. Pascal wrote in the 17th century: "Let us labour at trying to think clearly: herein lies the source of moral conduct." (Travaillons donc à penser bien: voilà le principe de la morale.) And in our own time George Orwell wrote: "We have sunk to such a depth that the restatement of the obvious has become the first duty of intelligent men."

References

Bauer, Peter T. *Dissent on Development*. Cambridge: Harvard University Press, 1972.

Bauer, Peter T. *Equality, the Third World, and Economic Delusion*. Cambridge: Harvard University Press, 1981.

Bauer, Peter T. *Reality and Rhetoric*. Cambridge: Harvard University Press, 1984.

Bauer, Peter T. "The Disregard of Reality." *Cato Journal* 7 (Spring/Summer 1987): 29–42.

Medawar, Peter. *The Art of the Soluble*. London: Methuen, 1967.

Wiener, Norbert. *God and Golem, Inc.* Cambridge: MIT Press, 1964.

3. The Poverty of Nations

Karl Brunner

The Condition of Poverty and the Creation of Wealth

Poverty remains an endemic state of man. The curse imposed by an angry god on Adam and his descendants describes the human fate. Man experienced over history, with rare exceptions, toil, hardship and oppression. The uncertain and stringent conditions of life challenged man's awareness. He sought for answers explaining this fate and these were couched in the form of myths and legends. An imaginative human mind invoked a fall from grace or a curse imposed by gods. Such orientations naturally affected man's expectations of liberation from the grinding burden of toil and hardship. The restoration of grace appeared to be the crucial condition for such liberation.

This elementary message emerged over the centuries in very different forms and in widely varying detail. The basic story of man's fate conveyed by ancient myths still persists with a subtle and pervasive influence. The dominant ideologies of our time promise the restoration of (at least secular) grace with the liberation from human bondage to poverty. This promise of liberation should be realized by a collective action imposing a set of explicitly designed *political* institutions as the dominant mechanism for the coordination of society.

The ancient themes still reverberate under new labels in various branches of sociology or social psychology. But their influential repercussions on the intelligentsia market have been challenged for

---

Karl Brunner was Fred H. Gowen Professor of Economics and Director of the Center for Research in Government Policy and Business at the Graduate School of Management at the University of Rochester. This chapter is reprinted, with some revisions by the editors, from the late author's article in the Spring/Summer 1985 *Cato Journal* (Brunner 1985). An earlier version of the paper appeared in the January 1985 issue of *Business Economics.*

200 years by the evolution of economic analysis. This analysis, initiated by the Scottish philosophers of the 18th century, offered a revolutionary insight into the social context of man's life. This insight has hardly been absorbed or understood by the educated middle classes of western societies and even less by the professional articulators.

The Scottish tradition of economic analysis explains the emergence of social groups and "great societies" extending social interaction far beyond face-to-face associations. It also explains the emergence of political structures without invoking metaphysical entities. This tradition shows in particular how the social structure emerges as resourceful human agents interact to improve their lot according to their judgment and understanding. The social structure appears in this manner as an important but quite unintentional by-product of this interaction.

The same analysis also addresses the condition of poverty and the creation of wealth. The wealth of nations, expressed by the standard of living, depends foremost on individual effort, ingenuity, and imaginative adaptation to the environment. The natural environment together with the resources provided by nature can make a substantial difference for a nation's opportunities. These opportunities offered by nature condition the pattern of activities and the use of available human and nonhuman resources. But the possessions of natural resources do not determine a nation's wealth and do not, per se, suspend Adam's curse. Nature's heritage forms, contrary to widely held beliefs well represented by the Brandt Report on the North-South dialogue, neither a necessary nor a sufficient condition for high or rising levels of wealth. More than 50 years ago Argentina was expected to evolve on the basis of its natural resources into one of the world's wealthiest nations. It approached in contrast a pattern of stagnation. Brazil should also be on this count among the wealthiest nations today. Switzerland, less favored with natural resources than Zaire, Nigeria, Mexico, and other nations, should appear among the poorer nations appealing for aid from Argentina, Brazil, Mexico and others. We may also compare Hong Kong, South Korea, Taiwan, and Singapore with more favored nations. Or consider the permanent stagnation of Tanzania and Zimbabwe in Africa or of Bolivia and Peru in South America.

Political power has frequently been singled out as a crucial factor of a more widely conceived "natural environment" which decisively affects the wealth of nations. The Brandt Report exemplifies once again this view. But history and economic analysis fail to support this claim. Nations with little power experienced over the past 100 years or more a remarkable increase in wealth. This accrual of wealth occurred moreover not at the cost of other (more powerful?) nations but contributed actually to benefit others through an expanded economic interaction.

Poverty is characterized by a low rate of production of goods and services. The creation of wealth involves an expansion of this production. Western nations experienced this process over the last 200 years on a scale never before recorded in history. Power can simply not explain this phenomenon. Power does not produce goods, it simply absorbs and uses goods to maintain the power apparatus—a *nomenklatura*. Power, however, may be applied to extract wealth from those who produced it, an exercise that does not create wealth but actually destroys it in the final analysis. The emphasis on power thus confuses the *creation* and the *redistribution* of wealth. It also fails to understand the longer-run consequences of redistributive power. The argument based on power frequently occurs in a context linking the accumulation of wealth in Western nations with colonialism. But Adam Smith already elaborated the crucial implications of colonialism. He recognized that colonialism meant a loss in wealth for the colonizing nation combined with a domestic redistribution favoring specific groups involved in the process. This redistribution, and not any general accrual of wealth, was the historical driving force of colonization. The exercise of power applied to colonial efforts thus imposed an economic burden on the mother country.

Our attention clearly must be directed beyond natural resources and power to human effort and resourceful ingenuity. The founding fathers of modern economic analysis recognized the central importance of human capital and investment in human capital as a condition of the wealth of nations. The development of the German economy after World War II dramatically confirmed this contention. But effort and resourceful ingenuity are not "sociological data" determined by the mysteries of a "mental attitude," a "religious commitment" or an inherited "work ethic." Customs, traditions, and cultural values may play a role for a while. However, they will diminish in importance and behavior will adjust once the supporting conditions have eroded. Economic analysis informs us that effort and resourceful probing emerge with substantially greater frequency and intensity when human agents expect to capture the benefits of their search activity and their ingenuity. Without the incentives of potential rewards, agents hardly will find it worthwhile to expend much effort and ingenuity. The magnitude and quality of effort and the intensity of search for imaginative innovations in types and use of resources is generally closely linked with the expectation of capturing the returns from these endeavors. The penalty-reward system thus conditions the current level of human endeavor. Economic incentives also shape the accumulation of human capital expressed by the level and quality of skills and the development of nonhuman resources with the productive modification of the environment.

The power argument outlined above fails to comprehend the central role of incentives and the close link between the investment of one's efforts and the capture of expected returns. It proceeds as if there operated no incentive feedback from the distribution of the product to its supply. The argument suggests on the contrary that all goods are to be grabbed by participants in a social game. The powerful acquire the lion's share of the economic pie and the losers get the crumbs. The natural conclusion from this romantic vision is that the balance of power needs to be changed.

The message conveyed by economic analysis thus directs our attention to the conditions that encourage the application of human effort and ingenuity to the inheritance determined by history and the environment. These conditions do not depend on nature. They are determined by the social organization characterizing a society. The prevailing sociopolitical institutions condition the potential opportunities facing human agents. They ultimately shape the incentives that guide human effort and ingenuity, and that evolve over time into customs, habits, and traditions. Such customs and traditions, however, can be destroyed by institutional changes that lower the expectation of a link between effort and real benefit. Thus we recognize in the pattern of existing sociopolitical institutions the crucial condition for both wealth creation and the persistence of widespread poverty. A stagnant economy and persistent poverty, therefore, do not express a curse of vengeful gods (in the heavens or in history) to be atoned by a purifying collective action. Rather, such stagnation and poverty result essentially from the inheritance of social institutions affecting individual behavior.

The Ambivalence of the Political Structure

The nature of institutions maintaining poverty or fostering wealth creation requires some further attention. The role of the political structure, and specifically of the state, needs to be clarified in this context.

The social productivity of the political structure is best understood in comparison with a state of anarchy. An agent arranging his affairs under anarchy has the following options for the use of his resources: he can invest in production, in trade, in attempts of robbery, and in defense against others. The exposure to potential loss of resources due to piracy by others lowers the incentive to invest in production. It also constrains the opportunity to trade. Under the circumstances productive activity addressed to wealth creation remains at a low level. All agents seem to be caught in the trap of a prisoner's dilemma. The repetitive occurrence of the basic social problem posed by anarchy, however, induces the interacting responses so well described by the founders of economic analysis and more recently elaborated by F. A. Hayek (1982). The evolution of political institutions offers in this respect a solution to the prisoner's dilemma inherent in a state of anarchy.

Consider the options available to an agent arranging his activities in the context of the political structure. He can invest his resources again in four different ways: in production, in trade, in the political process to redistribute wealth on his behalf, and in the political process as a defense against wealth redistribution schemes advanced by others. Anarchy and the political structure are thus not distinguished by presence or absence of a zero (or possibly even negative) sum game of social interaction. We recognize at this stage the peculiar ambivalence of the political structure. This structure establishes rules of the social game. Such rules substantially confine the wealth-impeding activities of anarchy but they never totally eliminate them, as exemplified by the Mafia and the Camorra. The rules therefore provide a "monopoly of violence" anchored by the political structure. This monopoly forms a necessary condition for the specification of property rights and their enforcement. Investment in production and in activities raising the level and quality of human and nonhuman resources is encouraged as a result of the greater expectation of capturing the returns under the rules of the social game. Specification and enforcement of property rights also encourage a wider range of possible transactions and provide new opportunities for mutually beneficial trade. The resulting increase in the creation of wealth expresses the remarkable productivity of a stable political structure that allows individuals to capture the benefits of increased economic efficiency.

The magnitude and extent of the benefits accruing from the political structure, however, depend on the institutional arrangements guiding the coordination of socioeconomic activities. In this context private property exhibits a crucial advantage that is not well understood by most professional articulators in the public arena. The assignment of property rights resolves a physical impossibility associated with potential social conflicts. Scarce resources cannot be controlled simultaneously by several persons. The structure of rights determines who can do what with respect to which scarce object. This structure fully reflects the inherited patterns of resources. It mirrors in this sense the constraints imposed by nature. All resources need be owned by some person and beyond this no rights should be assigned.[1] This condition rules out the wide array of market-closing and entry-restricting arrangements under any name. Private property rights also guarantee the important link between effort and reward that was emphasized above. Under such a system this link is actually generalized to transactors beyond the range of owners of nonhuman resources.

No rules of the social game however can preclude a new form of wealth-impeding activities from replacing the ancient patterns of anarchic wealth impediments. The problem actually adheres to any set of rules. All political structures determine potential opportunities for manipulation *within* the rules accepted for their operations. They unavoidably offer incentives to be used for purposes of wealth redistribution among the participants of the social game. There is hardly a political institution that does not have consequences for the distribution of wealth. Agents respond to this fact by investing resources in the political process in order to generate wealth transfers from others or to ward off attempted transfers by others. This aspect of the political structure involves basically a negative sum game within the context of the socially productive positive sum game provided by a stable set of rules. The incentives to invest in the political

[1]See Meckling and Jensen (1980).

process for purposes of acquiring wealth from others or for protective political actions lower the allocation of resources to socially productive activities. The taxes imposed by implicit or explicit wealth transfers occurring in one form or another lower moreover the incentive to invest in production, trade, and the accumulation of resources. These consequences determine the inherent ambiguity of the state expressed by the joint operation of a positive and negative sum game proceeding in the context of political institutions organizing the social interaction.

All political structure thus involves simultaneously a wealth-creating and a wealth-impeding dimension. In contrast to the state of anarchy, however, the wealth-obstructing activities proceed in accordance to a recognized and generally accepted set of rules. Political structure thus lowers, but does not remove, the uncertainty confronting agents' socially productive activities. The magnitude of the lowered uncertainty or, in other words, the extent of the wealth-impeding range of activities associated with the political structure depends crucially on the detail of the sociopolitical institution. Every set of political institutions produces its specific mix of positive and negative sum social games. The weight of wealth-impeding activities depends thus on the sociopolitical arrangements of nations.

The nature of wealth-fostering and wealth-impeding political institutions may be usefully described in rough outline. The distinction between the two dimensions of the state may be usefully introduced for this purpose. These dimensions refer to the "protective state" and the "redistributive state." This classification is essentially justified in terms of the purpose of political institutions but holds only approximately in terms of their consequences.

Robert Nozick (1974) and James Buchanan (1977) demonstrated the redistributive dimension unavoidably embedded in the protective state. The protective state encompasses a set of political institutions that define general rules offering a stable framework for agents' productive activities. Such rules involve most particularly the definition of private property, the protective arrangements of police and courts associated with this definition, enforceability of privately negotiated contracts, and stable and predictable fiscal procedures including monetary policy. The rules bearing on the government's financial affairs need explicit recognition in this context. Unpredictable explicit changes in taxation or implicit changes via erratic inflation in a world of tax rates addressed to nominal values can substantially lower the incentives of the positive sum social game. A rich variety of observations informs us that the detail of the political framework shaping the social institutions listed above substantially influences the productivity of the social game. Well-designed political structures foster the evolution of markets and improve their functioning. Moreover the higher level of predictability tends to encourage the accumulation of resources. These consequences are essential strands of a wealth-creating social process. This follows from the fundamental fact that the social institutions protected by the type of political structure under consideration assure, on average, a systematic link between effort and ingenuity applied on the one side and the resulting returns on the other. We may formulate this more generally as a set of institutions that raise the probability of a link between the consequences of actions and the agents committing these actions. They also lower the likelihood of market-closing and entry-restricting activities.

An alternative set of rules or institutions embodied in political structures represented by the redistributive state typically produce wealth-impeding consequences. The class of these political institutions exhibits a rich detail testifying to man's inventiveness. We may divide this vast detail into two broad groups for our purposes. One group involves constraints on choices bearing on contractual arrangements and the tenure of property. The other group contains structures with direct distributional consequences and associated distortions of incentives. Although this division is neither neat nor clean, a better organization of the material may emerge from further discussion.

The argument outlined above suggests that the creation of wealth or entrenched poverty is substantially conditioned by both levels of the political apparatus—the protective state and the redistributional state. Too little of the first and too much of the second obstruct wealth creation and maintain pockets of poverty or even mass poverty. An uncertain or more or less deliberate failure to exercise the basic protective function erodes the link between productive effort and capture of expected returns. This experience can be observed over history and continues in our time. Political instability and longer-run uncertainty bearing on important sociopolitical institutions provide few, or weak, incentives to create wealth through productive investment. Instead, incentives are directed toward the conquest of political control and the acquisition of the associated spoils. The resulting pattern of entrenched poverty cannot be alleviated by doses of foreign aid. Such aid essentially contributes to raise the resources available to the local *nomenklatura*. It cannot replace or offset the absence of an adequate protective state.[2]

The realization of the basic protective function may be offset to some extent by the state's redistributional activities. Constraints on contractual arrangements and the effect of sociopolitical conditions on property tenure exemplify this aspect. The usual textbook treatment of production obscures this important point. We read that output is linked with an array of inputs via a production function. This function purportedly represents the underlying technology. This interpretation is thoroughly misleading, however. The nature of the production function is sensitively conditioned by sociopolitical circumstances. The production function actually forms the outcome of agents' optimizing responses to these conditions. It follows that variations in the admissible range of contractual arrangements or associated organizational forms modify the production function. Constraints on admissible contractual arrangements tend to lower output for any given input. Consequently they impoverish a society and obstruct the imaginative search for new modes of wealth creation.

The imposition of self-management or codetermination illustrates the issue. The organizational forms may survive successfully in competition with the corporation and other forms. They may exhibit a comparative advantage for specific activities. Our experience clearly indicates, however, that this comparative advantage occurs over a very limited range. A coercive imposition of these forms forces, therefore, the organization of production into a mold less adapted to the coordination of resources in production. A comparative decline in output thus emerges. Detailed investigations of the incentives prevailing under self-management and codetermination confirm the results of economic analysis. These investigations also show that self-management in particular creates new social tensions and

[2]See Bauer (1978).

conflicts between younger and older workers, or between established workers and potential new workers entering the market.

Corporate governance is another fashionable issue that should be mentioned here. Modifications of governance are proposed in order to achieve purportedly desirable social goals. The sense of these proposals usually conveys that they impose *no* social costs and *will* achieve the desired effects. Economic analysis disillusions us on both counts. The social costs in particular will rise with the severity of constraints controlling corporate organizations.

The change in the law governing insolvency in Germany and the "comparable worth" movement in the United States offer further examples of contractual constraints. The assignment of priority rights to several months' salary beyond the date of filing for bankruptcy raises the cost of capital, impedes investments, and affects employment. A systematic application of "comparable worth" procedures would seriously impede the organization of production and impose social costs in terms of lessened output of goods and services.

Pharmaceutical regulations and the admissible range for the forms of property tenure are the last examples of constraints on the production function potentially lowering welfare. The prevailing regulation of pharmaceutical products confines both contractual procedures and the choice of production processes. It has increased the cost of operation and, via the reduction in the relevant economic duration of the patent, it has lowered the expected return. Moreover, the regulatory constraints have lowered new pharmaceutical innovation and thus the achievable state of health.

The modification of the patent's relevant duration actually abrogates established property rights. Constraints on the form of property tenure can significantly impair the nature of the social production function. In many countries around the world land is frequently tended by peasants under a usufruct system. Irrespective of the political motives behind this tenure system an examination of its operation reveals that it obstructs productivity of agricultural labor, obstructs investment that would improve the quality of land, and encourages population growth in the countryside. The collectivization of agriculture in the Soviet Union offers a particularly emphatic example of obstructive institutionalization. It eroded incentives to produce and raised incentives for a wasteful use of resources. Agricultural output naturally suffered.

The second strand of the redistributional state encompasses examples from the welfare system of Western societies, the oligarchic power structure of nations in the Third World, the *nomenklatura* of socialist countries, or some patterns of nonsocialist dictatorships. The welfare system of Western nations imposed a massively accelerated redistribution which lowered incentives to work, invest, and save. On the other hand it raised incentives to invest resources in the negative sum game of political processes.

The oligarchies of many nations in the Third World depend for their survival on a persistent redistribution of wealth from the countryside to the cities. Their political base is usually anchored with the populace in the cities. In order to maintain their power the ruling oligarchies find it advisable to impose low prices on agricultural products. This pattern destroys incentives to produce food, erodes incentives to invest resources in agricultural operations, and creates incentives to abandon fertile land and join the masses in the cities.

Most socialist countries operate a vast system redistributing wealth from the potentially productive sector to the *nomenklatura*—a socially unproductive sector composed of a huge military complex, an internal security and economic control apparatus. Once again this redistribution system lowers incentives for the productive use of resources. Nonsocialist military dictatorships also require for their survival a redistribution favoring the military apparatus with similar consequences for the wealth-creating dimension of the social process.

The evolution of labor markets reveals that Western nations participated in their own way to obstruct, usually with the best intentions, the wealth-creating process. Unemployment in European countries stayed very low until about the end of the 1960s. The pattern changed dramatically during the 1970s. Unemployment rates rose to the double-digit range. With the exception of Switzerland, almost all European nations experienced massive increases in measured unemployment. Politicians and the media frequently attribute this development to new technologies. In the public arena one also encounters comparisons with the Great Depression. This comparison fails however. The rising trend in European unemployment occurred, in contrast to the 1930s, during a period of expansionary financial policies. Moreover, as we learn from economic analysis, technology cannot explain this unemployment either. Technological innovations change opportunities. Old jobs disappear and new jobs emerge.

The American experience demonstrates that reasonably functioning market processes continuously create new jobs and offer new employment.

The crucial conditions pertain to the sociopolitical institutions under which markets operate. Most European countries experienced, in this context, major changes. A variety of arrangements affecting the operation of labor markets were introduced by European governments. These arrangements include measures of employment protection, liberalizations of unemployment support, increasing payroll and social security taxes imposed on employers, and similar measures. Employment protection, represented among other procedures by increased compensation payments upon dismissal, raised the expected real cost of employment relative to the real return expected from employment. The same result holds for increased payroll taxes and other obligations associated with employment. It follows that either net real wages fall or employment declines relatively. These adjustments are unavoidable. As it happened, the resulting adjustments occurred in most nations dominantly in the employment-unemployment dimension. No single step or single measure introduced in this evolution involved any dramatic or crucial changes. But their cumulative effect over time did change the operation of the economy. Whatever the motivation and intention of the political decisions shaping this evolution they produced a stagnant labor market. Vast human resources are poorly used, and nations are significantly poorer than they otherwise would be. The petrification of labor markets caused by a long sequence of political decisions also endangers the future course of Western societies. Technological innovations—a necessary condition of rising wealth in our history—will increasingly evolve as a social threat in the context of petrified labor markets. Under the circumstances the resulting political decisions tend to obstruct the wealth-creating process even further. Proposals to lower the working time per week to 35 or 25 hours illustrate this point.

The evolution of labor markets, however important, offers just one strand to our theme about the wealth and poverty of nations. The government's fiscal operations deserve some attention in this respect. In an investigation of the consequences of taxes and government expenditures on the pattern of resource allocation, it was estimated that the general welfare of the United Kingdom was lowered by about 8 percent. Thus taxes and most particularly expenditure patterns severely distorted the allocation of resources.

A reference also should be made to the rising tide of protectionism. The range of protectionist schemes has expanded and evolved in imaginatively subtle complexity. The rationale for and the welfare implications of protectionism have barely changed over the centuries. Protectionist policies continue to redistribute wealth, benefiting special groups at the expense of the rest of society. The highly visible benefit of the favored group in conjunction with the widely dispersed—and thus less visible—social costs misleads politicians and publicists into believing that protectionist institutions increase general wealth. The redistribution produced by such policies is typically associated with a comparative social impoverishment. The ideology and illusion of protectionism as a necessary condition for fostering wealth creation permeates influential groups in many nations.

Conclusion

History demonstrates, analogously to biological experimentation via mutation, an endless experimentation with social organizations and associated cultural terms, attitudes, and values. These organizations yield very different survival characteristics in competition with other social groups. They also determine the long-run chances of rising wealth or entrenched poverty and disease. The intentional, and frequently unintentional, evolution of the sociopolitical institutions decisively determines, ultimately, the conditions of poverty or wealth creation irrespective of the evolution's motivating conceptions. The role of political structure, represented by the state and its apparatus, thus deserves careful and intense attention in this context. The illusion is widely held that the state produces wealth, and, more particularly, that little wealth will be created without the detailed and controlling intervention of the state.

Another illusion dominating our time and well represented among the Christian churches holds that government intervention addressed to massive redistribution cannot affect the incentives guiding the social process of wealth creation. The translation of moral fervor "to help the poor" into institutional arrangements that lower opportunities and entrench poverty is one of the saddest ironies of our age. It is a small step from such beliefs to the view, implicit in the legal thesis of "tax-expenditures," that all wealth really belongs to the state and is conditionally and revocably leased to individual agents.

Our discussion reveals the nature of the misconception asserting a *direct* productivity of the state. The state is not a producer of wealth. It shapes *conditions* that encourage the creation of wealth. But it also frequently represents political institutions that impede expanding welfare. The state can, and frequently does, obstruct the wealth-creating process and contribute to sustained poverty. Its wealth-impeding activities yield an economic rent to a small group with access to the sociopolitical institutions. The emerging social organization of Western societies will thus determine whether a nation accumulates wealth or persists in poverty.

References

Bauer, Peter T. "Western Guilt and Third World Poverty." In *The First World & the Third World.* Edited by Karl Brunner. Rochester, N.Y.: University of Rochester Policy Center Publications, 1978.

Brunner, Karl. "The Poverty of Nations." *Cato Journal* 5 (Spring/Summer 1985): 37–49.

Buchanan, James M. *The Limits of Liberty: Between Anarchy and Leviathan.* Chicago: University of Chicago Press, 1977.

Hayek, F. A. *Law, Legislation and Liberty.* Reprint (3 vols. in 1). London: Routledge & Kegan Paul, 1982.

Meckling, William H., and Jensen, Michael C. "A Positive Analysis of Rights Systems." Working paper, University of Rochester, Graduate School of Management, 1980.

Nozick, Robert. *Anarchy, State, and Utopia.* New York: Basic Books, 1974.

4. The Transformation of Developing Economies: From Plan to Market

Deepak Lal

Economic development became a topic of widespread interest during the decolonialization that occurred after the Second World War. The mainstream view among economists, governments of newly independent countries, and international organizations soon after the war emphasized economic planning and an autarkic pattern of development as ways of achieving prosperity. Later the mainstream view changed completely, and it now emphasizes the market and integration in the world economy. Ideas and events alike have contributed to this remarkable transformation.[1]

The Postwar Dirigiste Dogma: Origins and Effects

The postwar story must begin with the long shadow the Great Depression cast on the minds of theorists and practitioners of economic development. The collapse of world trade and the drastic decline in the prices of primary products such as sugar, tin, peanuts, and iron ore fed a postwar export pessimism, which became the dominant assumption underlying the early theories of economic development. The interwar collapse of the international capital market, which had funnelled essential finance to the Third World through the relatively impersonal and arm's-length bond market, led to widespread default and the imposition by the United States of "blue sky" laws that prevented American financial intermediaries

---

Deepak Lal is the James S. Coleman Professor of International Development Studies at the University of California, Los Angeles. This chapter is an expanded version of an article written for the Bretton Woods Commission on the future of the Bretton Woods institutions (Lal 1994d) and updates Lal (1983).

[1]Lal (1992) collects the major readings on the subject that have appeared as journal articles. Comprehensive surveys are found in Chenery and Srinivasan (1988, 1989) and Meier (1989).

from holding foreign government bonds. In Europe exchange controls closed capital markets to the Third World—in Britain until 1979. It seemed natural therefore to assume that neither foreign trade nor foreign capital could fuel growth in the Third World, as they had done in the great worldwide boom of the mid-19th century, by providing an expanding world market for Third World products and foreign finance to help produce them.

Nor did the prospects of growth through agricultural development seem bright. The continuing stagnation of the countryside in the Third World was variously ascribed to backward peasants who were not economic men, feudal patterns of landholding, and the lack of any obvious signs of technological progress in tropical agriculture. Not surprisingly, development literature of the later 1940s and 1950s is filled with various "vicious circles" of poverty and stagnation.

Finally, there was deep pessimism about the supply of domestic entrepreneurs and growing economic nationalism fuelled by the emergence of colonies into nationhood in Asia and Africa. The leaders of the new countries sought to build nation-states out of the welter of groups with conflicting loyalties by extending the scope of the government's control over economic activity. This motive was similar to that which led many princes in post-Renaissance Europe to erect mercantilist systems of economic controls for nation-building (Heckscher 1955, Lal and Myint 1996).

The panaceas economists proposed to break out of the vicious circles concentrated on removing the limits of: (1) domestic demand (foreign demand was assumed to be price- and income-inelastic because of pessimism about foreign trade); (2) the low level of domestic savings (because of widespread poverty), which could no longer be supplemented by private foreign capital inflows, and (3) domestic entrepreneurship.

The stage was set for dirigiste policies that sought to deal with these dilemmas of development through a statist strategy of import-substituting industrialization. Agriculture, it was hoped, would eventually prosper from the backwash effects of industrialization, including the transfer to industry of most of the surplus labor purported to exist in agriculture. Some hope was placed on land reforms as a means of improving both efficiency and equality in Third World agriculture. In the interim, however, besides providing a perfectly elastic supply of labor, agriculture would continue to be the major source of foreign exchange (however limited because of inelastic world demand for primary products) and of savings required for industrialization. In accumulating savings for industrialization a colonial instrument, the marketing board, proved provident. Colonial governments had set up marketing boards in Africa and Asia to stabilize farmers' incomes by offering stable domestic prices for agricultural goods, in contrast to the unstable prices in world markets. As time went on, governments increasingly used marketing boards to tax agriculture by reducing average domestic prices paid to farmers below average world prices.

This direct tax on agriculture was supplemented by indirect taxes such as import controls and exchange controls to husband foreign exchange for "essential" purposes. The controls substantially raised the effective protection to domestic producers of industrial products. All users of industrial goods, in particular agriculture, bore the tax burden. The controls were usually formulated and justified in the framework of a Five-Year Plan, mimicking the instrument that many thought explained the successful transformation of the Soviet Union from a backward stagnant economy into an industrial giant. Soviet experience also provided a justification for the bias towards heavy industry that came into favor. If foreign exchange is limited because of inelastic world demand, so its supply cannot be increased by producing more or devaluing, and if imports are essential inputs in domestic production for which there are no domestic substitutes, then foreign exchange constrains economic growth independently of savings. This was the doctrine of the "foreign exchange bottleneck" (Chenery and Strout 1966, McKinnon 1964). Stalin's Soviet Union had faced a similar problem, less due to economics than to the politics of a trade embargo. A young Soviet theorist (G. A. Feldman) provided the solution to the bottleneck: foreign exchange should be used to only import essential raw materials, while the country produced domestically all the required industrial inputs, including heavy machinery. Stalin accepted the message but shot the messenger! Much later an Indian physicist (P. C. Mahalanobis) rediscovered the same model and provided the rationale for India's Second Five-Year Plan. The Indian plan epitomized the planning strategy characteristic of development economics until the mid-1960s (Bronfenbrenner 1960).

Apart from import and exchange controls, the instruments for implementing plans of this sort were industrial licensing, price controls, and state enterprises. Typically the plans were based on input-output tables that assumed that, for technological reasons, inputs were required in fixed proportions. The tables began with a desired rate of growth of aggregate consumption and derived from it the quantities of different commodities required in fixed proportions as inputs for production or outputs for consumption. Governments sought to legislate production of the outputs through a panoply of controls and state provision of goods that the private sector was considered unlikely to produce in the requisite amounts.

Planned, balanced growth of commodities was supposed to overcome the foreign-exchange bottleneck as well as the limitations of domestic markets. But some theorists argued for a policy of unbalanced growth, based on a Big Push in industrialization under state aegis, because of the purported indivisibilities and strategic complementarities in investment in much of modern industry (Hirschman 1958). Arguments for a Big Push were particularly persuasive in economies with abundant land and natural resources, such as Brazil and many other Latin American countries. But it was usually impossible for governments to obtain the resources required for a Big Push through normal taxation. They resorted to a combination of foreign borrowing and inflationary domestic financing, hoping to generate forced savings through levying the inflation tax.

Finally, foreign aid played an important role in the "policy package." Foreign aid was supposed to be doubly important. Besides supplementing meager domestic savings and meager foreign private investment, foreign aid provided the foreign exchange to break the foreign-exchange bottleneck. By contrast, the major form of private flows, direct foreign investment by multinational corporations, was discouraged except in so-called priority sectors because of fears it might engender a new colonialism.

The Neoclassical Resurgence

A few small countries on the Pacific Rim without much land or natural resources began to break away from this dirigiste consensus from the mid-1960s. Based more on pragmatism than theory, South Korea, Taiwan, Singapore, and Hong Kong (the Four Tigers) discovered that their domestic markets were too small to support policies of planned autarkic "balanced" growth. Moreover, their only resource was their people. They adopted "outward-oriented" development policies centered on promoting labor-intensive manufactured exports. They did so by allowing exporters (but not necessarily importers) to operate under conditions of virtual free trade (Little et al. 1970).

The results were stupendous. The Four Tigers achieved unprecedented growth rates of income and employment, based on explosive growth of exports. This belied the "export pessimism" which underlay conventional wisdom and its belief in the foreign-exchange bottleneck.

Remarkably, under U.S. leadership the West in a fairly short period of time succeeded in erecting a second great liberal economic order. Western governments progressively freed foreign trade from the controls and tariffs of the 1930s. They liberalized capital flows as the seeming success of the Bretton Woods system kept exchange rates fairly stable. The liberalization of Western trade and payments led to explosive growth in world trade and unprecedented rates of growth of world output.

The Four Tigers were the first group of countries to ride the wave of expansionary growth, but toward the late 1960s many other countries were beginning to follow. This was due to events and theoretical developments that undercut the intellectual basis of the "old development economics."[2]

The 19th-century classical liberal order was based on the twin policies of laissez faire and free trade. But starting with John Stuart Mill the arguments against laissez faire multiplied, as economists and politicians identified various forms of market failure that required government action. Starting with Alexander Hamilton and Friedrich List various arguments for protection, especially for protecting infant industries, also evolved. By the 1950s it seemed that neither laissez faire nor free trade had any intellectual justification in promoting economic development.

The modern (post-1950) theory of trade and welfare separated the case for free trade from the case for laissez faire. It demonstrated that most arguments for protection relied on the existence of some

[2]The seminal works in developing the new theory of trade and welfare were Meade (1955), Haberler (1950), Johnson (1965), and Bhagwati and Ramaswami (1966).

distortion in the working of the *domestic* price mechanism. The infant industry argument assumed that either the market interest rate used to determine the net present value of investment projects was much higher than the social cost of capital, or that there were externalities in labor training and dynamic economies of learning by doing (Baldwin 1969). The modern theory of trade and welfare demonstrated that while "domestic distortions" required government action, and hence a departure from laissez faire, restricting foreign trade was not the best way to deal with them, and could actually lead to lower welfare than doing nothing. The best way to deal with domestic distortions was to remove them by some suitable domestic tax-subsidy scheme that did not discriminate among goods and services by origin.

The intellectual case against protection was strongly buttressed by the disappointing results of the trade and industrial controls that were ubiquitous in the Third World by the early 1960s. In the postwar Golden Age the overall growth performance of most developing countries was respectable, but it was not as good or of the sort that theorists and policymakers had expected. Most developing countries substantially raised their domestic savings rates, and hence their investment rates, but there was wide variation in the efficiency of investment and resulting differences in growth rates. The differences in efficiency were moreover increasingly recognized to result from the dirigiste system of trade, industrial, and price controls, and the disappointing performance of state enterprises. Worse from the planner's viewpoint, actual industrial production diverged widely from planned production, because there was little relationship between the pattern of nominal protection designed to implement economic plans and the pattern of effective protection that resulted (Corden 1966). The pattern of effective protection usually had lower and sometimes negative effective rates on exportable commodities. That reduced their relative profitability and meant that export growth was not as high as it could have been. Chronic balance-of-payments problems were the result.

The pattern of effective protection also discriminated against agriculture. Agricultural growth was much lower than was feasible. By the late 1960s the "Green Revolution" made possible a large increase in the output of cereals where an assured water supply was present. Nor was it possible to argue that peasants were noneconomic men, when they reacted to the tax squeeze on agriculture (through the marketing boards, overvalued exchange rates that hurt exports, and industrial protection) by reducing agricultural supply, just as Western farmers would have done. Thus for example cocoa output and exports, and with it Ghana's output and incomes, collapsed as a result of Kwame Nkrumah's dirigiste policies.

Most heinous was the bias against employment that the dirigiste policy package entailed. The bias resulted from discrimination against labor-intensive agriculture and manufactured exports. Populations burgeoned in the Third World as death rates fell with the spread of modern medicine and sanitation. The resulting increase in the labor supply met the less than adequate increase in labor demand, leading to stagnant wage levels and the growth of what was labelled the urban "informal sector." Industrial wages, particularly in state enterprises, were set above market-clearing levels, inducing large migration from the country side to cities and underemployment of the "search" variety, whose physical manifestation was the slums that arose in many Third World cities (Harris and Todaro 1970).

The persistence of widespread poverty, despite seemingly respectable growth rates of output till the late 1960s, led many international agencies to advocate more direct attacks on poverty. One agency advocated redistribution with growth, another a "basic needs" program modelled on Western welfare states (Chenery et al. 1974, International Labour Organisation 1976). In primarily rural countries the major asset is land, so land redistribution was a major part of proposed programs of poverty alleviation. An empirical finding across many countries was that the productivity of land declined with the size of landholding (Berry and Cline 1979). Though this has been questioned more recently (Bhalla and Roy 1988), it provided the basis for promoting an agrarian structure which would promote *both* equity and efficiency by breaking up large farms into small family farms. Apart from Korea and Taiwan, which made land reforms under American tutelage soon after the Second World War, few other countries garnered the requisite political support for such reforms. Some, however, like Tanzania and China, did have the means, but their preferred agrarian structure based on their socialist ideology was the collective farm. Both attempts at collectivization ended in tears, with the implosion of the Tanzanian economy following "ujaamization," and the biggest famine in human history (estimated to have cost nearly 25 million lives) in China after it established its communes. Both disasters arose from the perverse incentives faced by peasants on collective farms (Collier et al. 1986, Lin 1990).

Meanwhile, the availability of Green Revolution technology and the partial removal of price incentives against agriculture led to rapid increases in agricultural output and income, to the surprise of many development economists. As much of this growth was labor-intensive, it benefitted the bulk of the poorest—those in rural areas, whose only asset was their labor—as real wages rose (Lipton and Longhurst 1989). Many countries also began to remove incentives against manufactured exports. This increased employment and the incomes of the poorest (Krueger 1983, Squire 1981). Gradually, promoting efficient labor-intensive growth through "getting prices right" was recognized as the most important means of alleviating poverty in the Third World.

At the same time, many countries went through the so-called demographic transition (Birdsall 1989). With birth rates declining after a lag with death rates, this meant that the fear of unbounded population growth in poor countries was also unfounded (Simon 1977, 1981).

Commodity Power, the Debt Crisis, and Structural Adjustment

Not everyone was convinced by these arguments and events. There was one last attempt at promoting dirigisme, this time at the international level, before the conversion to the market became ubiquitous in the 1980s.

The oil price rise of 1973 brought the postwar Golden Age to an end. Through the reactions it promoted, it also led to the final breakdown of dirigisme in the Third World. But initially, many in the Third World hailed OPEC as showing the route toward commodity power, and showing how to effect a massive transfer of resources from rich to poor countries. Third World countries demanded a new international economic order (NIEO), a world planned economy entailing massive international redistribution of income (Lal 1994a).

It has been known since John Stuart Mill that if a country has monopoly or monopsony power in its foreign trade, in the absence of foreign retaliation it can garner more of the gains from trade by levying a so-called optimum tariff to turn the terms of trade in its favor. This is what OPEC in effect did. Many other developing countries sought to do the same. Commodity power seemed to be the new Third World weapon in its ongoing skirmishes with the West. But as Alfred Marshall had noted, even though the elasticities of demand and supply for many traded goods were likely to be low in the short run, they were likely to be high in the long run. The massive rise in the price of oil promoted successful substitution through various conservation measures, and increased the returns from extending exploration, so that known reserves rose. Compared to oil, the elasticities of demand and supply for most other primary commodities were even higher. Nothing came of commodity power; its death knell was the decline in the real price of oil in the 1980s.

An enduring myth that fuelled NIEO, and the program for raising the prices of commodities formulated by the United Nations Commission on Trade and Development (UNCTAD) was the belief that the terms of trade between primary commodities and manufactures would inexorably decline (Singer 1950, Prebisch 1959). That implied that if developing countries kept relying on primary commodities as their main exports they would grow poorer relative to industrialized countries. Suffice it to say that as far as the *income* terms of trade of developing countries are concerned there is no such tendency (Grilli and Yang 1988). With the eventual collapse at most attempts at rigging international commodity markets (the latest being the collapse of the International Tin Agreement) the commodities issue seems dead, at least for the time being.

The 1973 OPEC price shock, however, also led to a large transfer of resources from oil-importing countries to OPEC members, whose ability to absorb the resultant foreign-exchange accruals in their domestic economies was limited. They had to find a home for this new-found wealth. They deposited much of it in Western banks, particularly in the offshore subsidiaries of those banks that formed the Eurodollar market. With the deflationary impulse transmitted by this transfer of resources from countries with low to high savings propensities, cries for recycling the OPEC surplus became clamorous. The banks obliged. The beneficiaries were Third World countries, particularly in Latin America, that had problems financing their budgets. They now found a new source of borrowing, at negative real interest rates! The seeds of the debt crisis were sown.

With the attempts to deal with the stagflation of the 1970s deriving from the oil price rise, there was a general tightening of macroeconomic policy in the West in the late 1970s. The resulting slowdown in world demand and rise in world interest rates dealt a double blow to the governments of heavily indebted countries. They had borrowed at floating interest rates themselves and had guaranteed loans by state enterprises and even the private sector. As real interest rates rose to new heights, to finance the large increase in debt service governments needed to raise the fiscal resources and to convert them into foreign exchange. Some countries, mainly in East Asia, managed this transfer problem in textbook fashion. They were helped by the capacity of their economies to convert domestic resources into foreign exchange because of their past outward-oriented trade policies, and because they had established viable fiscal systems. Many debtor countries in Latin America and Africa had neither attribute. The debt crisis created an acute fiscal crisis for them, often reflected in acute inflation. Given their past neglect of exports, the only way to obtain the necessary balance of trade surplus was through import compression, which in turn led to domestic recession. To deal with these joint fiscal, foreign debt, and balance-of-payments crises, they undertook economic liberalization, most often under the aegis of the World Bank and the International Monetary Fund (IMF).

The Revival of Classical Political Economy

World Bank structural adjustment programs and IMF stabilization programs increasingly embodied the intellectual consensus that emerged in the early 1980s in favor of markets against the plan. The final nail in the coffin of the "old development economics" was the realization, in theory and practice, of the immense corruption that a system of controls engenders. Some forms of corruption are a form of arbitrage, and aid efficiency, albeit illegally. However, the unproductive scramble for the valuable licenses on which the Permit Raj was based led to additional losses of economic welfare. An import quota, for example, is a license to print money for the lucky beneficiary, who can tax consumers by pocketing the difference between the price at which he imports the good and the higher domestic price at which he can sell it because of the quota restrictions. "Rent seekers" will tend to spend an amount equal to the total rent from the import quota, in the form of time and money (waiting in queues, lobbying, and bribery). Thus in addition to the loss consumers suffer from the higher price of the good, there will be a deadweight loss equal to the whole of the quota rents, as if the equivalent resources had been dumped into the sea (Tullock 1967, Krueger 1974).

Once it is recognized that, with the politicization of economic life, dirigisme necessarily breeds rent-seeking and its attendant losses, many of the prescriptions of so-called public economics, which supposedly provides the grammar of arguments for rational public intervention, also fall by the wayside. We have seen how the modern theory of trade and welfare argues for maintaining free trade but abandoning laissez faire. It recommends dealing with various domestic distortions through domestic tax-subsidies. But domestic subsidies will be subject to rent-seeking as much as tariffs and quotas. In that case the twin classical prescriptions of free trade and laissez faire seem the only workable ones to promote economic development (Lal 1994b).

As the classical economists were the first to point out, this does not imply anarchy or a neutered state. As Mill stated clearly in the textbook whose policy prescription remained the orthodoxy for half a century, the state has to provide the essential public goods (law and order, defense, a sound currency) and various merit goods (education, possibly health, and a social safety net to alleviate the poverty of the "deserving poor"). Beyond that, economic activities are best left to private agents. This is very much the conventional wisdom of the 1990s for promoting economic development.

The prescriptions of the classical economists were based on economics and on an understanding of the eternal dilemmas of politics. The most important change in thinking on economic policy in the Third World has been the recognition that the assumptions about the nature of the state that underpinned planning are unrealistic. It was implicitly assumed that the state was benevolent, omniscient, and omnipotent. Outside communist countries, any belief about the state's omnipotence was quickly shattered. Its omniscience is increasingly in doubt as planners have often shown a lack of foresight that would have swiftly bankrupted a private agent. But the assumption that the state, whether democratic or authoritarian, is a committee of benevolent Platonic Guardians has been more tenacious.

The so-called new political economy of recent decades, which resurrects the ideas of David Hume and Adam Smith, makes a more clear-headed appraisal of the motives of the state. Though there are some Platonic Guardian states or elements of it within most, many states are better viewed as being self-interested, even predatory. This realization has led to the search for a policy package serving the interests of the prey rather than the predator. A predatory state is interested above all in discretionary resources and hence will seek to maximize its revenues. The interests of the prey are to provide only enough revenues to finance the essential public goods. How to reconcile the differing ends remains controversial (Findlay 1990; Lal 1988, 1993).

There is more agreement on how to reverse the past dirigisme of the Second and Third worlds. Above all, it is essential to establish macroeconomic balance, ideally through a monetary constitution that prohibits any future levying of the inflation tax. The other components of the policy package include, first, converting import quotas into tariff equivalents, then gradually moving towards a low uniform tariff, ultimately as close to zero as possible. Second, removing price controls and all forms of industrial licensing. Third, liberalizing domestic capital markets by removing interest rate ceilings and centrally planned direction of credit. Fourth, removing exchange controls and maintaining realistic exchange rates. Fifth, privatizing state enterprises, not merely on grounds of efficiency, but on those of political economy: removing the State from areas where it has no role and to allow it to concentrate on the things only it can do.

As it is hard to undertake all these reforms simultaneously, lively but inconclusive debate continues about the appropriate sequencing of reforms (see Edwards 1984, 1992; Funke 1992; Lal 1993; Sell 1988).

The Political Economy of Reform

One lesson from past experience is, however, of importance. In reform, time may be of the essence. This is linked to the question of why self-interested predatory states, who have benefitted from their past dirigisme, should suddenly want to liberalize and serve the general weal. Here the parallel with the liberalization of the mercantilist "ancien regimes" in the late 18th and 19th centuries is instructive.

One unintended consequence of past mercantilism and contemporary neomercantilism is that, while both were motivated by the desire to establish "order" and thence "nations" by expanding the scope of government control, after a certain stage increased dirigisme bred disorder. As economic controls become onerous, people attempt to escape them through various forms of avoidance and evasion. This has a devastating effect on the state's fiscal base. The first sign of an impending crisis is fiscal, with the accompanying un-Marxian "withering away of the state." It is to regain control over what seem to have become ungovernable economies that economic liberalization is undertaken, to restore the fiscal base and government control. Once this crisis of the state seems to be manageable, there is no further incentive for the predatory state to continue with liberalization.

This suggests that a "crisis" provides an opportunity for liberalizers, but it may be short. A big bang may therefore be desirable to smash the equilibrium of rent-seeking interest groups who have a stake in maintaining the past system of dirigisme. To stiffen the government's spine in this unenviable task, sweeteners to ease its fiscal problems, in the form of soft loans or grants from multilateral and bilateral foreign governments, may be desirable. Beyond that the role of foreign assistance seems limited.

Good Governance

But it is still an open question whether once a market economy is established, it can be maintained against the unavoidable political pressures to subvert it. The sad fate of many constitutions shows how fragile a corset they are in constraining a predatory state. A political culture that internalizes classical liberal virtues may be a better bulwark. Questions concerning the appropriate institutions to create and foster the requisite character and culture have therefore come to the fore of the current debates on development.

As it is human to think that one's own "habits of the heart" are ideal, it is not surprising that the West is now promoting Western democracy in the Third World as the means of ensuring the good governance now generally recognized to be a prerequisite for economic development. Whatever the moral virtues of democracy, historical evidence does not support any necessary connection between democracy and prosperity. Even in the rocky transition from the plan to the market, as the contrasting experience of Russia and China shows, *glasnost* may not help *perestroika.*

The characteristics of good government are more important than its particular form. On this issue Hume and Smith remain relevant. While upholding benevolence as the primary virtue, they also recognized its scarcity. Fortunately, as Smith showed, a market economy that promotes "opulence" does not depend on benevolence for its functioning. It only requires a vast number of people, even without personal relationships, to deal and live together without violating the "laws of justice." The resulting commercial society promotes some virtues—hard work, prudence, thrift—which because they benefit the agent rather than others are inferior to altruism. But unintentionally these lower-level virtues do help other people by promoting general prosperity, and the resulting society is neither immoral nor amoral. Thus a good government is one that promotes "opulence" through a policy of preserving "natural liberty" by establishing laws of justice which guarantee free exchange and peaceful competition, leaving the improvement of morality to institutions outside the government. It would be inappropriate for the state to legislate morality.

The classical-liberal view of *civil association* sees the state as the custodian of laws that do not seek to impose any preferred pattern of ends (including abstractions such as the general welfare, or fundamental rights), but that merely facilitate individuals to pursue their own ends. A rival conception of society as an *enterprise association* sees the state as the manager of an enterprise seeking to use the law for its own substantive purposes, and in particular for the legislation of morality. As the British philosopher Michael Oakeshott has shown, both conceptions of the state have deep roots in Western thought, going back to ancient Greece in one case and the Judaeo-Christian tradition in the other (Oakeshott 1975, 1993).

Socialism is the major secular embodiment of society viewed as an enterprise association, with its desire to use the power of the state to equalize people. The demise of socialist economies does not mean the socialist impulse is dead, least of all in the First World. It continues to infect the design of an appropriate social safety net to protect the "poor." In combination with democratic politics it remains a continuing threat to the sustainability of a market order and to the classical-liberal view of civil society.

Welfare States for the Third World?

It is not surprising, therefore, that with the seeming victory of the market over the plan, the dirigiste bands have consolidated under the banner of "adjustment with a human face." They now seek to create Western-style welfare states in the Third and Second worlds.

But the Western welfare state is itself in trouble because of the dynamic costs of its inevitable enlargement in majoritarian democracies. Under factional pressures, politicians bid for votes by offering transfers of income to some sections of the populace at the expense of others. With the inevitable "universalization" of benefits, the middle class capture of the welfare state comes about, with a tendency for *net* transfers of income from the rich and the poor to the middle class. The same tendency occurs in developing countries such as Uruguay, Costa Rica, Sri Lanka, and Jamaica, which under the factional pressures of majoritarian democracy created and expanded their welfare states (Lal and Myint 1996). They financed benefits by taxing their major primary products. During booms in prices of primary products, tax revenues increased and political pressures led government to establish entitlements they could not repudiate when revenues fell during downturns. They increased taxes on primary products still further to close the fiscal gap, retarding growth and productivity in primary products and in some cases killing the goose that laid the golden egg.

Similar fiscal pressures have attended the universalization of benefits in Western economies (Lal 1994a). Political entitlements (mainly pensions and health care) whose extent depends more on demography than the state of the economy impose a growing tax burden that discourages productivity and growth. The reform of the welfare state is therefore at the forefront of public policy debates in the First World, just when many are seeking to establish or expand welfare states in the Third World.

Nevertheless, many classical liberals have recognized a role for the state in alleviating the inevitable vagaries of life and the persistent poverty of those incapable of earning a living. No ideal means are available to achieve this end. Ideally benefits should be targeted. But apart from the well-known perverse incentives this creates for the "able-bodied" poor, there will also be a tendency for them to be made universal in democracies. It is not surprising therefore that the most efficient poverty-redressal programs in the Third World have been in Pinochet's Chile and Lee Kwan Yew's Singapore (Casteneda 1992, Findlay and Wellisz 1993).

To overcome problems of moral hazard, adverse selection, and monitoring in relation to income transfers, there is fresh interest in using private associations (on the lines of British mutual aid friendly societies of the 19th century) for dealing with poverty caused by risks that could in principle be insured against (Green 1993). The task of dealing with the "deserving poor" could be devolved to private charities, possibly supplemented from the public purse on a matching basis. Using non-governmental organizations (NGOs) to deal with intractable problems of low-end poverty can also be a way of restoring civil association from the depredations it has suffered from the state as an enterprise association to alleviate poverty (Lal 1994c).

But the current flurry of interest in decentralizing and privatizing many of the tasks the state has taken on itself must be viewed with caution. Historically among the major NGOs involved in alleviating poverty have been churches. But whether in its Judaeo-Christian or Islamic form, these monotheistic, revelatory religious institutions have been at odds with the liberal notion of civil association. Churches have themselves been enterprise associations, which every so often have also sought to convert the state into one (a theocracy). It is debatable whether friends of the market should seek through public subsidy to strengthen an institution that historically has been, and in some cases continues to be, an enemy of the market. But there may be a case for using secular NGOs in servicing the poor.

Culture and Development

No form of government or agency for promoting good government is ideal. Ultimately, these forms are likely to be less important than the existing habits of a people (including habits that may evolve with modernization and industrialization). But habits relate to questions of character and culture. It is by no means self-evident, as the previous discussion has emphasized, that Western democracy necessarily promotes a market-friendly culture. Its uneasy tension between the rival notions of the state—as a civil association and as an enterprise association—can lead to decadence in private habits, which some have identified as a feature of many contemporary Western societies. By substituting public benevolence for private benevolence, the transfer state saps private benevolence, the highest private moral virtue for classical liberals. But every turn toward making the state an enterprise association saps the lower-level "vigorous virtues" of productivity, thrift, and self-reliance that classical liberals see as underpinning the market and "opulence" (Letwin 1992).

The Western impulse toward creating a state as an enterprise association has religious roots. But there are religions that have never sought to legislate morality. Hinduism and Confucianism, for instance, are ways of life (cultures rather than religions). They lack the centralized institutions of the various Christian or Islamic churches seeking to capture the state to serve their own substantive ends. They can provide the cultural sustenance for promoting the vigorous virtues, and unlike their Semitic counterparts, have done so without subverting the state as a civil association. Where the plan has replaced the market in the countries of these cultures, it is because the state has been captured by elites infected with the secular Western virus which views the state as an enterprise, whether it be Fabian socialism in India or Marxism in China.

Once it is realized that Western culture and Western forms of government have had an uneasy tension between the state as a civil association and as an enterprise association, mirrored in swings from market to plan to market, it is evident that merely transferring Western forms of governance and their attendant ideology is as unlikely to secure the market economy in the Third World as it is in the First World. It would be sheer arrogance to deny that there may be other cultures equally or even more compatible with the Western classical-liberal vision of the state as a civil association. The classical-liberal vision provides the general political underpinning but not necessarily a particular form of government to perpetuate the market economy.

Beyond this little can be said, for with the increasing compartmentalization of the social sciences, speculation and research on grand themes of culture and development undertaken by social scientists such as Alexis de Tocqueville and Max Weber has sadly atrophied. A revival of this grand tradition is a precondition for thinking sensibly about these unsettled questions concerning economic transformation and development.

References

Baldwin, R.E. "The Case against Infant-Industry Tariff Protection." *Journal of Political Economy* 77 (2) (1969): 295–305.

Berry, R.A., and Cline, W.R., eds. *Agrarian Structure and Productivity in Developing Countries.* Baltimore: Johns Hopkins University Press, 1979.

Bhagwati, Jagdish N. *Anatomy and Consequences of Trade Control Regimes.* Cambridge, Massachusetts: Ballinger for National Bureau of Economic Research, 1979.

Bhagwati, Jagdish N., and Ramaswami, V.K. "Domestic Distortions, Tariffs and the Theory of Optimum Subsidy." *Journal of Political Economy* 71 (1) (1966): 44–50.

Bhalla, S., and Roy, P. "Mis-Specification in Farm Productivity Analysis: The Role of Land Quality." *Oxford Economic Papers* 40 (1) (1988): 55–73.

Birdsall, Nancy. "Economic Analyses of Rapid Population Growth." *World Bank Research Observer* 4 (1) (1989): 23–50.

Bronfenbrenner, Martin. "A Simplified Mahalanobis Development Model." *Economic Development and Cultural Change* 9 (1) (1960): 45–51.

Castaneda, T. *Combating Poverty.* San Francisco: ICS Press, 1992.

Chenery, H.; Ahluwalia, M; Bell, C.L.G.; Duloy, J.H.; and Jolly, R. *Redistribution With Growth.* New York: Oxford University Press, 1974.

Chenery, H., and Srinivasan, T.N., eds. *Handbook of Development Economics,* vols. 1–2. Amsterdam: North-Holland, 1988, 1989.

Chenery, H., and Strout, A.M. "Foreign Assistance and Economic Development." *American Economic Review* 56 (September 1966): 679–733.

Collier, P.; Radawan, S.; and Wange, S. *Labour and Poverty in Rural Tanzania.* Oxford: Clarendon Press, 1986.

Corden, W. Max. "The Structure of a Tariff System and the Effective Protective Rate." *Journal of Political Economy* 74 (3) (1966): 221–37.

Edwards, Sebastian. "The Order of Liberalization of the External Sector in Developing Countries." Essays in International Finance 156. Princeton: Princeton University Press, 1984.

Edwards, Sebastian. *The Sequencing of Structural Adjustment and Stabilization.* Occasional Paper 34. San Francisco: International Center for Economic Growth, 1992.

Findlay, R. "The New Political Economy: Its Explanatory Power for LDCs." *Economics and Politics* 2 (2) (1990): 193–221.

Findlay, R., and Wellisz, S. *The Political Economy of Poverty, Equity and Growth: Five Small Open Economies.* Oxford: Oxford University Press, 1993.

Funke, N. "Timing and Sequencing of Reforms: Competing Views." Working Paper 552, Kiel Institute of World Economics, 1992.

Green, David. *Reinventing Civil Society: The Rediscovery of Welfare Without Politics.* Choice in Welfare Series 17. London: Health and Welfare Unit, Institute of Economic Affairs, 1993.

Grilli, E.R., and Yang, M.C. "Primary Commodity Prices, Manufactured Goods Prices, and the Terms of Trade of Developing Countries: What the Long Run Shows." *World Bank Research Observer* 2 (1) (1988): 1–47.

Haberler, Gottfried. "Some Problems in the Pure Theory of International Trade." *Economic Journal* 40 (June 1950): 223–44.

Harris, J., and Todaro, M. "Migration, Unemployment and Development: A Two Sector Analysis." *American Economic Review* 40 (March 1970): 126–42.

Heckscher, Eli. *Mercantilism*. 2d ed. London: Allen and Unwin, 1955.

Hirschman, Albert O. *The Strategy of Economic Development*. New Haven: Yale University Press, 1958.

International Labour Organisation. *Employment, Growth and Basic Needs*. Geneva: International Labour Organisation, 1976.

Johnson, Harry G. "Optimal Trade Intervention in the Presence of Domestic Distortions." In *Trade, Growth and the Balance of Payments: Essays in Honor of Gottfried Haberler*. Edited by R.E. Baldwin et al. Chicago: Rand McNally, 1965.

Krueger, Anne O. "The Political Economy of the Rent-Seeking Society." *American Economic Review* 44 (1974): 291–303.

Krueger, Anne O. *Trade and Employment in Developing Countries: Synthesis and Conclusions*. Chicago: University of Chicago Press, 1983.

Lal, Deepak. *The Poverty of "Development Economics."* Cambridge, Massachusetts: Harvard University Press, 1983.

Lal, Deepak. *The Hindu Equilibrium*, vol. 1. Oxford: Clarendon Press, 1988.

Lal, Deepak, ed. *Development Economics*, 4 vols. Aldershot, England: Edward Elgar, 1992.

Lal, Deepak. *The Repressed Economy: Causes, Consequences, Reform*. Aldershot, England: Edward Elgar, 1993.

Lal, Deepak. *Against Dirigisme*. San Francisco: International Center for Economic Growth, 1994a.

Lal, Deepak. "In Praise of the Classics." In *From Classical Economics to Development Economics*, pp. 28–50. Edited by Gerald Meier. New York: St. Martin's Press, 1994b.

Lal, Deepak. "Poverty and Development." In *The Ethical Foundations of the Market Economy*, pp. 147–73. Edited by Horst Siebert. Tuebingen: J.C.B. Mohr, 1994c.

Lal, Deepak. "From Plan to Market: Post-War Evolution of Thought on Economic Transformation and Development." In *Bretton Woods: Looking to the Future*, pp. C57–66. Washington: Bretton Woods Commission, 1994d.

Lal, Deepak, and Myint, Hla. *The Political Economy of Poverty, Equity and Growth: A Comparative Study*. Oxford: Clarendon Press, 1996.

Letwin, Shirley. *The Anatomy of Thatcherism*. London: Fontana, 1992.

Lin, Justin Y. "Collectivisation and China's Agricultural Crisis in 1959–61." *Journal of Political Economy* 98 (1990): 228–52.

Lipton, M., and Longhurst, R. *New Seeds and Poor People*. London: Unwin Hyman, 1989.

Little, Ian M.D.; Scitovsky, Tibor; and Scott, M.F. *Industry and Trade in Some Developing Countries*. Oxford: Oxford University Press, 1970.

McKinnon, Ronald. "Foreign Exchange Constraints in Economic Development." *Economic Journal* 74 (June 1964): 308–409.

Meade, James E. *Trade and Welfare*. Oxford: Oxford University Press, 1955.

Meier, Gerald. *Leading Issues in Economic Development*. 5th ed. Oxford: Oxford University Press, 1989.

Oakeshott, Michael. *On Human Conduct*. Oxford: Clarendon Press, 1975.

Oakeshott, Michael. *Morality and Politics in Modern Europe*. New Haven: Yale University Press, 1993.

Prebisch, Raul. "Commercial Policy in Underdeveloped Countries." *American Economic Review* 49(2) (May 1959): 251–73.

Sell, F. "True Exposure: The Analysis of Trade Liberalization in a General Equilibrium Framework." *Welwirtschaftliches Archiv* 124 (4) (1988).

Simon, Julian L. *The Economics of Population Growth*. Princeton: Princeton University Press, 1977.

Simon, Julian L. *The Ultimate Resource*. Princeton: Princeton University Press, 1981.

Singer, H. "The Distribution of Gains Between Borrowing and Investing Countries." *American Economic Review* 11 (May 1950): 473–85.

Squire, L. *Employment Policy in Developing Countries: A Survey of Issues and Evidence*. Baltimore: Johns Hopkins University Press, 1981.

Tullock, Gordon. "Welfare Costs of Tariffs, Monopolies and Theft." *Western Economic Journal* 5 (June 1967): 224–32.

5. Is Population Growth a Drag on Economic Development?

Julian L. Simon

This is the economic history of humanity in a nutshell: From 2 million or 200,000 or 20,000 or 2,000 years ago until the 18th century there was slow growth in population, almost no increase in health or decrease in mortality, slow growth in the availability of natural resources (but not increased scarcity), increase in wealth for a few, and mixed effects on the environment. Since then there has been rapid growth in population due to spectacular decreases in the death rate, rapid growth in resources, widespread increases in wealth, and an unprecedentedly clean and beautiful living environment in many parts of the world along with a degraded environment in the poor and socialist parts of the world.

That is, more people and more wealth have correlated with more (rather than less) resources and a cleaner environment—just the opposite of what Malthusian theory leads one to believe (see Simon 1994, 1995).

Misguided Attention

For many years until recently, it was thought by development economists that population growth is a drag on economic development in poor countries. And even after a considerable shift in professional opinion in the 1980s, population growth is commonly believed to hinder development.

In accord with the earlier professional opinion, since the early 1960s official institutions such as the U.S. State Department's Agency

---

Julian Simon is Professor of Business Administration at the University of Maryland. This chapter draws on a variety of his other writings that have touched on the subject at hand, especially Simon (1985a, 1985b). He thanks James Dorn, David Boaz, and Theordore W. Schultz for their comments and Stephen Moore who helped prepare the tabular material.

for International Development (AID), the World Bank, and the United Nations' Fund for Population Activities (UNFPA) have acted on the assumption that population growth is the key determinant of economic development. This belief has misdirected attention away from the central factor in a country's economic development: its economic and political system. This misplaced attention has resulted in unsound economic advice being given to developing nations. It also has caused (or allowed) the misdiagnosis of such world development problems as supplies of natural resources, starving children, illiteracy, pollution, and slow growth.

Since the 1970s the U.S. government directly and indirectly has been spending hundreds of milions of dollars annually in foreign assistance for family planning and other programs aimed at slowing population growth in the poorer countries. Not only could those funds have been put to other purposes, but in some cases, the population control programs funded by U.S. taxpayers have involved coercive policies designed to reduce birth rates in LDCs.

One reason that population growth has been viewed as a malefactor is that poor countries tend to have a high birth rate. It seems "common sense" that if fewer babies were born, there would be more of the supposedly fixed quantities of food and housing to go around. Furthermore, in earlier decades most economists did not have another persuasive explanation of growth and wealth. Population growth became the villain by default.

The belief that population growth slows economic development is not a wrong but harmless idea. Rather, it has been the basis for inhumane programs of coercion and the denial of personal liberty in one of the most valued choices a family can make—the number of children that it wishes to bear and raise. Also, harm has been done to the United States as a donor of foreign aid, over and beyond the funds themselves, by way of money laundered through international organizations that comes back to finance domestic population propaganda organizations (see Simon 1981, chaps. 21–22).

This paper makes two points. First, there is a persuasive explanation for why some countries grow faster than others, and the explanation has nothing to do with population growth. This factor leaves little room for population growth to be the cause of slow growth. Second, there is persuasive direct statistical evidence that population growth is not associated negatively with economic development in the short or intermediate run, and may well be a positive influence in the long run. A corollary is that a more dense population does not hamper population growth.

In the very short run, additional people are an added burden. But under conditions of freedom, population growth poses less of a problem in the short run, and brings many more benefits in the long run, than under conditions of government control.

The Role of the Socioeconomic System in Economic Progress

If there is another convincing explanation for the bulk of differences among countries in economic growth, then the likelihood that population growth is an important drag on development is logically diminished. The most powerful evidence explaining the rate of economic progress is found in the aggregate statistics which relate economic-political systems to their rates of economic growth.

Raymond Gastil categorizes the systems in his yearly publication, *Freedom in the World*. He grades each nation on three measures of liberty: political, civil, and economic. Economic liberty comprises two submeasures—the extent of government intervention in markets and the level of personal economic liberty. Gerald Scully (1988a, 1988b) related Gastil's data to economic results. Allowing for other relevant factors, he finds a strong relationship between each of the three liberty variables and the rate of economic growth during 1960 to 1980 among 115 nations. And when he folds all three measures of liberty into a single variable, he finds that nations characterized as "politically open, individual rights, and free market" had an average growth rate per capita of 2.73 percent, whereas those characterized as "politically closed, state rights, and command [economy]" had an average growth rate of 0.91 percent. This is a huge difference in performance.

Gary Becker (1989) deepens confidence in Scully's result with a study along the same lines which finds that "political democracy" is positively related to economic growth. And using somewhat different methods, Keith Marsden (1985) arrived at much the same now-solid conclusion.

Two other studies also point to a strong relation between economic freedom and economic prosperity. Bryan Johnson and Thomas Sheehy (1996) and James Gwartney, Robert Lawson, and Walter

Block (1996) offer the most comprehensive studies to date of the importance of free-market institutions for economic development.

The Chinese Experiment

The results in China's agricultural sector before and after the 1979–81 period are an important illustration of the decisive effect of the political and economic structure on economic development. Under a system of collective production where there was little incentive for farmers to work hard and take risks, but great incentive for them to loaf on the job, food production stagnated in the years before 1979. The combination of bad weather and The Great Leap Forward during the years 1959 to 1961 caused production to fall so drastically that 30 million people died of starvation. This was certainly the worst food-production performance of any country in modern times, and perhaps the worst ever.

Then the Chinese government undertook the largest and fastest social movement of all time. Within a period of three years, the 700 million people in the agricultural sector shifted from collective enterprise to individual enterprise. And since then Chinese agricultural production has skyrocketed. Per capita food production showed almost no increase from 1950 to 1978. But starting with the reform in 1979, per capita production almost doubled by 1985, a truly incredible increase, with continued growth since then and no limit in sight. Since then the visitor to China is confronted with bounteous appetizing food on every street corner, it seems, in the sharpest contrast to the situation as it was in the former Soviet Union until the 1990s and its breakup.

One may wonder whether the Chinese agricultural turnaround was "just" an isolated event, and could have other causes than the shift in social system. We may therefore consult a wider range of experience, though using prose accounts rather than statistical analysis.

Economic Stagnation under Socialism

Sven Rydenfelt (1983) analyzed the experience of 15 socialist countries on four continents and found a pervasive pattern of economic failure. However, each of these cases also can be "explained" on the basis of its individual culture rather than its socialist system.

Most vivid is the eyeball evidence. One need only have traveled by bus across the Karelian peninsula which was wholly within Finland until World War II. The part that was continuously within Finland has incomparably better roads and more modern shops and facilities than the part that was within the Soviet Union. Or compare the drive from West Berlin to East Berlin before the unification of Germany. Or the 1980's train ride from the mainland portion of Hong Kong across the border to China. The differences in favor of a free-enterprise, private-property society were literally unmistakable for all who were not entirely masked by ideological blinders. I am sure that the situation is still the same when passing from South to North Korea as of 1997.

Evidence that is both dramatic and powerful statistically arises from the unique experiment that the world's political system created following World War II. Three nations—China, Korea, and Germany—were split into socialist and nonsocialist parts, producing three pairs of countries whose members began with the same culture and language and history. The members of the pairs also had much the same standard of living when they split apart, and the same birth rates. Their subsequent histories enable us to determine the effect of economic system, because it is the only relevant variable that differs between the elements of each pair. These comparisons constitute a useful combination of scientific rigor with ease of communication and understanding.

Other than the case of Korea, which provides a continuing laboratory example to the world, the results are now in and are known to all (see Simon 1987, Simon and Moore 1990 for a full display of the data). The following standard measures of development show the huge differences in results with different socioeconomic systems.

Real Income per Capita. After World War II, China and Taiwan, North and South Korea, and East and West Germany began with roughly equal incomes per person. In each case, by the 1990s the communist country had a much lower per capita income. Taiwan's real income per capita was three or four times as high as China's; South Korea's was about twice as high as North Korea's; and West Germany's was vastly higher than East Germany's.

Differences in product quality are not reflected in the standard statistical comparisons, but are important. In East Germany the four-cylinder primitive Trabant was almost the only car one could buy.

A person had to work 3,807 hours to earn enough to purchase a Trabant, whereas in West Germany 607 hours work paid for a much better car. And people had to wait in line for 10 years to get a car in East Germany. A refrigerator required 293 hours of work in East Germany, but only 40 hours in West Germany; a suit required 67 hours of work, versus 13 hours in West Germany. Only 36 percent of housing facilities in East Germany had central heating, 60 percent an indoor toilet, and 68 percent a bath or shower. In West Germany the corresponding percentages were 70 percent, 95 percent, and 92 percent.

Life and Health. Goods only have value if one is alive to enjoy them. Concerning the number of years that a newly born person could expect to live, the free-enterprise countries did better in each pair, though each pair started out with much the same life-expectancy after World War II. The same is true of the results for infant mortality. These results are particularly interesting because public health had been one of the more-successful activities of socialized countries. And indeed, for a while the differences between the members of pairs were small. But throughout Eastern Europe, life expectancy actually fell in the last decades of the socialist experiment, and infant mortality increased. This reversal is not yet well-understood, but it certainly stemmed from a congeries of characteristics of a publicly run health system, and from the general poverty of socialized economies.

Proportion of the Labor Force in Agriculutre. The best long-run indicator of the extent of development of a society is the proportion of the labor force that is employed in agriculture. The fewer the people that are needed to feed the population, the larger the number of people that can be employed in providing other goods. The countries with freer markets—including freer labor markets and freer agriculture—needed fewer people to feed the rest.

Economic Infrastructure. The number of telephones is a good measure of the development of a country's infrastructure, and more particularly its crucial communications infrastructure. The communist countries lagged behind the development of the market-oriented countries.

These data for the paired-country experiments in political and economic systems provide evidence that is well-grounded scientifically as well as dramatic and easily understood. They prove that the socioeconomic system is the main determinant of economic growth. There is little other variation in developmental rates that might be explained by population growth.

Population Growth and Density as Influences on Development

There is a large body of scientific evidence to support the claim that population growth and density do not hamper development. The first row in Table 1 shows that in each split-country case the centrally planned communist country began with less population "pressure," as measured by density per square kilometer, compared to the paired market-directed, noncommunist country. And the communist and noncommunist countries in each pair also started with much the same birth rates and population growth rates. There is certainly no evidence here which suggests that population growth or density influences the rate of economic development.

Contrary to the idea that population growth necessarily inhibits economic growth, the free-market countries, each with faster expansion in population, experienced more rapid development—on a per capita basis—than their neighboring socialist nations. If anything, these data show that more people have a *positive* effect on development.

The most powerful evidence of the relationship between the rate of population growth and the rate of economic growth are the global correlations (see Simon 1989). There now exist perhaps a score of competent statistical studies, beginning in 1967 with an analysis by Simon Kuznets covering the few countries for which data were available over the past century, and also analyses by Kuznets (1967) and Richard Easterlin (1967) of the data covering many countries since World War II. The basic method is to gather data on each country's rate of population growth and its rate of economic growth, and then to examine whether—looking at all the data in the sample together—the countries with high population growth rates have economic growth rates lower than average, and countries with low population growth rates have economic growth rates higher than average. Various writers have used a variety of samples of countries, and they have employed an impressive battery of ingenious statistical techniques to allow for other factors that might also be affecting the outcome. The most recent, and the most comprehensive and econometrically resourceful such study ever done (Kelley and

TABLE 1
POPULATION DENSITY AND GROWTH, SELECTED COUNTRIES, 1950–83

	East Germany	West Germany	North Korea	South Korea	China	Taiwan	Hong Kong	Singa-pore	USSR	USA	India	Japan
Population per Sq. Km., 1950	171	201	76	212	57	212	2236	1759	8	16	110	224
% Change in Pop., 1950	1.2	1.1	−7.8	0.1	1.9	3.3	−10.4	4.4	1.7	1.7	1.7	1.6
% Change in Pop., 1955	−1.3	1.2	3.5	2.2	2.4	3.5	4.9	4.9	1.8	1.8	1.9	1.0
% Change in Pop., 1960	−0.7	1.3	3.0	3.3	1.8	3.1	3.0	3.3	1.8	1.7	2.0	0.9
% Change in Pop., 1970	−0.1	1.0	3.0	2.4	2.4	2.2	2.2	1.7	1.0	1.1	2.2	1.3
% Change in Pop., 1983	−0.3	−0.2	2.1–2.6	1.4–1.6	1.3–1.6	1.8	1.5	1.2	0.7–0.9	0.9	2.1–2.2	0.6

SOURCES: Population per square km.: United Nations Educational, Scientific, and Cultural Organization, *UNESCO Yearbook* (1963, pp. 12–21). Percentage change in population: U.S. Department of Commerce, *World Population* (1978); United Nations, Report on *World Population* (1984).

Schmidt 1994) has qualified the previous body of literature by finding an apparent reversal for the decade of the 1980s. But I (and they) believe that this single result should not be translated into a conclusion that population growth has a negative effect for a variety of reasons.[1]

The clear-cut consensus of this body of research is that faster population growth is not associated with slower economic growth. Of course one can adduce cases of countries that seemingly are exceptions to the pattern. It is the genius of statistical inference, however, to enable us to draw valid generalizations from samples that contain such wide variations in behavior. The exceptions can be useful in alerting us to possible avenues for further analysis, but as long as they are only exceptions, they do not prove that the generalization is not meaningful or useful (see Simon 1970).

It has been suggested (e.g., by Roger Conner 1984) that the studies showing the absence of a relationship between the population rate and the economic growth rate also demonstrate that additional people do not imply a higher standard of living in the long run. That is, because these studies do not show a positive correlation, one is said to make claims beyond the evidence if one says that over the very long sweep of human history a larger population in the world (or perhaps, in what is the developed part of the world at any moment) has meant faster rates of increase of technology and the standard of living.

It is indeed the case that the existing body of empirical studies does not prove that fast population growth in the more-developed world as a whole increases per person income. But this is not inconsistent with the proposition that more people do raise the standard of living in the long run. Recall that the studies mentioned above

[1]The reasons include the following: (1) The overall 1960–90 population growth effect is not negative, and that long-run assessment should provide the most reliable and general conclusion. (2) The multiple test effect: Examine enough cases of anything with variability and some will show a statistically significant effect just by chance. (3) If a negative effect is associated with lower income, as Kelley and Schmidt suppose, one would have expected to see the result they found for the 1980s in the earlier decades and then disappearing, rather than the opposite. (4) The results for the 1980s do not square with the long-run historical evidence as analyzed by Kuznets and later data as extracted from Maddison (1991). (5) There is an apparent logical contradiction between a negative growth effect and the density result discussed below. Lower growth means you get more slowly to a more desirable density.

do not refer to the very long run, but rather usually cover only a third of a century, or less than a century and a half at most. The main negative effects of population growth occur during the first quarter or half a century so that, if these effects are important, the empirical studies referred to should reveal them. These shorter-run effects upon the standard of living include the public costs of raising children—schools and hospitals are the main examples—and the costs of providing additional production capital for the additional persons in the work force. The absence of an observed negative effect on economic growth in the statistical measures therefore is enough to imply that in the very long run more people have a *positive* net effect. This is because the most important positive effects of additional people—improvement of productivity through both the contribution of new ideas, and also the learning-by-doing consequent upon increased production volume—happen in the long run, and are cumulative.

To put it differently, the statistical measurements of the relationship of population growth to economic growth are biased in favor of showing the shorter-run effects, which tend to be negative, and of not showing the longer-run effects, which tend to be positive. If such negative effects do not appear, one may assume that an unbiased measure of the total effect would reveal a positive effect of population growth on economic growth.

There is still another reason why the studies mentioned above do not imply an absence of positive effect in the long run: They focus on the process of population growth. If we look instead at the attained level of population—that is, the population density as measured by the number of persons per square mile—we see a somewhat different result. Studies of developed countries are lacking. But Everett Hagen (1975) and Charles Kindleberger (1965) show visually, and Simon and Roy Gobin (1979) show in multivariate regressions, that in LDCs higher population density is associated with higher rates of economic growth. This effect may be strongest at low densities, but there is no evidence that the effect reverses at high densities. And in their careful, comprehensive study of data for the three decades from 1960 to 1990, Kelley and Schmidt (1994) find the most consistent result to be the positive effect of density on economic growth. So again, the statistical evidence directly contradicts the common-sense conventional wisdom. That is, if you make a chart with population density on the horizontal axis and either the income level or the rate of change of income on the vertical axis, you see that higher density is associated with better rather than poorer economic results.

The data showing a positive effect of population density on economic growth constitute indirect proof of a positive long-run effect of population growth on economic growth, because density changes occur very slowly, and therefore the data pick up the very long-run effects as well as the short-run effects.[2]

Hong Kong is a vivid example of this phenomenon. In the 1940s and 1950s, it seemed impossible for Hong Kong to surmount its problems—huge masses of impoverished people without jobs, total lack of exploitable natural resources, and more refugees pouring across the border each day. Today, Hong Kong enjoys high living standards, low unemployment, an astounding collection of modern high-rise apartments and office buildings, and one of the world's most modern transportation systems. Hong Kong starkly demonstrates that a very dense concentration of human beings does not prevent comfortable existence and exciting economic expansion, as long as the economic system gives individuals the freedom to exercise their talents and to take advantage of opportunities. And the experience of Singapore demonstrates that Hong Kong is not unique.

[2]It may at first seem preposterous that greater population density might lead to better economic results. This is the equivalent of saying that if all Americans moved east of the Mississippi, we might not be the poorer for it. Upon reflection, this proposition is not as unlikely as it sounds. The main loss involved in such a move would be huge amounts of farmland, and though the United States is a massive producer and exporter of farm goods, agriculture is not crucial to the economy. Less than 3 percent of U.S. income comes from agriculture, and less than 3 percent of the U.S. working population is engaged in that industry. The capitalized value of all U.S. farm land is just a bit more than a tenth of just one year's national income, so even if the United States were to lose all of it, the loss would equal only about one year's expenditures on liquor, cigarettes, and the like. On the other hand, such a change would bring about major benefits in shortening transportation and communication distances, a factor that has been important in Japan's ability to closely coordinate its industrial operations in such a fashion as to reduce costs of inventory and transportation. Additionally, greater population concentration forces social changes in the direction of a greater degree of organization, changes that may be costly in the short run but in the long run increase a society's ability to reach its economic and social objectives. If we were still living at the population density of, say, 10,000 years ago, we would have none of the vital complex social and economic apparatuses that are the backbone of our society.

Check for yourself: Fly over Hong Kong—just a few decades ago a place seemingly without prospects because of insoluble resource problems—and you will marvel at the skyline of buildings. Take a ride on its excellent smooth-flowing highways for an hour or two, and you will realize that a very dense concentration of human beings does not prevent comfortable existence and a rapid rate of economic growth.[3]

At this point the question frequently arises: If more people cause there to be more ideas and knowledge, and hence higher productivity and income, why are not India and China the richest nations in the world? Let us put aside the matter that size in terms of population within national boundaries was not very meaningful in earlier centuries when national integration was much looser than it is now. There remains the question, however, why so many human beings in those countries produced so little change in the last few hundred years. Yes, low education of most people in China and India prevents them from producing knowledge and change (though we should note the very large, in absolute terms, contemporary scientific establishments in those two countries.) But though education may account for much of the present situation, it does not account nearly as well for the differences between the West and the East over the five centuries or so up to, say, 1850.

William McNeill (1963), Eric Jones (1981), and others have suggested that over several centuries the relative instability of social and economic life in Europe, compared to China and India, helps account for the emergence of modern growth in the West rather than in the East. Instability implies economic disequilibria, which (as Theodore Schultz [1975] reminds us) imply exploitable opportunities which then lead to augmented effort. (Such disequilibria also cause the production of new knowledge, it would seem.)

The hypothesis that the combination of a person's wealth and opportunities affect the person's exertion of effort may go far in

[3]Hong Kong is a special thrill for me because I first saw it in 1955 when I went ashore from a U.S. Navy destroyer. At the time I felt great pity for the thousands of people who slept every night on the sidewalks or on small boats. And it is this sort of picture that has convinced many persons that a place is overpopulated and should cut its birth rate (e.g., Paul Ehrlich [1968] at the beginning of *The Population Bomb*). But upon returning in 1983, I saw bustling crowds of healthy, vital people full of hope and energy. No cause for pity now.

explaining the phenomenon at hand. Ceteris paribus, the less wealth a person has, the greater the person's drive to take advantage of economic opportunities. The village millions in India and China certainly have had plenty of poverty to stimulate them. But they have lacked opportunities because of the static and immobile nature of their village life. In contrast, villagers in Western Europe apparently had more mobility, less stability, and more exposure to cross-currents of all kinds.

Just why Europe should have been so much more open than India and China is a question that historians answer with conjectures about religion, smallness of countries with consequent competition and instability, and a variety of other special conditions. This matter need not be pursued here. But we should at least mention Deepak Lal's book on India's economic development over thousands of years, which suggests that it was only the rapid population growth starting around 1921 that cracked the "cake of custom" and the Hindu caste system, and caused the mobility which allowed India to begin modern development (Lal 1989).

Most (if not all) historians of the period (e.g., Nef 1963, Gimpel 1976) agree that the period of rapid population growth from before A.D. 1000 to the beginning of the middle of the 1300s was a period of extraordinary intellectual fecundity. It was also a period of great dynamism generally, as seen in the extraordinary cathedral building boom. But during the period of depopulation due to the plague (starting with the Black Death cataclysm) and perhaps to climatic changes from the middle 1300s (though the change apparently began earlier at the time of major famines around 1315–17, and perhaps even earlier, when there also was a slowing or cessation of population growth due to other factors) until perhaps the 1500s, historians agree that intellectual and social vitality waned.

Henri Pirenne's ([1925] 1969) magisterial analysis of this period depends heavily upon population growth and size. Larger absolute numbers were the basis for increased trade and consequent growth in cities, which in turn strongly influenced the creation of a more articulated exchange economy in place of the subsistence economy of the manor. And, according to Pirenne, growth in population also loosened the bonds of the serf in the city and thereby contributed to an increase in human liberty (though the causes of the end of serfdom are a subject of much controversy).

A corollary, of course, is that once the people in the East lose the shackles of static village life and get some education, their poverty (absolute and relative) will drive them to an extraordinary explosion of creative effort. The happenings in Taiwan and Korea in recent decades suggest that this is already occurring.

This explanation would seem more systematic, and more consistent with the large body of economic thought, than are explanations in terms of Confucianism or of particular cultures, just as the Protestant-ethic explanation for the rise of the West (discussion of which goes back at least to David Hume) now seems unpersuasive in the face of religious counter-examples (e.g., the Catholic Ibo in Nigeria) and shifts in behavior of Protestant nations.

Though the statistical studies together with the historical analogies would seem to constitute persuasive evidence of the positive long-run effect of additional people, experience shows that it is not convincing to many. Perhaps a few thought experiments in the form of hypothetical comparisons will add conviction. Therefore, please ask yourself:

1. Would the world be in better or worse shape today if all the people who have ever lived in the area now called the Netherlands (or India, or China, or Portugal, or wherever) had never lived at all?

2. If you were colonizing another planet such as the moon or Mars or Saturn, would you prefer that ten, or a hundred, or a thousand, or a million, or ten million persons were also colonizing along with you? Under which condition would exploration and mapping of the resources of the colonized planet take place more rapidly? Under which condition would that planet be more rapidly rendered habitable so that one could travel safely, and find accommodations and a fast-food outlet?

3. If you were Robinson Crusoe, would you have preferred that the island on which you were cast away was not devoid of other humans, but rather contained some or many other persons? Under which conditions do you think that you would be in less fear of your life, and feel less need to erect fortifications and stand watch at night? Under which conditions would there be a greater pool of useful skills, and of the manpower to build a ship and leave the island? Would the "congestion" of more people outweigh the isolation of none?

4. Were the Pilgrims better or worse off for the the presence of Native Americans in the area when they arrived?

Conclusion

For years the World Bank, the State Department's Aid to International Development, the United Nations' Fund for Population Activities, and the environmental organizations have misanalyzed such world development problems as starving children, illiteracy, pollution, dwindling supplies of natural resources, and slow growth. Their "experts" have asserted that the cause of all those problems is population growth—the population "explosion" or "bomb" or "plague." That error has cost dearly. It has directed attention away from the factor that we now know is central in a country's economic development—its economic and political system.

Too much attention has been paid to population growth rather than to fighting tyranny and working for economic freedom. The perverse focus on population growth even has led some Westerners to condone and abet inhumane programs that prevent couples from having children in China and elsewhere. Perhaps the events in Eastern Europe in 1989 and 1990, and since then, will open minds to the irrelevance of population growth for intermediate-run economic development and reveal the key importance of the social and economic system.

References

Becker, Gary. "An Environment for Economic Growth." *Wall Street Journal,* 19 January 1989, p. A8.

Conner, Roger. "How Immigrants Affect Americans' Living Standard." A Debate Between Julian Simon and Roger Conner. Heritage Foundation, Washington, D.C., 30 May 1984.

Easterlin, Richard A. "Effects of Population Growth in the Economic Development of Developing Countries." *Annals of the American Academy of Political and Social Science* 369 (1967): 98–108.

Ehrlich, Paul R. *The Population Bomb.* New York: Ballantine Books, 1968.

Gastil, Raymond D. *Freedom in the World.* Westport, Conn: Greenwood, yearly.

Gimpel, Jean. *The Medieval Machine.* New York: Penguin, 1976.

Gwartney, James; Lawson, Robert; and Block, Walter. *Economic Freedom of the World: 1975–1995.* Vancouver, B.C.: Fraser Institute, 1996.

Hagen, Everett E. *The Economics of Development.* Home wood, Ill.: Irwin, 1975.

Johnson, Bryan T., and Sheehy, Thomas P. *1996 Index of Economic Freedom.* Washington, D.C.: Heritage Foundation, 1996.

Jones, Eric L. *The European Miracle.* New York: Cambridge University Press, 1981.

Kelley, Allen, and Schmidt, Robert M. "Population and Income Change." World Bank Discussion Paper 249, August 1994.

Kindleberger, Charles P. *Economic Development*. 2nd ed. New York: McGraw-Hill, 1965.

Kuznets, Simon. "Population and Economic Growth". *Proceedings of the American Philosophical Society* 11 (1967): 170–93.

Lal, Deepak. *The Hindu Equilibrium, Vol. 1: Cultural Stability and Economic Stagnation in India, 1500 B.C.–1980 A.D.* New York: Oxford University Press, 1989.

Maddison, Angus. *Dynanic Forces in Capitalist Development*. Oxford: Oxford University Press, 1991.

Marsden, Keith. "Why Asia Boomed and Africa Busted." *Wall Street Journal*, 3 June 1985.

McNeill, William H. *The Rise of the West: A History of the Human Community*. Chicago: University of Chicago Press, 1963.

Nef, John U. *Cultural Foundations of Industrial Civilization*. Cambridge: Cambridge University Press, 1958.

Nef, John U. *Western Civilization since the Renaissance*. New York: Harper and Row, 1963.

Pirenne, Henri. *Medieval Cities* [1925]. Reprint. Princeton: Princeton University Press, 1969.

Rydenfelt, Sven. *A Pattern for Failure*. New York: Harcourt Brace, Jovanovich, 1983.

Schultz, Theodore W. "The Value of the Ability to Deal with Disequilibrium." *Journal of Economic Literature* 13 (September 1975): 827–46.

Scully, Gerald W. "The Institutional Framework and Economic Development." *Journal of Political Economy* 96 (June 1988a): 652–62.

Scully, Gerald W. "Liberty and Economic Progress." *Journal of Economic Growth* 3 (November 1988b): 3–10.

Simon, Julian L. "The Concept of Causality in Economics." *Kyklos* 23 (2) (1970): 226–54.

Simon, Julian L. *The Ultimate Resource*. Princeton: Princeton University Press, 1981.

Simon, Julian L. "The War on People." *Challenge* (March / April 1985a): 50–53.

Simon, Julian L. "Why Do We Still Think Babies Create Poverty?" *Washington Post*, 12 October 1985b.

Simon, Julian L. "Population Growth, Economic Growth, and Foreign Aid." *Cato Journal* 7 (Spring / Summer 1987): 159–86.

Simon, Julian L. "On Aggregate Empirical Studies Relating Population Variables to Economic Development." *Population and Development Review* 15 (June 1989): 323–32.

Simon, Julian L. "More People, Greater Wealth; More Resources, Healthier Environment." *Economic Affairs* (April 1994): 22–29.

Simon, Julian L., ed. *The State of Humanity*. Cambridge, Mass.: Blackwell, 1995.

Simon, Julian L., and Gobin, Roy. "The Relationship between Population and Economic Growth in LDCs." In *Research in Population Economics,* vol. 2. Edited by J. L. Simon and Julie deVanzo. Greenwich, Conn.: JAI Press, 1979.

Simon, Julian L., and Moore, Stephan K. "Injecting Capitalism." *Journal of Corporate Governance* 11 (May/June 1990): 17–24.

United Nations. Department of International Economics and Social Affairs. *Concise Report on the World Population Situation in 1983: Conditions, Trends, Prospects, Policies.* New York: United Nations, 1984.

United Nations Educational, Scientific, and Cultural Organization. *UNESCO Yearbook.* Paris: UNESCO, 1963.

U.S. Department of Commerce. Bureau of the Census. *World Population 1977: Recent Demographic Estimates for the Countries and Regions of the World.* Washington, D.C.: Government Printing Office, 1978.

Part II

Institutional Choice and Economic Development

6. Institutions, Ideology, and Economic Performance

Douglass C. North

The central argument of this essay is that institutions and ideology together shape economic performance. Institutions affect economic performance by determining (along with the technology used) the cost of transacting and producing. Institutions are composed of formal rules, informal constraints, and characteristics of enforcing those constraints. While formal rules can be changed over night by the polity, informal constraints change very slowly. Both are ultimately shaped by people's subjective perceptions of the world around them; those perceptions, in turn, determine explicit choices among formal rules and evolving informal constraints. In succeeding sections I will develop this analytical framework, which I will use to diagnose the contrasting performance of Western market economies with those of Third World and socialist economies.

Institutions and Transaction Costs

Institutions are the rules of the game in a society; more formally, they are the humanly devised constraints that shape human interaction. Thus, they structure incentives in exchange, whether political, social, or economic. Institutional change shapes the way societies evolve through time and, hence, is the key to understanding historical change.

That institutions affect economic performance is hardly controversial. That differential performance of economies over time is fundamentally influenced by the way institutions evolve is also not

---

Douglass C. North is the Luce Professor of Law and Liberty in the Department of Economics and Director of the Center of Political Economy at Washington University. He is the co-recipient of the 1993 Nobel Memorial Prize in Economic Science. This chapter is reprinted from his article in the Winter 1992 *Cato Journal* (North 1992), which is drawn, in part, from North (1990b).

controversial. Yet Western neoclassical economic theory is devoid of institutions and, therefore, is of little help in analyzing the underlying sources of economic performance. It would be little exaggeration to say that while neoclassical theory is focused on the operation of efficient markets, few Western economists understand the institutional requirements essential to creating such markets, because they simply take them for granted. Entailed in such markets are both a set of political and economic institutions that provide for low transaction costs and credible commitment that makes possible the efficient factor and product markets underlying economic growth.

Four major variables determine the costliness of transacting in exchange. First is the cost of measuring the valuable attributes of the goods and services or the performance of agents in exchange. Property rights consist of a bundle of rights; to the degree that we cannot measure precisely the valuable attributes of the separable rights being exchanged, then the costs of transacting and the uncertainties associated with transacting rise dramatically. Measurement consists of defining the physical dimensions of the rights exchanged (color, size, weight, number, etc.) along with the property rights dimensions of the exchange (rights defining uses, income to be derived, and alienation). The immense resources that societies devote to organizations and enforcement would be superfluous in a world where measurement costs were zero. But because such costs are extremely high and, in consequence, the rights are imperfectly specified, other variables become important in the cost of transaction.

The second variable in the costliness of the exchange process is the market's size, which determines whether personal or impersonal exchange occurs. In personal exchange, kinship ties, friendship, personal loyalty, and repeat dealings will all play a part in constraining participants' behavior, and they will reduce the need for costly specification and enforcement. By contrast, in impersonal exchange, nothing constrains the parties from taking advantage of each other. Accordingly, the cost of contracting rises with the need for more elaborate specification of the rights exchanged. Effective competition acts as an essential constraint when the parties are engaged in repetitive dealings in impersonal markets.

The third variable is enforcement. In a world of perfect enforcement, ideally, a third party would impartially (and costlessly) evaluate disputes and award compensation to the injured party when contracts are violated. Opportunism, shirking, and cheating would never pay in such a world. But such a world does not exist. Indeed, the creation of a relatively impartial judicial system that enforces agreements has been a critical stumbling block in the path of economic development. In the Western world, the evolution of courts, legal systems, and a relatively impartial body of judicial enforcement has played a major role in permitting the development of a complex system of contracting that can extend over time and space—an essential requirement of a world of specialization.

If we retain the neoclassical behavioral assumption of wealth maximization, then these three variables alone will determine the cost of exchange. Thus, individuals would maximize at every margin (if cheating pays, one cheats; if loafing on the job is possible, one loafs; if one could with impunity burn down a competitor, one would do so). But it is hard to imagine that complex exchange and organization would be possible if this assumption accurately described human behavior. The costliness of measuring performance, of fulfilling contracts, and of enforcing agreements would foreclose a world of specialization and division of labor. But ideological attitudes and perceptions (the fourth variable) matter.

Ideology not only plays an essential role in political choices (see North 1990a) but also is a key to individual choices that affect economic performance. Individual perceptions about the fairness and justice of the rules of the game obviously affect performance. Otherwise, we would be at a loss to explain a good deal of schooling, as well as the immense investment made by politicians, employers, labor leaders, and others in trying to convince participants of the fairness or unfairness of contractual arrangements. The importance of ideology is a direct function of the degree to which the measurement and enforcement of contracts is costly. If measuring and enforcing contract performance can be done at low cost, then it makes very little difference whether people believe the rules of the game are fair or unfair. But because measurement and enforcement are costly, ideology matters.

Adaptive Efficiency

Efficient markets are a consequence of institutions that provide low-cost measurement and enforcement of contracts. This outcome is accomplished by rules that encourage adaptive efficiency, by complementary informal constraints, and by effective enforcement. I shall take each in turn.

Adaptively efficient rules provide incentives for the acquisition of knowledge and learning, induce innovation, and encourage risk taking and creative activity. In a world of uncertainty no one knows the correct solution to the problems we confront, as Friedrich Hayek has persuasively argued. Therefore, rules should encourage trials and eliminate errors. A logical corollary is decentralized decisionmaking that will allow a society to explore many alternative ways to solve problems. It is equally important to learn from and eliminate failures. The rules, therefore, must encompass bankruptcy laws and provide incentives to encourage decentralized decisionmaking and effective competitive markets, as well as provide low-cost measurement of property rights.

Formal rules are only part of the institutional matrix. They must be complemented by informal constraints—extensions, elaborations, and qualifications of rules that solve innumerable exchange problems not completely covered by formal rules and that have tenacious survival ability. Informal rules allow people to go about the everyday process of making exchanges without having to think out, exactly at each point and in each instance, the terms of exchange. Routines, customs, traditions, and culture are words we use to denote the persistence of informal rules or constraints. They include (a) conventions that evolve as solutions to coordination problems and that all parties are interested in having maintained, (b) norms of behavior that are recognized standards of conduct, and (c) self-imposed codes of conduct such as standards of honesty or integrity. Conventions are self-enforcing. Norms of behavior are enforced by a second party (retaliation) or by a third party (societal sanctions or coercive authority); their effectiveness depends on the effectiveness of enforcement.

Self-imposed codes of conduct, unlike conventions and norms of behavior, do not obviously entail wealth maximizing behavior but rather entail the sacrifice of wealth or income for other values. Their importance in constraining choices is the subject of substantial controversy—for example, in modeling voting behavior in the U.S. Congress (Kalt and Zupan 1984). Most of the controversy has missed the crucial reason why such behavior can be and is important: Formal institutions (rules) frequently deliberately, sometimes accidentally, lower the costs to individuals of such behavior and can make their normative standards, which are embodied in self-imposed codes of conduct, matter a great deal. Individual votes do not (usually) matter individually, but in the aggregate they shape the political world of democratic polities and cost the voter very little. By strategic voting, legislators commonly find ways to vote their personal preferences rather than those of the electorate (Denzau, Riker, and Shepsle 1985). Judges with lifetime tenure are deliberately shielded from interest group pressures so that they can make decisions on the basis of their interpretation (subjective models) of the law. In each case the choices that were made may be different from what they would be if the individual bore the full cost that resulted from these actions. The lower the cost we incur for our convictions (ideas, dogmas, prejudices), the more they contribute to outcomes (for empirical evidence, see Nelson and Silberberg 1987).

How effectively agreements are enforced is the single most important determinant of economic performance. The ability to enforce agreements across time and space is the central underpinning of efficient markets. On the surface such enforcement would appear to be an easy requirement to fulfill. All one needs is an effective, impartial system of laws and courts for the enforcement of formal rules, for the "correct" societal sanctions to enforce norms of behavior, and for strong normative personal standards of honesty and integrity to undergird self-imposed standards of behavior. The creation and enforcement of efficient property rights depend on the polity. However, it is difficult if not impossible to derive a model of a polity that produces such results as long as one retains the standard wealth maximization postulate and accepts the time horizons that characterize political decisions.

Modern Technology and Organization

The preceding paragraph highlights the major dilemma resulting from the revolutionary modern technology that underlies contemporary economic growth. It is easy to devise a set of property rights that, if enforced at low cost, would create an adaptively efficient economy. But as briefly noted earlier, the costs of measuring and enforcing agreements are fundamentally influenced by the informal constraints in an economy. This phenomenon occurs because the economies of scale of modern technology, which can be realized only by specialization and division of labor and of national and international markets, entail impersonal exchange. In such an exchange the parties are no longer constrained by forces that cement agreements in personal exchange—loyalty, kinship, reciprocity, and clientization. Moreover, the gains from defection, to use game theory terminology, rise dramatically. They rise because the gains from cheating, shirking, and stealing rise as well as the costs of monitoring and measuring performance.

The 19th-century revolution in technology fundamentally altered the performance of those economies that would take advantage of the new technology. This second economic revolution has equally radical implications for the organization of societies.[1]

The term "economic revolution" is intended to describe three distinct changes in an economic system: (1) a change in the productive potential of a society, which is a consequence of (2) a basic change in the stock of knowledge, and which entails (3) an equally basic change in organization to realize that productive potential. The change in the productive potential came about in the last half of the 19th century as a consequence of changes in the stock of knowledge arising from the development and implementation of modern scientific disciplines. These changes caused the systematic wedding of science and technology. The technology that characterized this revolution was one in which there were significant indivisibilities in the production process and large fixed-capital investment. The overall implications for economies that could take advantage of this technology were increasing returns and consequent high rates of economic growth; these features have characterized the Western world for the past century and a half.

To take advantage of this technology and realize this potential entailed fundamental reorganization of economies. In those Western economies that have, at least partially, realized the potential, the result has been stresses and strains that have threatened and do threaten their continued adaptive efficiency. For the remaining countries, the inability to reorganize has prevented them from realizing this productive potential and has produced underdevelopment and political instability. It is an extraordinary irony that Karl Marx, who

[1]The flat economic revolution was the development of agriculture, which is believed to have begun in the eighth millennium B.C. in Mesopotamia.

first pointed out the necessity for restructuring societies to realize the potential of a new technology, should have been responsible for creating economies that have foundered on this precise issue. We will examine the microlevel characteristics of the organizational requirements before turning to the macrolevel implications.

Realizing the gains from a world of specialization requires occupational and territorial specialization on an unprecedented scale; consequently, the number of exchanges grows exponentially. To realize the gains from the productive potential associated with a technology of increasing returns, one has to invest enormous resources in transacting. In the United States, for example, the labor force grew from 29 million to 80 million between 1900 and 1970. During that period, production workers increased from 10 million to 29 million, and white collar workers (the majority of whom are engaged in transacting) rose from 5 million to 38 million. In 1970 the transaction sector (that part of transaction costs that goes through the market) made up 45 percent of GNP (Wallis and North 1986).

Let me briefly describe some measurement and enforcement problems that underlie the size of the transaction sector. Control over quality in the lengthening production chain and a solution to problems of increasingly costly principal/agent relationships are necessary for realizing gains in a world of specialization. Much technology has been designed to reduce transaction costs by substituting capital for labor or by reducing the worker's degrees of freedom in the production process and by automatically measuring the quality of intermediate goods. An underlying problem has been that of measuring inputs and outputs so that one could ascertain the contribution of individual factors, the output at successive stages of production, and the final outcomes. For inputs, there was no agreed-upon measure of the contribution of an individual input. Equally, there was room for conflict over the consequent payment to factors of production. For outputs, there was not only residual unpriced output (waste and pollutants) but also complicated costs of specifying the desired properties of the goods and services produced at each stage in the production process.

Another characteristic of this new technology was that one had large fixed-capital investments with a long life and a low alternative scrap value. As a result the exchange process embodied in contracts had to be extended over long periods, which entailed uncertainty about prices and costs plus the possibilities for opportunistic behavior by one party or the other in exchange. A number of organizational dilemmas have resulted from these problems.

First, increased resources are necessary to measure the quality of output. Sorting, grading, labeling, trademarks, warranties, and licensing are all, albeit costly and imperfect, devices to measure the characteristics of goods and services. Despite their existence the dissipation of income is evident all around us in the difficulties of measuring automobile repairs, of evaluating the safety characteristics of products or the quality of medical services, or of measuring educational output.

Second, while team production permits economies of scale, it does so at the cost of worker alienation and shirking. The discipline of the factory is nothing more than a response to the control problem of shirking in team production. From the employer's perspective, discipline consists of rules, regulations, incentives, and punishment essential to an effective performance. Innovations such as time and motion studies are methods of measuring individual performance. From the worker's viewpoint, these methods are inhuman devices to foster speed-ups and exploitation. Since there is no agreed-upon measure of output that constitutes contract performance, both are right.

Third, the potential gains from opportunistic behavior increase and lead to strategic behavior both in the firm (such as labor-employer relations) and in contractual behavior between firms. Everywhere in factor and product markets, the gains from withholding services or altering the terms of agreement at strategic points offer large potential gains.

Fourth, the development of large-scale hierarchies produce familiar problems of bureaucracy. The multiplication of rules and regulations inside large organizations to control shirking and principal/agent problems results in rigidities, income dissipation, and loss of the flexibility essential to adaptive efficiency.

Finally are the external effects: the unpriced costs reflected in the modern environmental crisis. The interdependence of a world of specialization and division of labor increases exponentially the imposition of costs on third parties.

Adaptive Efficiency and Modern Technology

Marxists would contend that these problems are a consequence of capitalism and that the inherent contradictions between the new technology and the consequent organization of capitalism would lead to its demise. But Marxists are wrong; these problems are ubiquitous to any society that attempts to adopt the technology of the second economic revolution. However, as I have attempted to make clear, Marxists are correct in seeing a fundamental dilemma in the tensions arising between the new technology and organization. These tensions have been solved only very partially in the market economies of the Western world. The technology of the second economic revolution, the resulting enormous increase in specialization and division of labor, and the consequent radical alteration of relative prices have altered the traditional structure of society—not only the organization of the economy, but also that of the family and the polity. The growth of government, the disintegration of the family, and the incentive incompatibilities of many modern political and economic hierarchical organizations are all symptoms of the consequent problems besetting Western economies.

However, it has been the relative flexibility of Western institutions—both economic and political—that has been the mitigating factor in dealing with these problems. Adaptive efficiency, while far from perfect in the Western world, accounts for the degree of success that such institutions have experienced. The basic institutional framework has encouraged the development of political and economic organizations that have replaced (however imperfectly) the traditional functions of the family; mitigated the insecurity associated with a world of specialization; evolved flexible economic organization that resolved some incentive incompatibilities of hierarchies and that encouraged creative entrepreneurial talent; and tackled (again very imperfectly) the external effects that are not only environmental but also social in an urban world.

It is easy in the abstract to state the conditions that underlie adaptive efficiency. They consist of formal rules (both political and economic) that result in well-specified property rights, effective competition, decentralized decisionmaking, and elimination of failures. But such formal rules by themselves are no guarantee of adaptive efficiency. After all, many Latin American economies adopted the U.S. Constitution (or variants thereof) when they became independent; many economies have copied Western legal systems. In fact, the simple-minded notion that "privatization" is all that is needed to set faltering and failed economies on the path to growth is a travesty of institutional reasoning that reflects the primitive understanding of most economists about economic history and growth. Creating efficient factor and product markets is a complicated process about which we know all too little. But the one thing we do know is that formal rules must be complemented by informal constraints and effective enforcement to produce such markets. Shaping the choices about formal rules that a society adopts, the complementarity of informal constraints, the effectiveness of enforcement are the subjective frameworks that individuals employ to explain the world around them.

Ideology, Choices, and Adaptive Efficiency

Ideologies underlie the subjective frameworks that individuals possess to explain the world around them. Ideologies contain an essential normative element; that is, they explain both the way the world is and the way it ought to be. While subjective models may be, and usually are, a hodgepodge of beliefs, dogmas, sound theories, and myths, there are usually elements of an organized structure that make them an economizing device for receiving and interpreting information.

Ideology plays no role in neoclassical economic theory. Rational choice models assume that the actors possess correct models by which to interpret the world around them or receive feedback of information that will lead them to revise and correct their initially incorrect models. Actors and their organizations that fail to revise their models will perish in the competitive markets that characterize societies. At issue is the feedback of information that will lead individuals to update their subjective models. If, in fact, the instrumental rationality postulate of economic theory were correct, we would anticipate that false theories would be discarded and, to the extent that wealth maximizing was a basic behavioral trait of human beings, that economic growth would be a universal feature of economies. With a sufficiently long time horizon, that conclusion may be true, but in 10,000 years of human economic history we are still a long way from universal economic growth. The plain fact is that we do not possess the information to update our subjective theories to arrive at one true theory; in consequence no one equilibrium is the outcome; rather, multiple equilibria exist that can take us in many directions including stagnation and decline of economies. Ideology matters. But where do individuals' subjective models come from and how do they get altered?

The subjective models that individuals use to decipher the environment are partly a consequence of the growth and transmission of scientific knowledge and partly a consequence of socially transmitted knowledge that is the cultural heritage of every society. To the extent that the former type of knowledge determines choices, an instrumental rationality approach is the correct one in analyzing economic performance. But from the beginning of human socialization, people have created myths, taboos, religions, and dogmas to account for much of their environment that defied scientific explanation. They still do. Culture is more than a blending of different kinds of knowledge; it is value-laden with standards of behavior that have evolved to solve exchange problems (be they social, political, or economic). In all societies there evolves an informal framework to structure human interaction. This framework is the basic "capital stock" that defines the culture of a society. Culture, then, provides a language-based conceptual framework for encoding and interpreting the information that the senses present to the brain. As a consequence, culture not only plays a role in shaping the formal rules but also underlies the informal constraints that are a part of the makeup of institutions.

The ideological constructs that individuals possess to explain their environment do change. These constructs are clearly influenced by fundamental changes in relative prices, which result in persistent inconsistency between the perceived outcomes and the outcomes predicted by the subjective models that individuals possess. But that is not all. Ideas matter; what accounts for the evolving subjective models that shape choices in a society is the combination of changes in relative prices filtered through the culturally conditioned ideas that are generated.

The second economic revolution induced an equal revolution in individual perceptions. It questioned many traditional values and beliefs that had been associated with the traditional role of family, polity, and economic organization. The intellectual ferment of the past century and a half, including the diverse perceptions of economists from Marx to Keynes to Hayek, has been an integral part of this change in perceptions that has, in turn, shaped the ideological constructs and, therefore, the players' choices. But neither the constructs of economists nor the subjective perceptions of those making choices over political and economic institutions have been independent of the evolving external political and economic environment. Or to restate my earlier proposition, what shapes the evolving subjective models that humans use to make choices is the interplay among the evolution of culturally conditioned ideas, the constraints imposed by the existing institutional framework, and the consistency or inconsistency between perceived and predicted outcomes.

What characterizes the Western world is the institutional framework of market economies, which have adjusted to partially resolve the costs associated with the second economic revolution and have permitted the productive potential of the new technology to create high-income economies. For the Third World and socialist economies, the consequences of the institutional framework have been to incur the costs of the second economic revolution and to realize only very partially the productive potential of new technology.

The dramatic fall in information costs associated with this modern technology not only has sharpened the perceived inconsistencies between predicted outcomes and observed results, but also has made people acutely aware of alternative models that exist and that appear to offer improved solutions to economic problems. It is one thing to become disenchanted with the old subjective models that one has used; it is much more difficult to arrive at a new equilibrium in the context of rapidly changing external events. Feedback of information produces confused signals that can be interpreted differently by different individuals and groups. The reason for the confusion is the difficulty of fundamentally altering the path of an economy. An economy's organizations and the interest groups they produce are a consequence of the opportunity set provided by the existing institutional framework. The resulting network externalities reflect the symbiotic interdependence among the existing rules, the complementary informal constraints, and the interests of those members of organizations created as a consequence of the institutional framework.

A change in subjective perceptions about the efficacy of the existing framework will produce political and social fragmentation and political instability. For example, a change in the formal rules and, specifically, in property rights must be complemented by consistent informal constraints and effective enforcement to produce the desired results. But norms of behavior, conventions, and self-imposed codes of conduct change very slowly; moreover, enforcement would have to, at least partially, be undertaken by organizations and interest groups whose interests rested with the old institutional matrix.

A new, stable equilibrium would be one that produces new informal constraints (conventions, norms of behavior, and self-imposed codes of conduct) that solve the new problems of political, social, and economic interaction that emerge and are complementary to the new, formal rules that are devised.

References

Denzau, Arthur; Riker, William; and Shepsle, Kenneth. "Farquharson and Fenno: Sophisticated Voting and Home Style." *American Political Science Review* 79 (1985); 1117–34.

Kalt, Joseph P., and Zupan, Mark A. "Capture and Ideology in the Economic Theory of Politics." *American Economic Review* 75 (1984): 278–300.

Nelson, Douglas, and Silberberg, Eugene. "Ideology and Legislator Shirking." *Economic Inquiry* 25 (1987): 15–25.

North, Douglass C. "A Transaction Cost Theory of Politics." *Journal of Theoretical Politics* 4, no. 2 (1990a): 355–67.

North, Douglass C. *Institutions, Institutional Change, and Economic Performance.* Cambridge: Cambridge University Press, 1990b.

North, Douglass C. "Institutions, Ideology, and Economic Performance." *Cato Journal* 11 (Winter 1992): 477–88.

Wallis, John J., and North, Douglass C. "Measuring the Transaction Sector in the American Economy, 1870–1970." In *Long-Time Factors in American Economic Growth.* Edited by S. L. Engerman and R. E. Gallman. Chicago: University of Chicago Press, 1986.

7. Economic Growth and the Property Rights Regime

Alan Rufus Waters

> It is often nearer the truth to say that capital is created in the process of economic development than that development is a function of capital accumulation.
>
> —Peter T. Bauer and Basil S. Yamey
> *The Economics of Under-Developed Countries*

To those who depended on the assumption that capital accumulation is the cause of economic development—Marxists, social engineers, elitists of every ilk, and others—Peter Bauer's words must have seemed challenging if not offensive. The world has changed. We now recognize that if economic development means anything, it means that the parameters are changing; and the parameters are all those institutional benchmarks that many economists and other social scientists have chosen to hold constant—or at least to let vary with assured prescience (Bauer 1971, pp. 281–82). The lesson from the failed socialist economies is not that they lacked physical assets but that they destroyed, or failed to cultivate, the complex institutions needed for a successful market economy.

We have always known that a free and competitive market with minimal government participation would outperform a planned and centrally controlled one. During the past five decades immense intellectual energy has been expended by several generations of economists in trying to demonstrate the critical role of planners and those who supported interventionist policies. As with the demise of the Ptolemaic orthodoxy in Rome when faced with the challenge of the Copernican evidence of a better explanation for the cosmos, we must

---

Alan Rufus Waters is Professor of International Business in the Sid Craig School of Business at California State University-Fresno. This chapter is a revised version of Waters (1987).

not expect to see the intellectual establishment of the last half century leave the field with grace and resignation in the face of mere overwhelming evidence. We must go forward to continually improve our understanding of market-driven economic development and continually improve our ability to create policies that facilitate real economic development.

Unquestionably the chivvying interventionists have been horribly wrong. Cultural and ethnic differences do matter. For example, we cannot ignore the economic success of the overseas Chinese and other immigrant groups. Why is there a taboo against investigating the reasons for their success? Why have they been persecuted, discriminated against, and dispossessed by their host governments?[1] Conspiracies and ethnic factors have only been excuses for their persecution. Could it be that the success of immigrant groups is due instead to a sense of personal responsibility and a consequent high level of entrepreneurial activity?

Are cultural differences fixed? There is too much evidence to the contrary. Rather than using such differences as a reason for further intervention into and manipulation of the economy, we should seek to discover why some groups are so energetic and perform so constructively. This article offers the hypothesis that an important reason for group success can be found in the pattern of ownership and responsibility.

If, within some domestic minority, individual ownership rights predominate, with consequent personal responsibility for success or failure, intervention to restrain the success of that minority is not an appropriate government policy. The appropriate response—insofar as one is required—is to generalize the pattern of ownership rights that made success possible, and to take advantage of its "demonstration effect" to accelerate development for society as a whole. Above all, individuals are the key players in the process of economic development. Individuals and institutions, not circumstances, create development.

Before examining the role of the property rights regime in the process of economic growth, it is instructive to consider the meaning

[1]Would it be indecent also to ask why the World Bank and other agencies have funded expatriates to replace or fill the positions of the domestic Chinese minority in countries such as Malaysia? This is nothing but complicity in the very racism they frequently denounce.

of economic success and failure. The fundamental role of ownership and property rights in determining success or failure can then be fruitfully examined.

Economic Success and Failure

It is not enough to ask if individuals in a nation are better off now than they were several decades ago; that should be taken for granted. The past five decades have, after all, seen enormous preoccupation with economic development. Foreign aid and foreign advice have poured into the Third World. There has been an obsessive interest in developing ways to accelerate economic progress. Given these circumstances, it is much more relevant to ask why the less successful nations have not performed better. To raise such a question requires a comparison with an operating alternative and not some abstract ideal. A comparison of South Korea with Sri Lanka is useful.

Thirty-five years ago South Korea was thought to have few recognizable resources, and its capital stock had been destroyed by war. Its per capita income was comparable to that of India, Burma, Sri Lanka, and similar nations, and its Confucian culture was thought unlikely to adapt to modern competitive individualist business methods. Moreover, Korea itself had been sundered some 15 years earlier and the traditional industrial heartland had gone to the communists in the North. Large amounts of foreign aid to South Korea stopped in the 1960s.

Despite these unfavorable circumstances, South Korea has achieved sustained economic growth and is now a middle-income nation. Even with high population density and rapid population growth, it has flourished. The per capita gross national product is now almost 8 times that of India, and more than 11 times that of Burma. Life expectancy is now 12 years longer than in either India or Burma.

Sri Lanka and South Korea received their independence at approximately the same time. Sri Lanka inherited from Ceylon a stable administrative structure, established communications and transportation systems, and well-developed educational institutions. Ethnic and religious differences do exist in Sri Lanka, but the fact that almost a third of the people in nominally Confucian Korea were active Christians should not be ignored either.

In 1950 South Korea's gross domestic product per capita was just under 82 percent of Sri Lanka's, in 1963 it was just over 97 percent, and by 1973 it was over 186 percent (Kindleberger and Herrick 1977, p. 17, Table 1-2). By 1983 South Korea's gross national product per capita was over 600 percent of Sri Lanka's (World Bank 1985, pp. 6–9). This incredible divergence cannot be explained by war or external conflict because the victim of such disasters was the country that grew successfully. Foreign aid might be an explanatory factor since Sri Lanka continued to receive increasing amounts of foreign aid throughout the whole period, while Korea's receipts declined sharply in the late 1960s (USAID 1982). By this reasoning, however, foreign aid could only be said to have had a pernicious effect on the recipient.

Keith Marsden (1985) has looked at "Why Asia Boomed and Africa Busted." His comparison of the two continents highlighted the fact that countries starting from quite similar circumstances, but following distinctly different policies, have performed very differently in terms of the major development indicators. By the standard of South Korea, most of the Third World has failed.

An impressive range of hypotheses has been offered to explain relative economic failure: vicious cycles of poverty, population density or rapid population growth, cultural factors such as religion, the choice of economic structure, and, always, a lack of capital. Conspiracy theories by structuralists and others abound but do not warrant serious consideration. Foreign aid was, and often still is, the eternal anodyne for every successive failure. By and large, external and exogenous factors have been the principal excuses. Flagrant misgovernment, faulty economic policies, and meddling intervention have only recently begun to be taken seriously as possible sources of economic failure. "A country, whatever its stage of development, can be well or poorly governed. . . . But with the Third World, the notion of responsibility for bad results disappears completely," notes Jean-Francois Revel (1981).

So many elegant technical explanations for failure have turned out to be nothing more than intellectual curiosa. Consider the example of immiserizing growth that once absorbed so much intellectual interest in trade circles, but which, as a practical matter, contributed nothing. There is the unavoidable feeling that many technical arguments about economic progress were similar to the debate about neoclassical growth models and capital theory between the two Cambridges in the 1960s and 1970s—one side trying to destroy capitalism and the other trying to demonstrate its own mathematical virtuosity.

A Return to the Market Mechanism

Ultimately, the best explanation of any phenomenon must be in accord with observed outcomes. The theories that underpinned economic development planning and the role of government as entrepreneur have now had their run. Every success cannot be a special case; every failure cannot be due to random and external events. Economies in the Third World can be grouped into those that are market oriented and those that are more regulated and centrally controlled. The more market-driven economies have consistently outperformed the others.

With the collapse of the various forms of socialism and statism, markets are back in vogue. The Third World, for example, is making moves to allow prices to signal scarcities and surpluses and to allocate rewards. There is even talk of competition as a goad to action in lethargic societies. Privatization is now proclaimed as a viable purgation by governments with distended portfolios seeking relief by eliminating their less defensible activities. We may even yet discover that disguised unemployment can and does exist, but only in the government sector. Finally, James Buchanan (1983) and the public choice school have countered the paradigm of market failure with that of government failure within a democratic setting, pointing out that even imperfect markets may outperform "well-intentioned" government planners. It is now quite usual to see international agencies agreeing with such research conclusions as: "The study finds that rapid economic growth depends on policies, not circumstances" (IMF 1985, p. 61).

The implication of the emerging enthusiasm for markets, however, has not been fully recognized—namely, that the beneficial results of competition and price signals cannot be achieved unless effective ownership rights are established. As Armen Alchian (1967, p. 6) pointed out two decades ago:

> Every question of pricing is a question of property rights. . . The existing system of property rights establishes the system of price determination for the exchange or allocation of scarce resources. Many apparently diverse questions come down to the same element—the structure of property rights over

> scarce resources. In essence, economics is the study of property rights.

Property Rights

What are property rights and how do they influence economic growth? Property rights are the rights of human beings to control and dispose of property as they see fit. Property rights are human rights over property, as against state ownership and hence detailed rights over humans. Property rights are what people are entitled to do with things they control: who will be allowed to claim the rewards of wise decisions and who will bear the costs of misfortune or irresponsibility.

To fulfill their role effectively, property rights must be exclusive, transferable, partitionable, and perceived to be permanent. They should be exclusive; the definition of property rights should be clear as to whom the owner may or may not exclude. Exclusion is seldom, if ever, complete. The owner of an automobile may be able to exclude others from using the car without his consent under normal circumstances. In times of war the government may be entitled to requisition the vehicle.

Unless property rights are transferable we cannot shift resources from lower- to higher-valued uses. Property rights should be partitionable; it should be possible to divide up the collection of rights that goes with any particular element of property. In this way property may be used economically for a wide range of different purposes under differing circumstances. Rights to mineral resources are the simplest example. The owner of a piece of land may wish to use it for cultivation. At the same time he may wish to allow someone else to pay for the right to search for minerals under the land. This is possible because property rights over the land are partitionable.

Property rights must be perceived to be permanent while belonging to any individual. As Roland McKean (1964) has noted, if individuals cannot capture the net benefits they could produce, they cannot be expected to produce those incremental benefits. Or, consider Richard Posner's (1975, p. 12) example:

> Imagine a society in which all property rights have been abolished. A farmer plants corn, fertilizes it, and erects scarecrows, but when the corn is ripe his neighbor reaps and sells it. The farmer has no legal remedy against his neighbor's conduct since he owns neither the land that he sowed nor

> the crop. After a few such incidents the cultivation of land will be abandoned and the society will shift to methods of subsistence (such as hunting) which involve less preparatory investment.

It must be clear that ownership refers to the rights to use assets and resources, and that all such rights are inevitably circumscribed in some way. The right to use one's own mind and body for certain activities is restricted by law. Similarly, the ownership of resources does not carry the right to inflict the results of their use on a neighbor. That also is restricted by law. Nevertheless, the broader the range of rights that are embodied in ownership and the broader the range of opportunities open to the owner, the more valuable the owned resource will be (Alchian and Demsetz 1973).

Because the bundles of ownership rights determine the value of any type of property, it matters little how the property is classified in traditional terms. Property may be tangible or intangible, for example, physical assets or things such as the accumulated goodwill that go with a particular firm or product. It does, however, matter greatly whether property yields pecuniary rewards (money), or nonpecuniary rewards that may have to be consumed in the form of services and other goods.

To capture pecuniary rights the owner of property must be able to sell the stream of services it generates or to capitalize the stream by selling the property itself. Where the rights to sell or capitalize are constrained, by law or by other institutional arrangements, the property value will decline. For example, a government official is delegated the right (and duty) to distribute valuable property such as licenses to buy foreign exchange. The licenses are limited in number as a means to ration scarce foreign exchange. They are typically distributed by a government official free to successful applicants, rather than sold by the government to the highest bidder, so they are worth more to the chosen buyers than they cost. Under these circumstances the official has no ownership rights. The official has an incentive to shift some of the value of the licenses to himself in nonpecuniary form—such as by distributing licenses to a particular category of people in a manner that would reflect favorably on him within his own social circle. There are many other ways he could accomplish the same end without resorting to legally corrupt behavior. Due to the nature of the property rights that go with the licenses, the official's estimate of their value will be below that estimated by the purchaser. This wedge between the value that the two parties put on the thing being transferred may lead not only to the transfer of nonpecuniary rewards to the official, but also to the possibility of outright corruption.[2]

Another example of the attenuation of property rights can be found in the universal response to rent controls. Where apartment owners are not allowed to charge occupants the full value of their apartments, there has been visible change in the owners' patterns of behavior. Maintenance declines and the number of apartments available for the public is reduced as owners rent to relatives and friends and as they convert their apartments to business or other uncontrolled uses. The effect of rent controls is a partial transfer of property rights from the owners of the buildings to the present group of tenants—with slums being the ultimate result (Furubotn and Pejovich 1972).

Property Rights and Incentives

The pattern of property rights and the cost of marketing those rights will determine what is possible and profitable. If economic growth is the goal, then the structure of property rights should induce people to do those things that lead to economic growth. Economic growth is a long-term process and is more likely to be sustained if people have a strong stake in the future. The way in which ownership is defined determines the expected future income stream from particular kinds of property and thus determines people's vision of the future.

Assurances about future property rights determine both the quantity and kind of wealth people will accumulate. The relative success of South Korea when compared with Sri Lanka may be in large part attributed to the way successive Sri Lankan governments avowed that their policy was to reduce private property rights in the name of socialism. Until 1977 Sri Lanka's various governments pursued policies that centralized economic power, intervened widely in markets, and moved the country toward a stated goal of complete

[2]The distinction between pecuniary and nonpecuniary rewards stands on the microeconomic argument that pecuniary rewards (money) will always be preferred to nonpecuniary rewards of the same value because money is fungible and tastes differ (Sanchez and Waters 1974).

socialism. Private property was threatened and confiscated, creating an atmosphere of uncertainty about the future. Since few people wanted to acquire or create assets with a low probability of yielding a return in the future, the value of productive assets declined. In the process there occurred a shift from saving to current consumption and consequent reduction in the overall rate of economic growth. Since 1977, however, Sri Lanka has reversed its economic policies and undertaken a free-market approach. Nevertheless, great harm must be undone before Sri Lanka and other such countries become recognizably market driven, but they have begun (Subasinghe 1986).

Private property rights permit the holder to transfer the results of his efforts to future generations of his choice. This reinforces the family as a social unit. On the other hand, the absence of such well-defined private property rights diminishes the economic importance of the family and reduces the incentive to make provision for the future. In all this is a self-fulfilling prophecy: if the state attenuates private property rights, people will reduce their time horizon and their savings, in turn paving the way for the state to step in with forced saving and government-determined investment.

One way the state can attenuate private property rights is through the tax system. Consider the case of Jamaica. The Jamaican government chose an economic system in which people received free food and other services if they made US$1,200 per year. At $1,300 per year they moved into an escalating tax structure that reached a marginal rate of almost 58 percent at an income of only $2,500 (Reynolds 1985). Understandably, under this structure the returns on productive activity were very low, and the benefits from remaining in poverty were very high. What kind of wealth could one acquire under these circumstances? As McKean (1964, p. 243) observed, "The higher the cost of pursuing one objective, the less of it one will try to achieve." We would then anticipate that not only current activities but also the creation of future wealth would take the form of untaxed activities. We might expect, for example, to see emigration as a means to increase the return on intellectual capital in various forms. The net return on illegal activities—after discounting for the risk involved—would increase, and there would be less respect for the law. We might expect to find existing capital poorly cared for and maintained. All of this was seen in Jamaica, and the effect on Jamaica's economic progress was obvious.

Economic growth means constant and pervasive change. Economic change results in continual reevaluation of assets in which some people gain and some lose. A strong system of private property rights permits individuals to diversify the inevitable time-related risks by holding a variety of assets. This risk-reducing aspect of property rights can be particularly significant in societies where shifting risks to the government has become an accepted doctrine. Risk is inevitable in economic growth; learning to accept and plan for risk is another key to economic progress. Policies that discourage the emergence of various forms of insurance or the growth of futures markets will retard economic growth.

Restricted ownership of real property—as with land in many less developed countries—will cause a shift to investment in human capital. Schooling and certification will replace other productive activity. However, human capital has several disadvantages in this situation. Human capital normally has a finite life; it deteriorates in later years. It can only be passed on to others at a relatively high cost. If investment in human capital is undertaken voluntarily because the returns are higher than for any other form of property, the outcome will be to the benefit of the individual and society. If, however, people invest in human capital because they are not allowed to invest in other assets, or because the government has subsidized human capital, the benefits to both the individual and society are likely to be overestimated.

It must also be stated that foreign aid has no effect on the structure of property rights and is therefore largely irrelevant from the standpoint of economic growth. Foreign aid may, however, be used to sustain patterns of property rights inimical to economic growth. In such cases aid can do substantial harm, as, for example, when it is used to keep alive otherwise failing cooperatives, government farms, and state production and credit institutions. In this respect the World Bank and the international aid donors bear a heavy responsibility for various agricultural credit banks and marketing boards created for the administrative convenience of the lender or donor. World Bank loans to bus companies in Bombay and Tunis, for example, were required to be filtered through additional government institutions when they could have been made directly to the borrower.

Property Rights and Individual Responsibility

Outsiders—both domestic and foreign—have tended to concentrate on the role of positive incentives in the economic growth process. In several less successful societies it is clear, albeit surprising, that almost nobody is personally responsible for anything that goes wrong. Some collective entity is always at fault, and as a result little can be done to correct the situation. Since outside forces caused the problem, the usual recourse is to ask outside forces for help. In more successful societies, on the other hand, there is a sense of personal responsibility. No individual is responsible for every failure that occurs, but people are certainly responsible for those things that they own or have certain rights to use. Herein lies a fundamental aspect of economic growth.

Economists have long ignored the role of negative incentives and penalties in the overall economic learning process. Nevertheless, much of the discussion about capturing externalities is necessarily about the assignment of personal responsibility. Well-defined property rights tie people to the way assets are used. Ownership is an important factor in making people responsible for the outcome of their action or inaction. Furthermore, private ownership ensures in a way like nothing else can that people bear the costs of their actions.

People who own their assets—their intellectual skills or their land—will themselves have to bear the cost of their behavior in terms of the reduced value and productivity of their assets (Shlapentokh 1986). In this sense, with the erosion of the concept of property rights as a natural right, we have lost a great deal. With no personal ownership there is little personal responsibility for what happens, and even less incentive to cooperate with others for mutual benefit. This is the basis of the enigma so often observed by foreign visitors to the United States: social cohesion and cooperation among individuals is greater in societies based on individualism than in others based on collectivism. The urge to cooperate is seen formally in the formation of mutual insurance and futures markets. It is more easily seen in the multitude of mutual aid organizations, churches, and social clubs. The tendency to seek shared responsibility and joint protection from risk is important for economic growth, but this pattern of voluntary cooperation is not to be found in North Korea or Cuba, to say nothing of a whole group of socialist economies that collapsed in the late 1980s. Ownership (and, therefore, responsibility) under socialism lay always with the distant and impersonal state.

A free-market economy in its operating form is not atomistic or anarchic. There are substantial incentives to cooperation in defining and enforcing limits to the use of private property and to sharing mutual risk. Externalities do exist, but they can frequently be internalized or eliminated through trade and mutually beneficial negotiation among property owners. Since such action would increase the value of each individual's property or it would not be undertaken, people will form cooperative arrangements for various purposes in protection of their property rights.

With private property, be it personal, intellectual, or business, there is a unity of purpose not existing with collective ownership. Self-interest and the profit motive are clear goals. Under these circumstances management is more effective than where property is collectively owned, and there may be a range of often conflicting objectives (Bryce 1960, p. 52). Effective private property rights do not only apply to large blocks of obvious property. The smallest entrepreneur—such as the shoeshine boy on the street in Nairobi—makes economic calculations at the margin and relies for his livelihood on a simple set of property rights and contracts (Elkan, Ryan, and Mukui 1982). It is reasonable to argue that secure private property rights are more valuable to the person who seeks to create wealth than to the existing rich—assuming the marginal unit of wealth is worth more to the person having less at the start. Ownership of trading licenses, permits, and other permissions to operate may be of vital significance to the small trader, as may access to a preferred spot in the marketplace. The way such assets are created and allocated has significant implications for economic growth.

Competition thrives where well-defined property rights exist. Those rights might facilitate trade and create a wider range of owned assets with which to compete. Competition is the engine of economic growth and change for several reasons. It provides clear criteria for the use of existing resources and drives the continuing search for new resources. It propels the search for new and appropriate technologies and ways to do both complex and simple tasks. Finally, it rewards applied research and product development that are patently lacking in less developed countries. Competition also plays a beneficial social role. Since there is no wedge between buyer and seller, competition generates courtesy to and respect for customers and potential customers. In a competitive situation customers have an alternative, in dealing with government they do not.

The Role of Failure in Economic Progress

I have already argued that private property rights define personal responsibility. Put another way, private property rights specify who may reap the rewards and who must bear the cost of failure. The cost of failure due to misfortune or irresponsible behavior cannot be shifted if property rights are well defined.

The entrepreneur has reemerged as the central figure in economic growth. We still have to overcome the widely held view that entrepreneurs are born with a special talent that cannot be learned or improved upon later. The image is, of course, false. Entrepreneurs learn their skill by interaction with their competitors and with their environment.

Few entrepreneurs succeed at the first attempt. They frequently assert that they have learned more from past failures than from any subsequent success. This message should not be lost on those who seek rapid economic growth. Failure is a necessary part of change, and it is a powerful teacher. Furthermore, there must be failures if an economy is growing and new activities are being introduced. It may be said of the less developed countries that they have avoided many small failures at the cost of some truly national ones. Their rulers do not seem to grasp that failure is a part of success. Nor do they appear to have noticed that a high proportion of all new businesses started in any given year in the United States, for example, fail.

Given a well-defined system of private property rights, there is little to fear from failure. With sound and flexible bankruptcy laws, administered with due haste and at low cost, failure can be used to great advantage. Bankruptcy does not destroy assets; it releases them from one firm for use in another, and potentially more profitable, venture. Thus, bankruptcy eliminates mistakes quickly and allows new entrants to the business world a chance to seek success. It is in this sense that failure is the basis for ultimate success.

Because private property rights are partitionable and therefore can be widely held, business failures may appear dramatic; but their collective effect will be offset by their benefits to society. It is the lack of bankruptcy and business failure in the government sectors of the less developed nations that should be of greater concern. The cost to the economy of assets retained in less productive activities may be a luxury that a rich nation can afford; it may be disastrous to a poor country.

Business failures create flexibility for the introduction of new technologies and new institutional arrangements. The financial community can discover a whole new range of potential markets for its services in the process of failure and reconstruction. The lack of this mutual learning experience may be one of the factors causing the slow emergence of organized financial markets in less developed nations.

The Evolution of Property Rights

Much of modern development economics is devoid of institutional content. This is not true, however, of Bauer's work, which is full of forthright demands that attention be paid to the institutional framework. Adam Smith carefully examined the alternatives of public and private ownership under various institutional arrangements (Clarkson 1975). The key to economic growth in this respect is that the institutional arrangements should be easily rearranged so that those that most readily capture new gains and exclude new losses will survive. Private property rights offer the greatest flexibility in this respect.

There is no conflict between the idea of assured ownership rights and flexibility as long as such rights can be freely divided, combined, exchanged, and traded. One of the most important functions for any government is the establishment and monitoring of an evolving legal system that facilitates trade in property rights. On one hand, technology continually changes the nature of property, making some assets more valuable and others less so. On the other hand, technology continually improves the ability to measure and control property so that it may be more effectively traded at lower cost. There is little of this process of evolution in the public sector and even less in those countries committed to socialist ownership (Demsetz 1967).

Additionally, demographic changes are inevitable during economic growth. Private property rights are a more effective adjustment mechanism than any administered scheme for redistribution of wealth. Widespread distribution of tradable assets permits more flexible provision for retirement by individuals than do fixed-age pension schemes. Both the United Kingdom and Chile have recently moved to provide private alternatives to a state monopoly of social security (Goodman 1983). There is every logical reason why that pattern should spread. Privatization would reduce the burden on younger generations who support government pension schemes with their taxes. Also, as the role of women in society changes, a flexible system of private pensions would accommodate the acquisition and creation of wealth by new entrants better than any assurance of "public employment." Finally, privatization would create greater pressure and opportunity for old elites to dispose of their assets and hence make way for new groups in society.

Creating a New Pattern of Property Rights

No nation starts with a clean slate. No existing pattern of property rights is of itself satisfactory or unsatisfactory. The crucial element, missing in the socialist case, is the process by which a given system of property rights may evolve in the face of market forces. The change from a collective or public ownership to private property rights is a move from rigidity to flexibility and responsiveness—it is the introduction of a process where none existed before. The transfer can be undertaken in two ways. First, all new enterprises can be created on the basis of free and tradable property rights. Second, the existing system of state enterprises and state ownership can be dismantled.

At the heart of the process of change must be a reform of the legal system. For economic success, there must be a judiciary that is responsive and evenhanded in adjudicating disputes over matters of contract law. The process of registration, licensing, and other forms of regulation must be streamlined so that all parties can be assured of quick decisions at the lowest possible cost. The appalling cost of over-regulation and turgid legal systems is seldom realized. Outsiders rarely come into contact with the full scope of the regulatory and legal systems of Third World nations; the local people are accustomed to their environment and frequently do not realize that it could be improved. The work of Hernando De Soto in Peru, for example, revealed that it took the equivalent of 289 work days, 81 meters of forms, and 8 overt bribes to legally establish a small clothing factory (O'Shaughnessy 1985). How much further need we go to find a key reason for economic stagnation? The governments of the Third World must undertake legal and regulatory reforms (Bauer and Yamey 1972).

Dismantling the present structure of collective ownership requires an active policy of privatization. Governments are currently producing and distributing goods and services that the private sector could handle more economically if allowed to compete. There is a growing body of literature on privatization, and there are numerous historical examples of success.[3]

Privatization can take the form of donation to some existing group such as employees, or sale to the same group or to the public. Whatever the method chosen, there will have to be considerable research and substantial involvement of the private sector in every case. A bold first step by the successful free-market economies would be the elimination of institutionalized foreign aid. As those who control the U.S. Agency for International Development (USAID) have now clearly demonstrated, it is not possible for a government agency—staffed by even the most dedicated people—to bypass the governments of the aid recipient nations and transfer money directly to the high-risk entrepreneurial private sector. The property rights within USAID institutions are not appropriate for the ends they have sometimes proclaimed. USAID is better at disaster relief, and focuses on that function, but perhaps others could do even that better and at a lower cost? It is not enough to talk about the obvious success of free markets. The people who control and benefit from government-led development institutions must be divested of their power and resources if we are to see the emergence of economies based on clearly defined property rights and personal responsibility.

Conclusion

Private property rights focus on individual responsibility for action or inaction. Furthermore, well-defined private property rights permit flexibility in the development process and allow for the rapid emergence of failures as they occur. Finally, private property rights increase the flexibility with which resources can be channeled into more productive activities and to new groups in society. Effective private property rights are essential to long-run economic growth.

References

Alchian, Armen A. *Pricing and Society*. London: Institute of Economic Affairs, 1967.

[3]Japan underwent a massive privatization phase during the reconstruction of its economy in the face of financial collapse during the late 1870s (Reischauer 1981, pp. 129ff). Modern examples from the United Kingdom and the United States abound (Pirie 1985, Roth 1985).

Alchian, Armen A., and Demsetz, Harold, "The Property Rights Paradigm." *Journal of Economic History* 33 (March 1973): 16–27.

Bauer, Peter T. "Some Aspects and Problems of Trade in Africa." In *Markets and Marketing in Developing Countries*, pp. 48–69. Edited by Reed Moyer and Stanley Hollander. Homewood, Ill.: Richard D. Irwin, 1968.

Bauer, Peter T. *Dissent on Development: Studies and Debates in Development Economics*. London: Weidenfeld and Nicholson, 1971.

Bauer, Peter T., and Yamey, Basil S. "Industrialization and Development: The Nigerian Experience." *Economic History Review* 2d ser., 25 (November 1972): 674–89.

Bauer, Peter T., and Yamey, Basil S. *The Economics of Under-Developed Countries.* Cambridge: Cambridge University Press, 1957.

Bryce, Murray D. *Industrial Development: A Guide for Accelerating Economic Development*. New York: McGraw-Hill, 1960.

Buchanan, James M. "The Achievement and Limits of Public Choice in Diagnosing Government Failure and in Offering Bases for Constructive Reform." In *Anatomy of Government Deficiencies*. Edited by H. Hanusch. Berlin and Heidelberg: Springer-Verlag, 1983.

Clarkson, Kenneth W. "Property Rights, Incentives, and Economic Development." *Growth and Change* 6 (April 1975): 23–28.

Demsetz, Harold. "Toward a Theory of Property Rights." *American Economic Review* 57 (May 1967): 347–73.

Elkan, Walter; Ryan, T.C.I.; and Mukui, J.T. "The Economics of Shoeshining in Nairobi." *African Affairs* 81 (April 1982): 247–56.

Furubotn, Eirik G., and Pejovich, Svetozar. "Property Rights and Economic Theory: A Survey of Recent Literature." *Journal of Economic Literature* 10 (December 1972): 137–62.

Goodman, John C. "Private Alternatives to Social Security: The Experience of Other Countries." *Cato Journal* 3 (Fall 1983): 563–79.

IMF. International Monetary Fund. *IMF Survey*. Washington, D.C., 17 February 1986. Review of Helen Hughes, "Policy Lessons of the Development Experience." Group of Thirty, Occasional Paper No. 16, New York, 1985.

Kindleberger, Charles P., and Herrick, Bruce. *Economic Development*. 3d ed. New York: McGraw-Hill, 1977.

Marsden, Keith. "Why Asia Boomed and Africa Busted." *Wall Street Journal*, 3 June 1985.

McKean, Roland N. "Divergences between Individual and Total Costs within Government." *American Economic Review* 54 (May 1964): 243–49.

O'Shaughnessy, Hugh. "A Positive View of Peru's Informal Economy." *Financial Times*, 3 July 1985.

Pirie, Madsen. *Dismantling the State, the Theory and Practice of Privatization*. Dallas: National Center for Policy Analysis, 1985.

Posner, Richard. "The Economic Theory of Property Rights." In his *Economic Theory of Law*. Boston: Little, Brown, 1972. Reprinted in Posner's *Economic*

Foundations of Property Law. Edited by Bruce A. Ackerman. Boston: Little, Brown, 1975.

Reishauer, Edwin O. *Japan: The Story of a Nation*. 2d ed. New York: Alfred A. Knopf, 1981.

Revel, Jean-Francois. *Wall Street Journal*, 5 November 1981.

Reynolds, Alan. Quoted in *Manhattan Report* 5 (3)(1985): 8.

Roth, Gabriel. *Private Provision of Public Services in Developing Countries*. Washington, D.C.: World Bank Economic Development Institute, May 1985.

Sanchez, Nicholas, and Waters, Alan Rufus. "Controlling Corruption in Africa and Latin America." In *The Economics of Property Rights*, pp. 279–95. Edited by Eirik G. Furubotn and Svetozar Pejovich. Cambridge, Mass.: Ballinger, 1974.

Shlapentokh, Vladimir. "Soviet Ideas on Property Invite Abuse of Capital Stock." *Wall Street Journal*, 20 March 1986.

Subasinghe, Devinda R. "Now, A Sri Lankan Free Market Economic Miracle." Heritage Foundation Asian Studies Center. *Backgrounder*, No. 27. Washington, D.C., 7 May 1986.

USAID. United States Agency for International Development. *U.S. Assistance Loans and Grants, and Assistance from International Organizations*. Statistical Annex I to the Annual Development Coordination Committee Report to Congress, prepared by the U.S. Agency for International Development, September 1982.

Waters, Alan Rufus. "Economic Growth and the Property Rights Regime." *Cato Journal* 7 (Spring/Summer 1987): 99–115.

World Bank. "Statistics on 189 Countries and Territories." *World Bank Atlas*. Washington, D.C., 1985.

8. Institutional Choice and Public Choice: Lessons for the Third World

Charles K. Rowley

A fundamental postulate of this essay is the notion that individuals desire to be wealthy and to be free, with freedom defined in the negative sense of absence of coercion by other individuals. However, this postulate does not necessarily imply that each individual desires other individuals to be wealthy and to be free. Nor does it imply that all individuals balance wealth and freedom commensurately either for themselves or for others. Differences in the weighting of these values may be significant within a country. They tend to be highly significant in cross-country comparisons. Historically, such differences have played a major role in the forging of the political institutions of specific societies, in effecting the institutional choices that determine whether a country will be classified as advanced or underdeveloped.

A second fundamental postulate of this essay is the notion that institutions matter, that a decisive factor determining whether an economy will grow, stagnate or decline is the quality of its constitution or the set of rules and constraints that serve to regulate the behavior of its political markets. A constitution, in this perspective, may be written or unwritten; it may have evolved or it may have been constructed, by consent or by imposition. It may be self-reinforcing or it may be policed. What matters, for wealth and for liberty, is that it should effectively protect individual and civil liberties and economic liberties (private property rights) for all citizens. Since these liberties are all negative (freedom from coercion by other individuals) an effective constitution must constrain the size of

---

Charles K. Rowley is Professor of Economics at George Mason University and General Director of the Locke Institute. He gratefully acknowledges financial support from the Lynde and Harry Bradley Foundation.

government, ideally to that of the minimal, nightwatchman state, empowered to recognize private property rights, to maintain internal law and order and to protect the borders from outside intervention.

Third World countries, by definition, are not wealthy, and, in practice, are not free in the sense defined above. If they have constitutions at all, such constitutions tend to be poorly crafted and to be even more poorly enforced. They fail to protect individual and civil liberties and show no comprehension of the concept of economic liberties. Third World countries are impoverished and unfree, not by bad luck or poor endowments, but by the deliberate design of the dictators, oligarchies, and one-party systems that control their destinies. Redemption, for the most part, lies exclusively in the hands of such leaders, or in the hands of citizens that oust them in successful revolutions, and not in the continued flow of para-statal aid that serves only to enrich the coffers of the few and to prolong the existence of inefficient and corrupt institutions.

Evidently, it is not necessary to be free in order to be wealthy. The Pacific Rim's Four Tigers—Taiwan, South Korea, Singapore, and Hong Kong—testify to the ability of autocracies that protect property rights to raise the per capita income of their citizens. Ultimately, of course, the economic liberties that underpin such achievements will be as long- or short-lived as the benevolent dictator or oligarchy that controls them. Evidently, also, countries that protect individual and civil liberties, but that fail to respect economic liberties may condemn themselves to poverty. India is the stellar case of such democratically endorsed immiseration, despite being the major single Third World recipient of international charity.

This essay makes use of ideas from public choice relevant to the shaky democracies, one party governments, oligarchies, and autocracies of the Third World to explain why most Third World countries fail to develop and to define the key institutional changes that must be made if their citizens are to have any realistic expectations of rising living standards.

The Ubiquity of Homo Economicus

In analyzing the behavior of private markets, economics successfully has focussed on the private, self-seeking motivation of all actors. Individuals are viewed as utility maximizers constrained by budgets; firms are viewed as profit maximizers constrained by bankruptcy. This approach has been immensely productive, both in explaining and in predicting market behavior. Arguably, it constitutes one of the most successful research programs in all of science; and this is a spectacular achievement, given that it deals with human beings and not inanimate objects as the fulcrum of its analysis.

Surprisingly, prior to 1957, economists stopped short when confronted with political markets, abandoned homo economicus, and fell back upon notions of impartial, omniscient, public interest motivated government, despite millennia of history that clearly invalidated such premises. In large part, this bifurcation in the research program reflected the utility perceived by economists from their role as philosopher-kings, an elite with acknowledged special access to their sovereign. Juvenile as this perception now seems, it was the dominant view among economists prior to the public choice revolution. It remains the dominant view, unfortunately, among the Ivy League elite that still controls the debate on the economics of underdevelopment.

In 1957, Anthony Downs launched the public choice revolution by denying the validity of the philosopher-king mind-set and by recognizing the ubiquitous presence of homo economicus in political markets. Focussing exclusively on democratic political markets, Downs reversed the traditional political science presumption, asserting that political parties advocate policies designed to win elections, rather than seek to win elections in order to implement preferred policies.

Downs outlined the framework for a rational choice theory of politics, a theory in which politicians broker policies designed to maximize votes and in which voters demand policies designed to maximize their utilities. Because of inescapable indivisibilities, political markets predictably do not clear as efficiently as private markets. For example, voters rarely confront incentives to become well-informed as to the policy platforms and past policy provisions of competing politicians. The lacunae presented by widespread rational voter ignorance was not viewed as particularly serious by Downs, who assumed that voters would rely on party ideologies as an effective information substitute. As the research program developed, however, other scholars began to take a much more pessimistic view of the implications of rational ignorance, recognizing the opportunities thus provided for other rational self-seeking actors.

Specifically, if many voters are rationally ignorant, politicians may fare well electorally by pursuing policies that concentrate benefits on a few well-organized recipients while disbursing costs widely across the general population. Mancur Olson in 1965 presented a rational choice theory of interest groups designed to explain how such well-organized recipients emerge as a significant factor on the demand side of political markets. Arguing against the then prevailing viewpoint in political science that interest groups easily emerge as information conduits in political markets, Olson argued that the public good (bad) characteristics of important interest group objectives implied that members confronted free-riding incentives of varying degree.

To the extent that certain kinds of interest groups could overcome this free-rider problem more effectively than others, they would exert a differential impact on political markets. Olson suggested that small, homogeneous groups, groups that could coerce the supply of their members' efforts, and groups that could provide selective benefits to members would exert the most effective demand on political markets. Rationally ignorant voters and less effective interest groups would "supply" political transfers brokered by vote-seeking politicians (Crew and Rowley 1988).

Politicians broker wealth transfers through legislative action. Legislation must be enforced by bureaus located in the executive branch of government. Bureaus typically are subjected to oversight and budget appropriation control by the legislature (or by committees and subcommittees of the legislature). In the traditional political science literature, bureaus were viewed as the faithful servants of their political masters. Such a naive view could not survive the rational choice revolution. Following initial contributions by Gordon Tullock (1965) and by Downs (1967), Niskanen (1971) developed a thorough-going rational choice theory of bureaucracy initially asserting that senior bureaucrats are motivated to maximize the size (or rate of growth) of their budgets subject to covering costs with revenues. In 1975, Niskanen revised this maximand (responding to criticism) to assert that senior bureaucrats seek to maximize the size of their discretionary budgets (Niskanen 1994).

Niskanen demonstrated, on this basis, that senior bureaucrats would out-maneuver the oversight and appropriations committees in budget negotiations, partly because they are better informed and partly because they devote more effort to their highly specific causes. Typically, bureau outputs will be higher than the median voter would prefer and typically bureaus will be technically inefficient in supplying their outputs. In such circumstances, the public sector will tend systematically to be too large and public sector outputs will tend systematically to be too costly even in competitive democratic political markets.

By 1971, therefore, all the essential pieces were in place. Public choice offered a consistent rational choice theory of democratic politics in which political markets, primarily though not exclusively, were viewed as agents of wealth transfers and in which all the significant principals and agents in political markets were viewed as being motivated by narrow self-interest. In this perspective, traditional welfare economics essentially was destroyed. It is pointless and even dangerous to proffer advice to politicians crafted from the high principles of Paretian welfare economics. For such advice will simply be emasculated and transformed to suit the self-seeking interests of those who serve in political markets more or less exclusively in pursuit of private benefits. Those who seriously seek to influence political markets from the vantage point of high theory now must be exceptionally well-versed in public choice and skilled in traversing the thickets and land-mines of terrain marked out as a major battlefield over wealth distribution.

The Rent-Seeking Insight

Even if political markets are vehicles for wealth redistribution rather than wealth enhancement, it might be thought that they would act efficiently, moving resources from one group to another at minimum deadweight cost (Becker 1983). After all, why would rational individuals long tolerate a redistribution mechanism that actually destroys wealth? Tullock (1967a) offered a depressing insight into the cost of transfers in 1967, essentially denying the validity of the efficient political market hypothesis.

Tullock's point of departure was the conventional deadweight loss to monopoly associated with Arnold Harberger's famous triangle (Harberger 1954). Estimates of this welfare loss had been quite remarkably low (of the order of one-tenth of 1 percent of U.S. GNP), arousing his suspicion. If the expected profits from monopoly (the income transfer that a successful monopolist could extract from its customers) were high, surely such prospects would induce would-be monopolists to invest accordingly in the activity of monopolizing. Indeed, risk neutral entrepreneurs should be willing to invest resources in attempts to form a monopoly until the marginal cost equals the property discounted marginal return.

If the resources dedicated to such rent seeking were dissipated without providing any social product, then the real cost of monopoly would be several times that calculated by Harberger. If the monopoly is sought through the regulatory powers of government, Tullock's insight about rent seeking pinpoints a potentially serious inefficiency in the use of political markets. If government, more generally, is viewed as an instrument for wealth redistribution, then rent seeking must be viewed as a pervasive phenomenon of political markets.

In 1971, Tullock returned to the theme of his 1967 paper, this time focussing attention specifically onto the cost of transfers. Like Chinese beggars who mutilate themselves in order to become attractive objects of private charity, Tullock observed that government transfer programs encourage rent seekers to render themselves into pitiful objects "deserving" of such transfers. Competitive lobbying of politicians occurs between those who seek to extract government transfers and those who seek to protect them. The fact that the transfer game itself is clearly negative sum in nature does not imply that those who engage in such political battles are behaving irrationally. It is an example of a prisoner's dilemma that is not easily resolved.

Tullock (1975a) extended his analysis of transfers to demonstrate that wasteful competition over transfers is not restricted to individuals but also occurs among the various levels of government in a multilayer system. Specifically, where higher level government programs provide assistance to lower level systems, the lower level governments respond by neglecting their own responsibilities in order to qualify for higher level subsidies, again behaving much like the Chinese beggars, mutilating themselves in order to become objects of pity. In competing for aid, lower levels of government waste scarce resources and degrade their assets.

A major activity of modern government is the granting of special privileges to various groups of influential individuals. As Tullock (1975b) observed, the profit record of such protected organizations does not appear to differ systematically from that of the unprotected sections of the economy. This observation led Tullock to develop a theory of the transitional gains trap.

> My thesis is that there are only transitional gains to be made when the government establishes privileges for a group of people. The successors to the original beneficiaries will not normally make exceptional profits. Unfortunately, they will usually be injured by any cancellation of the original gift. It would seem, as David Friedman has put it, that "the government cannot even give anything away" [Tullock 1993, p. 66].

The problem posed by the transitional gains trap is the ratchet-like nature of rent seeking. Once a rent has been attained through government lobbying, it is very difficult to remove even after it ceases to produce positive profits for those who have paid prices for the assets that capitalize the rent values. Its elimination imposes capital losses on such owners and, for that reason, will be opposed by rent-protection outlays (Rowley and Tollison 1986). The transitional gains trap insight is a warning of the difficulty of deregulating once rents have been created, whether under conditions of democracy or of autocracy.

Fred McChesney (1987) identified yet another rent-seeking problem by integrating the role of the politician into the basic rent-seeking, rent-protection model. Political office confers a "property right" not just to legislate rents but also to impose costs. Politicians can extract rent-seeking outlays merely by forebearing from imposing burdensome restrictions on private actions. When the Mafia indulges in such a protection racket, it is referred to as extortion. When governments follow suit it is usually depicted in less pejorative terms. McChesney uses the term "rent extraction" to depict such behavior. An interesting facet of rent extraction is that there are no evident signs of government activity. Successful rent extraction leaves no trace, no legislation or regulation to highlight the event that triggers the transfer of monies from private to political pockets.

Inefficient Political Markets in the Third World

Those countries that have been rendered Third World by the adoption of communism will not be evaluated in this paper. For the most part, their leaders have learned their lessons or have been ousted or assassinated in the wake of the collapse of the Soviet Union. Although their economies are in chaos, their market route to salvation, whether through democracy or autocracy, is well-charted, and many of the institutional obstacles to reform have been obliterated.

The noncommunist underdeveloped countries, especially those in Africa, however, face far more pernicious problems of institutional rigidity that threaten to prolong poverty and to deny freedom for many of their peoples for generations to come. It is on the countries of Africa that attention is focussed throughout the remainder of this essay.

Africa is the richest of all the continents in terms of natural resources and mineral wealth (Lamb 1984, p. 20). According to George Ayittey (1992, pp. 2–3),

> It has 40 percent of the world's potential hydroelectric power supply, the bulk of the world's diamonds and chromium, 30 percent of the uranium in the noncommunist world, 50 percent of the world's gold, 90 percent of its phosphates, 40 percent of its platinum, 7.5 percent of its coal, 8 percent of its known petroleum reserves, 12 percent of its natural gas, 3 percent of its iron ore, and millions of acres of untilled agricultural land. In addition, Africa has 64 percent of the world's manganese, 13 percent of its copper, and vast bauxite, nickel, and lead resources.

Yet in 1990, sub-Saharan (black) Africa was home to 24 of the world's 36 poorest nations. With a population of 450 million, sub-Saharan Africa has a gross domestic product of only $135 billion, which is about the same as Belgium, with a population of only 10 million (Ayittey 1992, p. 9).

The institutional problems that underpin the current catastrophe date back to 1884 when Belgium, France, Britain, Germany, and Portugal were staking out colonial claims on the African continent. To lay down rules to govern, an international conference was held in Berlin under the chairmanship of Otto von Bismarck. On February 26, 1885, the *Berlin Act* was passed, promulgating the rules for partition. Africa was divided up into colonies and transformed into appendages of the European powers. Boundaries were drawn up with little regard to demographic configurations. Africans were widely (though not universally) denigrated as inferior and were subjected to cultural and emotional humiliation.

Africa's colonial heritage is an important factor to be considered in understanding the political institutions that emerged in the postcolonial era. First, colonization coercively integrated different ethnic groups with distinct cultures and social systems. The boundaries of many colonies were artificially drawn, usually to facilitate European development of the resources of the African territories (Mbaku 1993, p. 24). Second, in order to achieve internal stability, the imperial powers only rarely (mostly the British) encouraged the development of participatory forms of government. Mostly, they employed force to regulate the relationship between the different ethnic groups. The process of decolonization typically accentuated conflict as ethnic groups battled each other to control the apparatus of government.

Third, colonial rule typically failed to treat ethnic groups equally, with damaging consequences for post-independence. Most of the educated, highly skilled individuals in the country at independence had been cultivated in the European languages and had embraced European culture. They would seize the apparatus of government and dominate many of the post-independence political markets. This concentration of political power boded ill for the establishment of efficient political institutions (Mbaku 1993). Fourth, those potential leaders who had been educated in European (especially in British) elite universities had been indoctrinated in socialist ideology and in the economics of John Maynard Keynes (1936). This disastrous political economic legacy from the colonialist era accentuated the movement toward highly centralized government and highly politicized economic markets.

In such circumstances, it is not surprising that many black African countries abandoned the institutional framework of parliamentary democracy imposed on them by the colonial powers in favor of some form of statism. Parliamentary democracy typically was abandoned in favor either of one-party government or of military dictatorship, periodically punctuated by coup d'état. A good example is that of Ghana (Krauss 1983, p. 30). Between independence in 1957 and 1982, Ghana was to reel through five military coups and three civilian governments. It is an example par excellence of a Third World country where socialism and centralized government made totalitarianism a recurrent aspect of political life. The collapse of real output, under such circumstances, is a predictable outcome of public choice.

The Vote Motive

Even in well-established Western democracies, public choice scholars do not place great confidence in the vote motive as a key demand variable in political markets, as the rational ignorance hypothesis (Downs 1957, Tullock 1967b) clearly indicates (Rowley 1984). In the case of underdeveloped countries, this weakness is at least an order of magnitude more pronounced, even where democracy in one form or another exists.

For most individuals in underdeveloped countries, primitive transportation systems and bureaucratic voting mechanisms ensure that voting is a time-consuming exercise, even though opportunity costs may not always be high. Undoubtedly, this factor will deter many citizens from going to the polls. Perhaps more serious, however, is the high incidence of illiteracy or semiliteracy that ensures that most individuals remain rationally ignorant of the newspaper and written propaganda debates between the competing political parties, even when their political interest is sufficiently aroused.

The widespread absence of television, even of radio facilities, among the poor rural population further stifles the flow of relevant political market information. Though word of mouth transmission may be relatively sophisticated, under such circumstances, the opportunities provided for misinformation remain high, especially among populations prone to manipulation by religion, witchcraft, and voodoo.

Given that the democratic political markets of underdeveloped countries, when they exist, systematically favor the elites cultivated under colonial rule, the expected benefits of political participation, for the relatively disadvantaged, are further diminished. In such circumstances, differential absenteeism, combined with electoral fraud, all but guarantee elite domination of the election box. If the nonelite achieves electoral victory, rent-seeking military intervention predictably protects the privileges of the elite population, thus further discounting the expected benefits of voting in democratic elections.

In such circumstances, even two party parliamentary democracies will not satisfy the median voter theorem set out by Downs (1957). Figure 1 illustrates the predictable bias of political party representation.

In Figure 1, the characteristic position of the right-leaning party is well to the tail of the distribution of voter preferences over government spending, though it is somewhat closer to the median than that of the left-leaning party. In part for reasons outlined above,

FIGURE 1

THE OUTCOME OF TWO-PARTY ELECTIONS IN UNDERDEVELOPED COUNTRIES

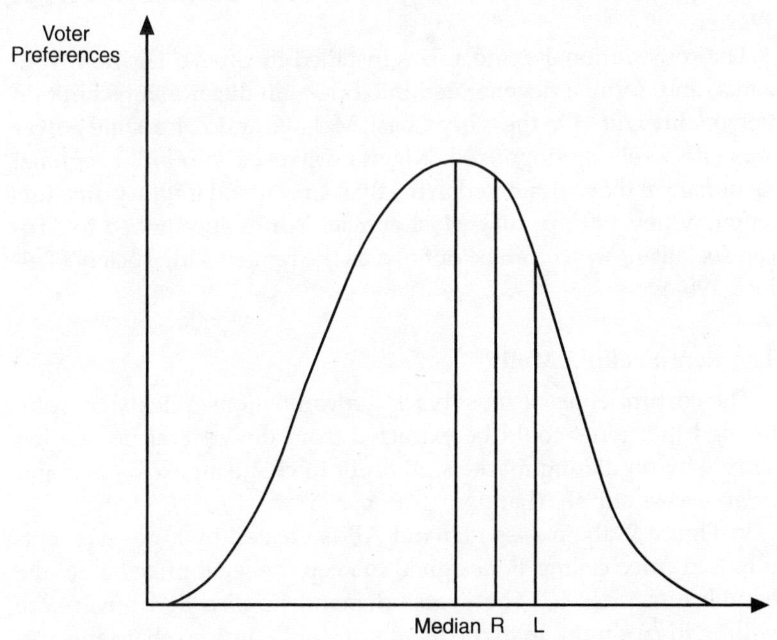

proximity to the median is no guide to electoral success. As Niskanen (1993) has noted for U.S. elections, the popular vote is a vote for a package of conditions specific to each party. Parties that approve high levels of government spending can usually be elected if their performance or position on other important conditions is satisfactory.

This is especially true in underdeveloped countries where the behavior of party activists and the amount of financial contributions are especially important, and where the decision to vote is primarily an expressive act (endorsement of democracy) rather than an investment decision. The agenda setters in the political establishment and military elite systematically bias electoral outcomes in favor of high levels of government spending and high levels of regulation for rent-seeking reasons.

In such circumstances, democracy is extremely vulnerable and, indeed, has been short-lived or sporadic through most of post-independence sub-Saharan Africa. Democratic structures established by the departing colonials were perceived by the new leaders as Western.

The constitutional democracies installed in Ghana, Uganda, Tanzania, and Zambia degenerated into one-man dictatorships built on personality cults. On the Ivory Coast, Malawi, and Zaire, state power was effectively monopolized. Nigeria collapsed into bitter regional factionalism that culminated in the Biafran war and military dictatorship (Ayittey 1992, p. 101). Most of black Africa succumbed to African socialism, which can be defined as the rent-seeking society (Tullock 1987).

The Rent-Seeking Motive

The corrupt elites of most black African nations quickly comprehended that rents could be extracted from the general population simply by regulating markets, in order to create an excess demand or an excess supply (Landau 1990, p. 575).

In Figure 2, the excess demand AB is created by a government-imposed price ceiling P_1 designed to keep the legal price below the equilibrium price P_0. The excess demand implies that buyers are willing to pay more than the legal price of P_1, indeed that rents can be appropriated by the government equal to the present value of the rectangle P_1ACP_2, simply by selling the Q_1 on a black market. These rents may take the form of direct payments, such as bribes, to the ruling elite or indirect payments, such as political support. In this way, running the government of an underdeveloped country can be extremely profitable.

Landau (1990) identifies several key areas commonly, though not universally, manipulated by ruling elites in underdeveloped countries as a basis for extracting rents. They include foreign currency markets, agricultural price controls, industrial regulations, and public enterprise. Let us review each of these in turn.

Many underdeveloped countries regulate the foreign currency market, setting the price of foreign currency below the free-market equilibrium. This policy is designed to create a shortage of foreign currency. In response to such a shortage, the government institutes foreign currency controls, typically requiring individuals and firms

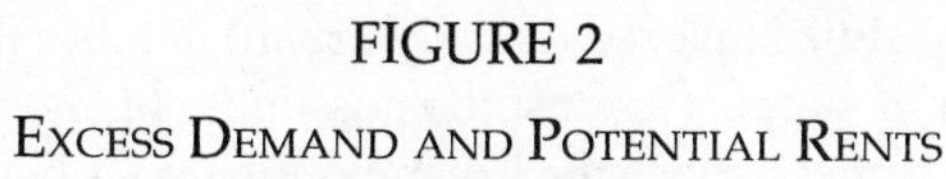

FIGURE 2

EXCESS DEMAND AND POTENTIAL RENTS

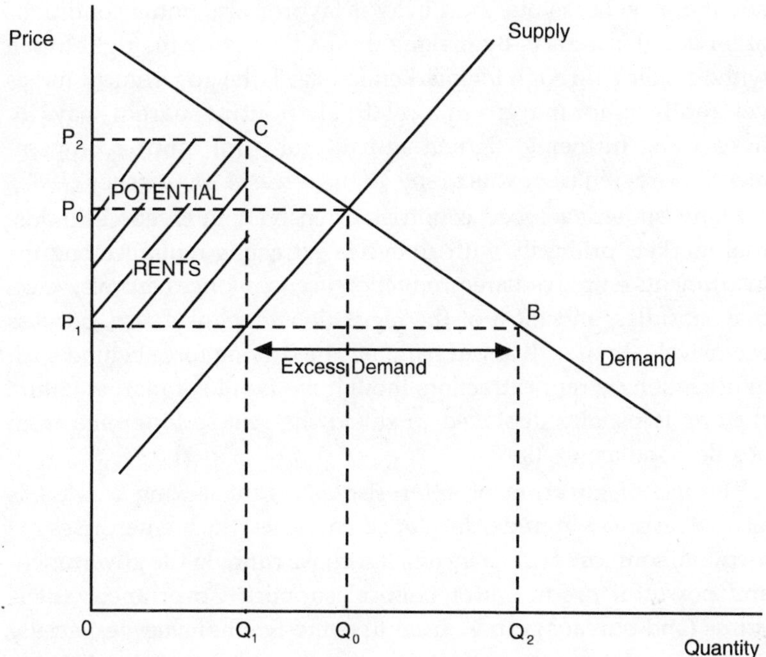

SOURCE: Landau (1990, p. 515).

to hold a license to have access to foreign currency. Since these licenses are valuable, they can be sold, either openly or covertly, to those who wish to gain privileged access to imported commodities. Such licenses can also be used selectively to protect domestic producers from foreign competition, once again in return for political favors. The threat to withhold a license can also be used to extract rent in the sense explained by McChesney (1987). In contrast, floating exchange rates, though much more efficient, create no rents and are politically unattractive to a corrupt government.

Many underdeveloped countries manipulate their agricultural markets, typically by lowering the prices received by farmers below the free-market equilibrium, often through the medium of marketing boards. At one level, this policy is a disguised form of taxation. It also opens up opportunities for government, through selective price controls, to subsidize favored (usually urban) families thus building up a reservoir of support against the possibility of any violent overthrow of government. Since the urban population is better educated and more likely to vote, this device is favored also under conditions of limited democracy. By making it possible to buy the right to sell without going through the marketing board, the government mines yet another rent margin in a relatively nontransparent way. By threatening further to tighten agricultural price controls, government once again can extract rents in the sense of McChesney (1987).

Many underdeveloped countries extensively intervene in industrial markets primarily with an eye to extracting rents. Among the instruments employed are production licenses, price controls, selective subsidies, and most of the regulations deployed also, but less extensively, in the advanced nations. The driving force behind such interventions is rent extraction, though the facade of market failure rhetoric is usually deployed to shield the rent-seeking elite from hostile popular reaction.

The use of government enterprise as a rent-seeking conduit is also widespread in underdeveloped countries. Such enterprises are lucrative sources of direct income for those running the government and powerful producers of political support. Government enterprises (and bureaus) can be used to overpay employees (especially management drawn from the educational and cultural elites) and to provide secure employment for lower level government supporters. They can be used selectively to assist private firms in return for political support and bribes. They are often used selectively to provide essential infrastructure to privileged localities, once again in return for political support and bribes.

What is impressive about underdeveloped countries is not the fact that such rent extraction devices exist—for they exist in all countries whether advanced or poor, democratic or autocratic—but the magnitude and pervasiveness of their deployment. It is no exaggeration to suggest that the best brains and best entrepreneurial talents of the educated population are diverted from wealth creation to wealth destruction in the rent-seeking societies of most black African countries.

Nor can the outcome be passed off as redistribution from poor to rich as, superficially, might seem to be the case. For most of the transferred wealth ultimately is dissipated on the network of regulatory bureaucracies necessary to extort the rents and the military-police-spy networks necessary to protect the extracted rents from expropriation. What is left typically leaves the country for numbered bank accounts in Switzerland and elsewhere. Herein lies the explanation why potentially rich nations are condemned to seemingly perpetual poverty in marked contrast to the continuing wealth-creation of the advanced nations.

What Can Be Done?

Most underdeveloped countries are characterized, at best, by very marginal forms of democracy, that are highly vulnerable to elimination by well-established, brutal rent-seeking elites. Autocracy is the rule rather than the exception throughout the underdeveloped world. Even in those rare exceptions, such as India, where multiparty democracy appears to be well-entrenched, the colonial legacy, together with ethnic and caste rivalries, leaves such countries open to widespread rent-seeking waste and corruption (Rajan 1988).

By now, international agencies and governments of the advanced nations should have learned, though for the most part they have not, that aid further accentuates the institutional weaknesses of such economies, creates additional rents that feed the rent-seeking frenzy of the educated elites, and maintains in power corrupt and ill-intentioned governments. Tullock's (1975b) insight into the nature of the transitional gains trap advises just how fiercely successful rent seekers will lobby to protect their rents from market-based reforms, if necessary by resort to military intervention. This trap is all the more sharply sprung since government is the primary rent seeker in underdeveloped countries and not simply the broker of rents fought over by rent-seeking interest groups. To review the prospects for internal reform, in such circumstances, from a public choice perspective, comes close to a counsel of despair.

Of course, one should never rule out hope for reform given unknowability about the future and given the will to survive of the human gene. As the collapse of the Soviet Union demonstrated, it is possible that a tired, corrupt elite may well walk away from a government machine that has so looted and pillaged its peoples that rents are all but completely dissipated, and that subsistence levels of output are in jeopardy (Brennan 1990). It is possible even before that fateful moment, that an enraged population may overcome the free-rider problem (Tullock 1974) and rise up in revolution to eliminate the elite that exploits it, in the hope, if not the expectation, of a freer and wealthier future. With very low probabilities, such an event may pave the way for serious institutional reform.

How then might a newly enlightened people draft a constitution for a nation or republic emerging into freedom? Let me draw broadly on recent work in constitutional political economy (Siegan 1992) to offer realistic solutions to a seemingly intractable problem of statism in the underdeveloped world.

A major concern of constitution framers is to determine how much power government should possess. For most underdeveloped countries the answer has been simple. Government should have absolute power. For the United States in the late 18th century, blessed with great constitutionalists as Founding Fathers, the answer was entirely different. The state exists only for the benefit of the people. Government should have only strictly enumerated powers sufficient to secure the people's life, liberty and property, their inalienable rights that precede the formation of civil society (Locke [1690] 1991).

For the framers of the U.S. Constitution, the separation and enumeration of powers of the federal government, the checks and balances between government branches, and the provision for judicial review to secure liberties were specifically designed to protect the individual from government oppression. Subsequent amendments in the form of a Bill of Rights were designed to fortify the supremacy of the individual over the state and to ensure that, even if checks and balances failed, the individual would have constitutional protection against a would-be Leviathan state. Such a constitution is a necessary, though not a sufficient, condition for any nation to emerge into freedom from statist tyranny.

Of course, not all the advanced countries have adopted the American system of separation of powers. Many have followed the British example of the parliamentary system; others have combined elements of both. In the case of underdeveloped countries, with their lengthy histories of statism, it is essential that they adopt the American model. The parliamentary system simply vests excessive power in a single body. There is an enormous risk that such powers will be exercised tyrannically. If government power instead is fractionalized into legislative, executive, and judicial branches, no single group of individuals can impose its unchecked will on the general population. Untidy and slow though a fractionalized system may be, it protects liberties more than any unitary system can guarantee.

Within a separation of powers system of government, the primary purpose must be to restrain the legislature, which imposes the greatest threat to liberty. This is especially important in underdeveloped countries, with their lengthy histories of ethnic and racial conflict. It is important, to this end, to establish a bicameral legislature, with each chamber elected (or appointed) for differing terms and on a different basis of representation.

The lower chamber—the engine of the legislature—arguably should be elected for short terms on the basis of proportional representation. This will ensure that all minorities gain representation and will limit the risk of a tyranny of the majority. The upper chamber—the brake of the legislature—should be appointed for longer terms by the regional or provincial governments and should overrepresent the small regions and provinces. This will ensure that regional minorities gain protection against discriminatory legislation. The legislature should be obliged to act with due process and to uphold the rule of law, as set out in the constitution.

In a government based on separation of powers "the President is the Chief executive officer of the nation, charged with implementing the nation's laws" (Siegan 1992, p. 18). It is arguably useful, in addition, to vest the office with some legislative authority such as the power of the veto and the formulation and conduct of foreign policy. Although the power of the veto may appear to give the presidency monarchial powers, it is an essential element of the separation system. Moreover, a president who is elected is essentially accountable to the people. Underdeveloped countries would do well to subject the presidency to election by universal suffrage, using the plurality system, and to limit an elected president to a single four year term in office.

Under a separation of powers system, the senior executives will be appointed by the president subject to confirmation by a majority of the upper chamber of the legislature. The legislature will write the rules by which the executive branch must operate and will appropriate annual departmental budgets. Nevertheless, the senior executives should reflect the political views of the president.

The protection of liberty requires an independent judiciary powerful enough to monitor the legislature and executive to ensure compliance with the constitution. It must be empowered to annul unconstitutional laws and to require compensation for unconstitutional actions. Individuals who are aggrieved must have reasonable access to the courts to protect their constitutional rights. The judiciary, in interpreting the constitution, should be empowered only to negate laws and not to impose them. The power of final judgment should be lodged in a supreme court of general jurisdiction whose members should be appointed for life by the president subject to confirmation by the upper chamber of the legislature.

In the case of underdeveloped countries, with lengthy histories of abuse of arbitrary powers and, at best, with only a skeletal respect for the system of common or civil law inherited from the colonial powers, it is essential that a bill of rights should be incorporated into the constitution. The bill of rights should enumerate and protect the liberties (negative freedoms) of individuals from "oppressive, arbitrary, confiscatory and capricious laws and regulations" (Siegan 1992, p. 34). This enumeration should help to ensure that the judiciary does not undervalue such liberties in its judgments of legislative and executive branch behavior.

The world is rarely blessed with such constitutional scholars as James Madison and Alexander Hamilton. More rarely do such scholars gain the opportunity to draft constitutions for nations newly emerging into freedom. Yet, the underdeveloped world has the example of the U.S. Constitution before it when contemplating constitutional reform. If the peoples of such countries value freedom and prosperity, they would do well to give serious consideration to the parchment that retained its texture for some 150 years before disintegrating under the rent-seeking pressures of special interests (Wagner 1993) much as Madison (*Federalist* No. 51) feared would ultimately come to pass.

References

Ayittey, George B.N. *Africa Betrayed.* New York: St. Martin's Press, 1992.

Becker, Gary S. "A Theory of Competition Among Pressure Groups for Political Influence." *Quarterly Journal of Economics* 63 (1983): 371–400.

Brennan, H. Geoffrey. *The Tale of the Slave-Owner: Reflections on the Political Economy of Communist Reform.* Fairfax, Va.: Center for Study of Public Choice, 1990.

Crew, Michael A, and Rowley, Charles K. "Toward a Public Choice Theory of Monopoly Regulation." *Public Choice* 57 (April 1988):49–68.

Downs, Anthony. *An Economic Theory of Democracy.* New York: Harper and Row, 1957.

Downs, Anthony. *Inside Bureaucracy.* Boston: Little Brown, 1967.

Harberger, Arnold C. "Monopoly and Resource Allocation." *American Economic Review* 44 (1954): 77–87.

Keynes, John M. *The General Theory of Employment, Interest and Money.* London: Macmillan, 1936.

Krauss, Melvyn B. *Development Without Aid.* New York: University Press of America, 1983.

Lamb, David. *The Africans.* New York: Random House, 1984.

Landau, Daniel. "The Pattern of Economic Policies in LDCs.: A Public Choice Explanation." *Cato Journal* 10 (Fall 1990): 573–601.

Locke, John. *Two Treatises of Government* [1690]. Reprint. Edited by Peter Laslett. Cambridge: Cambridge University Press, 1991.

Mbaku, John M. "Rent Seeking and Democratization Strategies for Africa." Weber State University Working Paper, 1993.

McChesney, Fred S. "Rent Extraction and Rent Creation in the Economic Theory of Regulation." *Journal of Legal Studies* 16 (January 1987): 67–100.

Niskanen, William A. Bureaucracy and Representative Government. New York: Aldine-Atherton, 1971.

Niskanen, William A. "The Reflections of a Grump." *Public Choice* 77 (September 1993): 151–58.

Niskanen, William A. *Bureaucracy and Public Economics.* Aldershot, U.K.: Edward Elgar, 1994.

Olson, Mancur. *The Logic of Collective Action.* Cambridge: Harvard University Press, 1965.

Rajan, Roby. "Entrepreneurship and Rent Seeking in India." *Cato Journal* 8 (Spring/Summer 1988): 165–84.

Rowley, Charles K. "The Relevance of the Median Voter Theorem." *Journal of Institutional and Theoretical Economics* (March 1984): 104–35.

Rowley, Charles K., and Tollison, Robert D. "Rent-Seeking and Trade Protection." *Swiss Journal of International Economic Relations* 41 (September 1986): 141–66.

Siegan, Bernard H. *Drafting A Constitution for a Nation or Republic Emerging into Freedom.* Fairfax, Va.: The Locke Institute, 1992.

Tullock, Gordon. *The Politics of Bureaucracy.* New York: University Press of America, 1965.

Tullock, Gordon. "The Welfare Costs of Tariffs, Monopolies and Theft." *Western Economic Journal* 5 (1967a): 227–32.

Tullock, Gordon. *Towards A Mathematics of Politics.* Ann Arbor: University of Michigan Press. 1967b.

Tullock, Gordon. "The Cost of Transfers." *Kyklos* 24 (1971): 629–43.

Tullock, Gordon. *The Social Dilemma: The Economics of War and Revolution*. Blacksburg, Va.: Center for Study of Public Choice, 1974.
Tullock, Gordon. "Competing for Aid." *Public Choice* 21 (1975a): 41–52.
Tullock, Gordon. "The Transitional Gains Hypothesis." *Bell Journal of Economic and Management Science* 6 (Autumn 1975b): 671–78.
Tullock, Gordon. *Autocracy*. Boston: Kluwer, 1987.
Tullock, Gordon. *Rent Seeking*. Aldershot, U.K.: Edward Elgar, 1993.
Wagner, Richard E. *Parchment, Guns and Constitutional Order*. Aldershot, U.K.: Edward Elgar, 1993.

9. Tribal Ownership: A Curse on Native Americans' Economic Development

Steve H. Hanke and Barney Dowdle

The Failure of Communal Ownership: The Case of Indian Reservations

There are roughly 1.5 million American Indians in the United States. Approximately half reside on or near publicly owned reservations. Indian reservations cover a total 52.5 million acres, which is about the size of Kansas. The reservations are held in trust by the Federal government and are managed by the Bureau of Indian Affairs (BIA).

Even though the reservations have broad powers of sovereign, self-governing "nations," the Federal government, through the BIA, has traditionally played a large role in all aspects of American Indian life. Indeed, the economic affairs of most tribes are micro-managed by the BIA. The BIA typically negotiates contracts, determines natural resource use, makes investment decisions, manages tribal financial records, and determines tribal employment policies. As an indicator of the government involvement in Indian affairs, consider that the Federal government spends upwards of $3 billion annually, or almost $2,000 per capita, on American Indians. This $3 billion is roughly evenly split between the BIA and Indian Health Services (United States Budget, Fiscal Year 1995). In addition, there are numerous other smaller programs specifically designed to aid the Indians. Likewise, the $3 billion figure does not include the various more general kinds of welfare payments for which the Indians are eligible.

Economic development on Indian reservations, when it occurs, is limited. (The recent gambling boom on some reservations is an

Steve H. Hanke is Professor of Applied Economics at The Johns Hopkins University, and Barney Dowdle is Professor of Forestry at the University of Washington.

exception.) Indian reservations resemble many less developed countries. Unemployment rates on reservations are, on average, about four times higher than the overall U.S. rate. Moreover, government make-work programs account for a great deal of the employment. Average family incomes are about 70 percent of the national average, and nearly one-third of all Indians live in poverty. Not surprisingly, American Indians suffer many of the ills that accompany poverty: high rates of alcoholism, criminality, familial instability, and general poor health. If this were not enough, corruption is widespread on reservations (*The Economist* 1989).

Indian reservations represent man-made disasters of the first order. Communal ownership and widespread government failure have provided the impetus for this sad state of affairs.

Indian Reservations and Privatization

To remedy the economic maladies that afflict Indians, the Presidential Commission on Indian Reservation Economics (United States 1984, p. 41) recommended a sweeping privatization program. The commission concluded that

> extensive tribal government management and involvement in business development activity contributed to the failure of tribal enterprises. Merely separating the corporate functions of tribal enterprises from interference by tribal government and employing competent management will not achieve a privatization of tribal enterprises capable of offering profit motivation, private property ownership, nor individual freedom.
>
> Private ownership of tribal enterprises contemplates ownership of the means of production, private management, for-profit motivation and freedom for individual Indians or groups of Indians who have or share an interest in participating in business activity on an Indian reservation. Tribes could just as easily lease tribally held assets to their members as they presently do to nonmember businesses which use their resources. Existing businesses could be sold to tribal members, or ownership transferred by way of stock transfers, rather than per capita distributions of corporate retained earnings. Employee stock participation plans could also be offered. There is no one correct approach to privatizing tribal enterprises. There are, however, many possibilities for offering individual Indians incentives. There is no difference

> between a per capita payment from a tribal enterprise, a judgment fund, a mineral royalty or bonus, and a welfare distribution, where no opportunity exists for individual Indians to self-actualize or to succeed through individual effort.

The presidential commission, therefore, advocated privatizing communally owned reservation resources as a necessary means to start economic development.

Since land resources comprise a significant portion of the assets on most reservations, we will focus on these resources throughout the remainder of this chapter. The present bureaucratic arrangements for managing communal Indian lands lead to a massive amount of economic waste. For example, Indian grazing lands are typically overused, while timberlands are underused.

In the pages that follow, we present an analysis of Indian timberlands, and conclude that the privatization of the timberlands under study would increase their value by a factor of about 2.7. Consequently, the privatization of Indian lands would stimulate economic growth and go a long way toward alleviating poverty on Indian reservations.

To understand why the uneconomic use of public lands occurs, it is instructive to consider why we should expect private lands to be used in an economically efficient manner. Private owners stand to gain enhanced wealth from prudent improvements on their property, reductions in production costs, proper land use and the like. Indeed, private owners are "residual claimants" who have a strong interest in maximizing the residual profit or capital gain arising from land ownership. Public owners, by contrast, lack a "residual claim" in any meaningful sense. Consequently, we should expect public lands to be used in an uneconomic manner. Our observation is, of course, not new. Adam Smith (1776, Book V, chapter ii, part II, article I) concluded that, "The attention of the sovereign can be at best a very general and vague consideration of what is likely to contribute to the better cultivation of the greater part of his dominions. The attention of the landlord is particular and minute consideration of what is likely to be the most advantageous application of every inch of ground upon his estate."

The use of public lands is usually governed by two quite different methods. One method is the "rule of capture." Under this rule, individuals can establish private rights on publicly owned resources by "capturing" the resources. The other method is a "bag limit rule." Under this rule, individuals can establish private rights on publicly owned resources by obtaining a "bag permit" (use permit) from the proper governmental authorities.

Public grazing lands are subject to what is called the "tragedy of the commons," a condition that has occurred many times in human history. It is characterized by overuse and a loss in land productivity because public grazing lands are subject to the "rule of capture." This tragedy would be eliminated if the land were privatized, because private owners have a residual claim on their land assets. Consequently, private owners have a strong incentive to exclude nonowners and to use grazing lands economically.

The following story illustrates the economics of the tragedy of the commons. Suppose a group of youngsters is given a free soda and straws. With the soda "owned" in common, the straws will enter the soda and each youngster will attempt to capture the maximum amount of soda as fast as possible before others can lay claim to it. The rule of capture will be at work. Consequently, the soda will be rapidly depleted. Under these rules, each youngster knows that a new soda will be depleted in the same manner as the first one. Hence, no one has an incentive to invest in another soda. The only way the soda supply can be maintained is for the youngsters to convince an outsider to replenish it.

The soda analogy reflects the fate of lands held in common ownership and managed by the rule of capture. For example, Gary D. Libecap and Ronald D. Johnson (1980) found a tragedy of the commons on the Navajo reservation, the largest in the United States. They found that common property (vague tenure) arrangements on the reservation have resulted in rapid increases in the number of sheep and goat herders. Consequently, overgrazing has occurred and the land quality has declined through a loss of palatable plant species and severe wind and water erosion. The result has been high livestock mortality, low lambing rates, poor wool production, and a fall in livestock-based income. To maintain their livestock, the Navajo have had to rely on feed-grain subsidies from the Federal government.

We now turn from grazing to timberlands. Indian timberlands, rather than being subject to the rule of capture, are subject to a timber-harvesting rule (or in some cases, a modification thereof) called "nondeclining even flow." This harvesting rule operates like a "bag limit" and is imposed on Indian tribes by the BIA.

Nondeclining even flow requires annual timber harvests not to fall below an initially established level. With even flow, the timber-harvest rate is determined by inventory volumes and timber-growth rates. Hence it is a physical rather than an economic concept. Economic costs and demands are not part of the determination of harvest rates. Consequently, a policy of even flow results in the uneconomic underuse of timberlands.

Uneconomic use does not occur on private timberlands because individuals have residual claims on them. Private owners treat their lands as capital assets and view them as an investment or capital management problem in which capital costs (interest costs) are part of the true cost of growing timber. The nondeclining even-flow principle does not take capital costs into account. The result is that harvest ages for public timber are much too long, timber is allowed to become "overripe" in an economic sense, and too much timber is held in inventory. A corollary problem results: current output from public timberlands is too low.

The problems caused by the even-flow principle and its lack of consideration for capital carrying charges on timber inventories are most pronounced when applied to "old-growth" timber (forests that have never been cut before). In old-growth forests, growth rates range from negligible to negative. It would be economic to cut old-growth, overmature timber rapidly, and then to replant the forests. The even-flow method, however, does not allow for this type of inventory adjustment. In economic terms, it imposes excessive opportunity costs (capital carrying costs) on timberlands. By idling capital resources, the even-flow principle turns forestlands into resources roughly analogous to the Hindus' sacred cows.

If this were not bad enough, overmature forests create environmental problems as well. They are more prone to attack by insects, parasites, and disease. Aged trees tend to blow down, creating a fire hazard. Blown-down trees make it difficult for large game to traverse an old forest's floor. Also, since old forests have high, thick canopies that restrict light from reaching ground level, they contain little plant life to provide food for game animals, which, in turn, provide food for predators. Consequently, public timberlands underproduce both marketable timber and many types of environmental outputs.

The even-flow principle also creates economic instability in the regions where public ownership of timberlands is dominant. With even flow, the amount of timber marketed annually is more or less constant. Prices must, therefore, bear the burden of fluctuating demand. During periods of weak demand, prices for timberland plummet, and during periods of strong demand, prices soar.

The Pacific Northwest, a region in which public ownership accounts for about 75 percent of the timber inventories, is paying dearly for even flow (Dowdle and Hanke 1985). The even-flow policy has not allowed for an economic liquidation of overmature timber. This, in turn, has resulted in an artificial shortage of timber going to market during periods of strong demand. Moreover, even flow has caused excessive price volatility in the region. To avoid artificial shortages and price volatility, the wood-processing industry of the Pacific Northwest has been migrating to the South, where most timberlands are privately owned.

Given this dismal record, why have Indians refused to advocate privatizing publicly owned Indian lands? The major obstacle has been many Indians' perception that past efforts to privatize Indian lands—most notably the Dawes Severalty Act of 1887—were failures. Consequently, most Indians view private property as an institution that favors the white man and believe that it is not well suited to Indian culture. But the real and imagined failure of privatization under the Dawes Act had little, if anything, to do with the institution of private property per se.

The Dawes Severalty Act of 1887 and Privatization

Throughout the 19th century, Indian policymaking was characterized by simplistic diagnoses of Indian problems, easy "solutions," and stereotypes of Indians as uncivilized savages. During the early decades of the century, Indian policy was influenced primarily by missionaries who believed that the teachings of the Bible and acceptance of the Sabbath were the best means for civilizing Indians and integrating them into society.

The lack of success of the missionary approach led to the domination of policymaking by 19th-century liberals. They believed that exposing Indians to private property rights and a laissez-faire economic system would enable them better to adjust to a civil society. The latter approach, as well as Indian stereotypes characteristic of the era, are well captured in the views of Merrill E. Gates, president of Amherst College and of the Lake Mohonk Conference of the Friends of the Indians. In his presidential address at the 1896 annual meeting of the conference, he observed that there was a "need of awakening in the savage Indian broader desires and ampler wants. . . . Discontent with the tepee and the starving rations of the Indian camp in winter is needed to get the Indian out of the blanket and into trousers." Moreover, he argued, these trousers needed to have "a pocket in them . . . a pocket that aches to be filled with dollars" (cited in Berkhofer 1978, p. 173).

The Dawes Severalty Act of 1887 was a product of such thinking. Most influential people thought that hard work, thrift, and a system of private property rights would encourage and enable Indians to acquire wealth and become integrated into society. The Dawes Act authorized the President to allot land on Indian reservations to individual Indians. Heads of families were to receive 160 acres, while others were to receive smaller allotments. Indians were to receive full citizenship with the land transfers. Titles were to be held in trust by the United States government for 25 years, and then the land could be freely transferred. "Surplus" land—land left over after the allotments had been made—was to be sold on the open market.

Since there were considerably more "Indian lands" than acreages that qualified for Indian allotments, almost half of the land controlled by Indians was declared "surplus" and removed form their control. Also, many Indians who qualified and received allotments sold their newly acquired lands. This further reduced lands under Indian ownership and control. In addition, and perhaps most important, Indians (as well as many white homesteaders) were not afforded common-law protections that accompany property and contracts. Property rights and contracts were often neither enforced nor protected. William T. Hagan (1956) has reported that many Indians lost their lands "through tactics that ranged from deceit and duplicity to murder."

With the passage of the Dawes Act in 1887, the land area controlled by Indians was reduced by 50 percent. Then, between 1887 and the so-called Indian New Deal of 1934, which reversed the policies set in motion by the Dawes Act, about 38 percent of the acreage that had been allocated to Indians under provisions of the act was transferred through sales and other means to non-Indians. Moreover, much of the land that the Indians retained was semiarid or desert land in the Southwest. This, along with the fact that the average parcel awarded to an Indian was 160 acres and farm prices were declining, resulted in a great deal of Indian ownership that was not economically viable.

The experience of the Dawes Act has led Indians to distrust private ownership. However, private property had little to do with the failure of the Dawes Act. Rather, the act failed as the result of a poorly conceived Federal privatization policy and a frontier justice system that did not properly recognize and use the common law of property and contracts. In a misguided effort to ensure that they would not be exploited by private property institutions, Indians have favored public ownership. In turn, public arrangements have ensured that the Indians would misuse their lands.

Privatization and the Siletz Indians

Indian views are neither monolithic nor static, however. The Siletz Indians, for example, have endorsed privatization. In the mid-1800s, the Siletz were moved from their native lands and relocated on a 1.2 million acre reservation located on the central Oregon coast. Subsequently, most of this land was transferred from reservation status to other types of non-Indian ownership and use. By 1900, little of the original reservation was left.

In 1954, Congress formally terminated all relationships between the Federal Government and the Siletz. Remaining reservation lands were transferred to the Federal Government, and the Siletz no longer qualified for programs administered by the BIA. With the adoption of the Siletz Restoration Act of 1977, however, the relationship between the Federal Government and the Siletz was restored. Moreover, this act instructed the Secretary of the Interior to develop a plan for reestablishing a new reservation.

After the Secretary's plan was presented, Congress reestablished the Siletz Tribal Reservation in 1980. The new reservation consists of 3,628 acres of land in Lincoln County, Oregon. These lands were previously part of the public domain. Most of the area consists of scattered parcels of timberlands located two to 25 miles from Siletz, Oregon. Government Hill, which is part of the reservation and the location of Siletz Tribal Headquarters, is a 36-acre parcel located within the city limits of Siletz.

There are 12,000 acres of public-domain lands in Lincoln County, Oregon. They are similar to the lands in the existing Siletz Tribal Reservation and are scattered throughout Lincoln County in 90 separate parcels that range from 20 to 520 acres. These lands are owned by the Federal government and managed by the U.S. Bureau of Land Management (BLM).

The Siletz have proposed that the Federal government privatize its public-domain lands in Lincoln County. Under the Siletz proposal, the 12,000 acres of public-domain lands would be transferred to a private corporation established by the Siletz. The initial distribution of equity shares in this corporation would be made to members of the Siletz and could subsequently be freely exchanged.

Three aspects of this proposal merit comment. First, it is not a proposal to privatize Indian lands per se. Rather, it is a proposal to privatize public-domain lands by transferring them to a private corporation that is originally owned by members of the Siletz tribe. Second, the economics of privatizing public-domain timberlands, such as those in Lincoln County, are similar to the economics of privatizing Indian lands because the BIA imposes the same timber management rules on Indian lands as other Federal agencies impose on public-domain timberlands. Hence, the results of our benefit-cost analysis could be applied directly to the privatization of Indian lands themselves. Third, our analysis of the privatization proposal only considers whether privatizing the timberlands would generate net economic benefits. We do not consider the possible terms for a privatization transfer or whether the transfer of resources from the Federal government to the Siletz is, or is not, justified on noneconomic grounds.

A Benefit-Cost Analysis of Alternative Property Rights Arrangements

To conduct a benefit-cost analysis of privatizing public timberlands, we compute the present value of the timberlands with public ownership and the present value of the same lands with private ownership. The difference between the two values is the net benefit from establishing private property rights.

In western Oregon, public timberlands typically consist of old-growth timber. The economic problem concerns the rate at which the timber on these lands should be liquidated and the cut-over lands converted to "second-growth" tree farms. In other words, the problem is one of moving from a "mining" operation to a "farming" operation. This type of transition characterizes the situation on the public-domain lands contained in the Siletz proposal.

To analyze the economics of the timberlands in the Siletz proposal, we use a two-step approach, which allows us to compute separately the net present value of liquidating (mining) the old-growth timber and managing a second-growth tree farm. The total net present value of the timberlands is obtained by summing the two components. The formulas and calculations are contained in the appendix to this chapter.

Table 1 contains the empirical results obtained by applying our analysis to timberlands in Western Oregon. We compare public ownership and private ownership of the same timberlands to determine whether a transfer of public-domain lands to private ownership would increase or decrease the value of the timberlands in question.

To conduct our analysis, we assume the following:

1. The initial timber stand consists of 100 acres of old-growth timber.

2. The old-growth timber volumes and soil productivity are constant across all acres.

3. The price received per million board feet (MBF) of old-growth timber is the same.

4. Annual management and administration costs are $20 per acre for public ownership and $7.50 per acre for private ownership. The difference is consistent with data from comparative cost studies for timber management in the United States and Europe and with cost data from studies of private versus public provision of other goods and services (Hanke 1987). Annual management and administration costs used do not include costs for the amortization of road construction and annual road maintenance. We have not included these costs because the roads on the timberlands under study are already in place. We have, therefore, assumed that there is no difference in the costs associated with roads on public land compared to private land. Our treatment is biased against private ownership to some extent because there would, no doubt, be some savings in road costs if the timberlands were privately owned. Furthermore, if we were analyzing a case in which new roads were required on timberlands,

TABLE 1
NET PRESENT VALUES FROM PUBLIC AND PRIVATE TIMBER OWNERSHIP
(1989 DOLLARS)

Data	Public	Private
Total acres	100	100
Old-growth timber (MBF/acre)	60	60
Old-growth timber price ($/MBF)	$250	$250
Cost of management ($/acre/year)	$20	$7.50
Cost of planting ($/acre)	$250	$125
Second-growth harvest age (years)	100	40
Second-growth harvest volume (MBF/acre)	50	30
Second-growth timber price ($/MBF)	$200	$175
Discount rate (%/year)	5.5%	5.5%
Calculations		
A. Disaggregated (two-step) approach:		
Net present value of old growth	$242,131	$601,168
Net present value of second growth	($10,684)	$12,226
Total net present value	$231,447	$613,394
B. Ratio of private to public total net present values	2.7:1	

road costs would have to be analyzed because the public-private road cost differential would be very large and would favor private ownership.

5. The planting costs per acre are $250 for public and $125 for private ownership. Again, the public-private cost differential is consistent with data from comparative cost studies of private versus public supply (Hanke 1987).

6. Old-growth timber is liquidated over a 100-year period for public and a 40-year period for private ownership. These time periods are also equal to the second-growth harvest ages for public and private ownership, respectively. The longer periods under public ownership result from the fact that public timber is managed on nondeclining even-flow basis. Recall that this rule does not consider capital carrying charges on standing timber inventories. Private ownership requires that capital carrying charges be considered. Consequently, the liquidation of old-growth timber under private ownership is more rapid

than under public ownership. Moreover, second-growth harvest ages are less for private than for public ownership.

7. The second-growth harvest volume per acre is higher for public ownership than for private ownership because trees are harvested at older ages for public than for private ownership. Note that old-growth harvest volumes per acre for both private and public ownership are equal and exceed even those for second-growth public ownership because the harvest age for old-growth stands exceeds the harvest age for public second-growth timber (100 years).

8. The second-growth timber price for public ownership exceeds that for private ownership. This occurs because the quality of wood from older trees is superior to that from younger trees. Note that it also explains why the prices of old-growth timber exceed those for second-growth timber.

9. The discount rate is a real rate, i.e. adjusted for inflation.

The results show that under public ownership the net present value per 100 acres of western Oregon timberlands is $231,447, or about $2,314 per acre. This value can be broken down into a positive $242,131 per 100 acres for liquidating old-growth timber and a negative $10,684 for second-growth tree farms. Although the net present value obtained under public ownership is positive, it is deceptive because the positive net present value from liquidating old-growth timber masks the negative value from the tree farming (second-growth) operation. This uneconomic outcome (cross-subsidization) results because public harvests are too slow and costs too high.

Under private ownership, the net present value per 100 acres is $613,394, or about $6,134 per acre. This is broken down into a positive $601,168 per 100 acres for liquidating old-growth timber and a positive $12,226 for second-growth tree farms.

Private ownership is clearly superior to public ownership of timberland. Transferring ownership from public to private would add about $3,820 per acre to the value of timberland. Under private property rights, timber is liquidated more rapidly and at a lower cost than under public ownership. This allows for a higher present value from liquidating old-growth timber and a positive present value from establishing a tree farm.

Conclusion

The transfer of public timberlands to private ownership increases their value by 165 percent. Hence, privatization of public timberlands (and Indian timberlands, which are managed under the same rules that govern public lands) is economic. Indeed, private property rights create wealth.

The Siletz Indians' proposal to have 12,000 acres of public-domain timberlands in Lincoln County, Oregon, privatized is also economical. The value of these lands under public ownership is about $27.8 million, whereas under private ownership the same lands would have a value of about $73.6 million.

Indian policies in the United States are now in a state of ferment. It appears that, with the privatization proposal of the Siletz, we are witnessing, at least in some parts of "Indian Country," the acceptance of an observation made by John Maynard Keynes (1936, p. 374):

> There are valuable human activities which require the motive of money-making and the environment of private wealth-ownership for their full fruition. Moreover, dangerous human proclivities can be canalized into comparatively harmless channels by the existence of opportunities for money-making and private wealth, which, if they cannot be satisfied in this way, may find their outlet in cruelty, the reckless pursuit of power and authority, and other forms of self-aggrandizement. It is better that a man should tyrannize over his bank balance than over his fellow citizens; and whilst the former is sometimes denounced as being but a means to the latter, sometimes at least it is an alternative.

Appendix: Benefit-Cost Analysis

The two-step procedure for computing the net present value of timberlands is expressed as

(1) $NPV = PV_0 + PV_s$

where:

NPV = total net present value,
PV_0 = net present value of old growth, and
PV_s = net present value of second growth.

PV_0 is equal to the present value of net cash flows generated from liquidating old-growth (naturally endowed) timber stands over a period of T years, less management and administration costs of carrying old growth timber inventories over time.

Formally:

$$(2)\quad PV_0 = \int_0^T [R_0 - (A - ht)]e^{-it}dt$$

where:

R_0 = annual revenues from liquidating old-growth timber,
A = total annual management and administration outlays,
h = annual management and administration outlays for the acreage cut-over annually,
i = interest (discount) rate,
T = harvest age for second-growth timber, which is also equal to the time required to liquidate the old growth, and
t = time.

Equation (2) reduces to

$$(3)\quad PV_0 = (R_0 - A)(1 - e^{-iT})/i + h[1 - e^{-iT}(1 - iT)]/i^2.$$

PV_S is the present value of net cash flows generated from tree farming. The revenue portion of PV_S begins in T, while the relevant outlays for stand establishment (tree planting) and annual management and administration begin in time 0.

Formally:

$$(4)\quad PV_S = \int_T^{\infty} [R_S - (C + A)]e^{-it}dt - \int_0^T (C + ht)e^{-it}dt$$

where variables are as defined in equation (2) above, and

R_S = annual revenues from harvesting second-growth timber, and
C = annual planting (stand establishment) outlays.

Equation (4) reduces to

$$(5)\quad PV_S = [(R_S - A)/i]e^{-iT} - C/i - h[1 - e^{-iT}(1 - iT)]/i^2.$$

References

Berkhofer, Robert Jr. *The White Man's Indian.* New York: Random House, 1978.

Dowdle, Barney, and Hanke, Steve H. "Public Timber Policy and the Wood-Products Industry." In *Forestlands: Public and Private*: 77–102. Edited by Robert T. Deacon and M. Bruce Johnson. Cambridge, Mass.: Ballinger Publishing Company, 1985.

The Economist. "Indians: In the Red." 25 February 1989: 25–6.

Hagen, William T. "Private Property: The Indian's Door to Civilization." *Ethnohistory* 3 (2) (1956): 126–37.

Hanke, Steve H., "Successful Privatization Strategies." In *Privatization and Development:* 77–86. Edited by Steve H. Hanke. San Francisco: Institute for Contemporary Studies Press, 1987.

Keynes, John Maynard. *The General Theory of Employment, Interest and Money.* New York: Harcourt, Brace and Co., 1936.

Libecap, Gary D., and Johnson, Ronald N. "Legislating Commons: The Navajo Tribal Council and the Navajo Range." *Economic Inquiry* 18 (January 1980): 9–86.

Smith, Adam. *The Wealth of Nations [1776].* New York: Random House, 1937.

United States. Presidential Commission on Indian Reservation Economies. *Report and Recommendations to the President of the United States.* Washington, D.C.: Government Printing Office, 1984.

United States. *Budget, Fiscal Year 1995.* Washington, D.C.: Government Printing Office, 1994.

10. Property Rights and the Economic Development of the Sahel

Wayne T. Brough and Mwangi S. Kimenyi

> Few sights were more appalling at the height of the drought last summer than the thousands upon thousands of dead and dying cows clustered around Sahelian boreholes. Indescribably emaciated, the dying would stagger away from the water with bloated bellies and struggle to fight free of the churned mud until they keeled over. . . . Enormous herds, converging on the new boreholes from hundreds of miles away, so savaged the surrounding land by trampling and overgrazing that each borehole quickly became its own little desert forty or fifty miles square.
>
> —Claire Sterling

Drought and Property Rights

Claire Sterling's graphic description refers to the drought that gripped the Sahel region of Africa from 1968 to 1973 (Sterling 1972, p. 102). The five-year drought had the greatest impact on eight countries along the southern border of the Sahara desert: Senegal, Mauritania, Mali, Burkina Faso, Niger, Chad, Sudan, and parts of Ethiopia. According to the World Bank (1994), seven of the eight countries had a per capita income of $675 or less per year in 1992. They are among the poorest countries in the world. Many depend on international aid for even their food sources.

The Sahel has not always been in such poor condition. It was once the home of vast trading empires with trade routes connecting savanna towns in the south to desert cultures in the north. The social order was crucially dependent on trade and market processes.

Wayne T. Brough is Director of Research for Citizens for a Sound Economy in Washington, D.C., and Mwangi S. Kimenyi is Associate Professor of Economics at the University of Connecticut.

Although drought and famine did occur periodically, the people were relatively prosperous and always managed to recover from the whims of nature. That era contrasts sharply with the stark poverty and the arid, barren lands so prominent in the Sahel today.

During this century, the fragile ecological zone next to the Sahara has been gradually consumed by the desert. Some people have claimed that the desert is advancing as much as 30 miles per year (Glantz 1977). Two theories have become popular in explaining desertification. The first and most extravagant is that a major climatic change is shifting the arid desert zone further south. More recent studies suggest a second theory that the region may be gradually growing drier through a long-term process that began in 4000 B.C. and has led to slight long-term fluctuations in climate (OECD 1988). The long-term trend has been accompanied by short-term fluctuations resulting in periodic droughts, which, in recent years, has led to erosion of valuable farmland as the desert encroaches even further south. Recent satellite data suggest the Sahara expanded southward from 1980, expanding by 15 percent at the drought's peak in 1984. The desert receded as rainfall increased, but the Sahara remains larger than it was in 1980 (Tucker et al. 1991).

These natural phenomena have been held as the causes of the Sahel's great drought, which reached its peak in 1970–73. The catastrophe repeated itself again in the 1980s, reaching its worst in 1984. In both periods the toll on human life was in the thousands, and the loss of cattle even greater. The causes researchers have suggested for these disastrous occurrences seem inadequate. Researchers need to look at changes in the social order, which for many years had insulated the inhabitants from massive catastrophes, even in periods of adverse weather conditions.

The 1968–73 drought was not the worst in the Sahel's history. In fact, the drought of 1913 is considered by those who remember it to have been far worse than more recent droughts (Le Houerou 1977). Furthermore, there are accounts of terrible droughts throughout the region's history. Eyewitness accounts from 1639–43 and 1738–56 depict times of severe drought (OECD 1988). Yet the increase in desertification associated with previous droughts was less severe than in recent years. Strictly climatological explanations of the calamity in the Sahel do not offer any insight into the real problem. As a World Bank report (Cleaver and Schreiber 1994, p. 27) indicates:

"Changes in land surface are partly caused by reduced rainfall itself, but human activity, notably deforestation and removal of vegetative cover on rangeland and cropland, has a considerable impact."

Our purpose here is to examine the process of human occupation or, in more familiar terms, to examine the social order of the indigenous population to gain a better understanding of the human role in desertification. We will begin by examining the social order as it existed before French colonization of West Africa. In particular, we will analyze the importance of trade and property rights, their role in maintaining the balance between humans and the environment, and how they contributed to the existence of trading empires that were relatively prosperous. Next we will examine the impact of French colonization and how colonial policies altered the existing social order. We will argue that the present failure to cope with the drought and the advancing desert originated in the French disruption of the system of property rights and market interactions. We will then look at the policies adopted by the independent governments, and investigate policies that may contribute to desertification. Because many countries in the region continued colonial policies after independence, they have extended the impact of policies introduced by colonial governments. Finally, we will consider policies that have been used by other nations to help the countries of the Sahel; we will critically examine the effectiveness of international aid. We will argue that some forms of aid have contributed to desertification and have actually led to more problems.

We stress property rights and the dynamic capabilities of the market process as engines of growth and development. Before French colonization, the market process did, indeed, provide a basis for economic development. As Friedrich Hayek (1978) emphasized, the market is a discovery process, and it was through the market that the indigenous population discovered an effective balance between humans and the environment. Because of this balance, the region became relatively prosperous. Although there were periods of drought, the system of property rights and the market process that existed mitigated the severity of famine. Yet beginning with French colonization, the market process was gradually restricted, upsetting the fragile balance and leading to the Sahel's current problems. The change resulted from the disruption of a previously efficient system of property rights and market relationships.

The Pre-Colonial Sahel

In analyzing the origins of the Sahel's drought and desertification problems, we will examine the history of the peoples of the region. The examples are from specific groups in the region; however, the examples can be generalized (see, for example, Swift 1977).

Two distinct populations inhabit the region below the Sahara: pastoralists (nomads) and sedentary farmers. Although each group had its own cultures and social orders, their lives were inextricably bound together by a market order. The ecological zone in which they lived was extremely fragile; consequently, an intricate structure of exchange and division of labor emerged between the two groups, allowing them to use existing resources without destroying the environment.

The nomads moved along a network of north-south trade routes in conjunction with the weather. They raised cattle and brought to the southern towns of the savanna desert goods such as salt and dates. Some tribes also brought goods from the Arab nations on the other side of the desert. The routes by which the nomads traveled were by no means random (Sterling 1974). They followed strict routes from well to well, allowing their herds to graze for specified durations at the various wells.

The nomads moved the herds with the arrival of the rains. As a rule of thumb, the northward journey in the rainy season continued as long as the grass ahead was greener than the grass behind. The upper boundary of movement was the Sahara Desert. When the rains ceased, the nomads reversed their journeys and moved south into the savanna, the land of the farmers. It was in the south that major markets were established. The nomads arrived after the harvest, and the cattle would feed on the stubble left in the farmers' fields. The nomads benefitted from the source of cattle feed, while the farmers gained manure for their fields—a good example of mutually beneficial exchange that existed between the two groups.

The nomads remained in the savanna throughout the dry season. When the rains returned, they again started north. They repeated the cycle year after year, allowing the indigenous population to survive in the harsh climate of the Sahel.

It is important to examine the symbiotic relationship between the nomads and the farmers in more detail; in particular, the structure of property rights and the social order. To do so, we will use the

Tuareg and the Hausa as an example of how different groups interacted in the pre-colonial Sahel. Our main focus will be on how property rights and market exchange adequately preserved an environmental balance and insulated the inhabitants of the region from the famines so common today.

The Tuareg were a nomadic tribe whose income was derived from cattle and trans-Saharan trade. Indigenous to the Sahel, they populated the more fertile areas of the region. The basic organization of the tribe was in clans, each clan having its own political power. The Tuareg were a martial people, and their supremacy in military affairs gave them the ability to dominate the Sahel. The hierarchy within the clan was a pyramid, with nobles on the top of a strict caste system. The nobles established the territory for the clan; there were no individual property rights in land. The nobles also invested any surplus the clan generated. Because of this structure, many researchers have equated the clans to business firms, with the nobles acting as managers (Curtin 1971). Water wells were owned by the clan that dug them, and the use of water was strictly regulated. A clan's leaders determined the length of time spent at the well and contracted with other clans, granting them rights to use its wells in exchange for the right to use the wells of other clans. Thus the Tuareg had a network of wells to support their cattle as they moved along their trade routes.

The Tuareg were not self-sufficient. Although the clan occupied relatively fertile areas on the desert edge, the land could not support them all; therefore, they relied on market exchange with farmers, particularly the Hausa who populated the regions further south. The Tuareg purchased grains from the savanna farmers and were involved with the caravan trade that passed through the Sahara from North Africa into the cities of the Sudan. The Tuareg maintained the wells that provided water for travelers from and into North Africa and the Sudan. The very harshness of the environment led these groups to a market society. As Lovejoy and Baier (1976, p. 150) emphasized,

> Since the desert sector could not grow beyond a certain point, the forging of close links with the savanna and ever-expanding investment there were inevitable. The commercial networks uniting desert and savanna assumed a critical importance in bad times, serving as a safety valve for people of

> the desert by providing a framework for their escape from an environment temporarily unable to support them.

While in the savanna the Tuareg bought stocks of millet for their desert sojourn. Yet the exchange system went far beyond simple barter for foodstuffs:

> [The Tuareg] invested in diverse activities ranging from stock breeding to transport, trade in salt, dates, grain, and manufactures, land ownership, slave labor, the finance of craft production, and commercial brokerage. . . . Investments crossed cultural boundaries, however defined, so that Tuareg firms were heavily committed to the economic well-being of the whole Central Sudan, not just to the desert edge where nomads concentrated [Lovejoy and Baier 1976, p. 146].

The sedentary Hausa, too, were a vital element in the market process. They were a "population of landlords, urban middlemen, brokers, and farmers" (Meillassoux 1971). The typical picture of the region's nomads and farmers eking out a living at the subsistence level does not fit the social order that existed. In fact, there was always a migration of nomads from the Sahel down to the savanna, where they became involved in market activities other than cattle or transport. In prosperous times many would invest in land in the savanna, giving up the nomadic life to till the soil. In times of drought, some nomads—usually the ones with smaller herds and, therefore, a comparative disadvantage in cattle raising—would opt out of the cattle trade and remain in the urban Hausa centers as merchants. The market not only allowed existence in a harsh environment but also provided a means to escape the nomadic lifestyle. In sum,

> The extent of interaction clearly establishes that the Tuareg were market-oriented, not in some peripheral way as the stereotype of pre-colonial Africa would suggest, but to a degree that helps to demonstrate the importance of market forces in the Central Sudan [Lovejoy and Baier 1976, p. 150].

The pre-colonial Sahel had its problems. Several factors limited the development of the Sahel's economy. There were periods of political instability and wars that caused famine and economic stagnation. Lovejoy and Baier (1976), however, offer the hypothesis that fighting occurred on the east and west frontiers of the region where trade was not as important a factor as it was elsewhere.[1] Although political instability contributed to famines in some way, the impact was minimal compared to the recent tragedies in the Sahel.

Another influence that limited development was the system of property rights. In the case of the Tuareg, although the wells and pasture lands were controlled by the clans, there was private ownership of cattle. The pasture was a public good, while the cattle were private; communal ownership of the pasture led to overgrazing, although limits on the length of time spent at each well constrained the number of cattle individual households could own.

Generally, however, the relationship that existed among the peoples of the Sahel was that of interdependence in a market system. Though there was not a clearly defined system of property rights, there was an efficient organization that not only provided the inhabitants with a livelihood, but fostered environmental preservation. As Richard Franke and Barbara Chasin (1980, pp. 61–62) remark,

> The overall picture that emerges from the available historical documents is one of relatively prosperous and stable communities. However, a contradiction developed between the farmers and herders, who created an ecologically sound production system toward excessive output to support the lavish lifestyles of the courts. The elite also sometimes caused the ruin of a particular region in the course of war. The balance, nonetheless, was clearly on the side of environmental preservation.

Although a system of fully defined property rights was lacking, the system of ownership in pre-colonial Sahel was relatively efficient and insulated its people from natural catastrophes. The rules that governed issues such as land use and wells evolved to meet the needs of the people at that time, and changes in the system of property rights adjusted to changes in economic conditions.

French Colonialism

The arrival of the French in West Africa in the late 19th century had great impact on the development of the Sahel. French colonialism

[1]This argument gives credence to the theories of Thomas Sowell and Alvin Rabushka, who claim that market activity alleviates conflict between different cultures. See Rabushka (1974) and Sowell (1994).

provided some benefits, yet few of the benefits were directed toward the Sahel (Miracle 1971). The French had two basic objectives in West Africa: to ensure military security within the colonies, and to promote economic development for French capital (Swift 1977). Both had adverse effects on the population of the Sahel, eventually weakening traditional society (OECD 1988).

There were many confrontations between the French and the nomads. The French fought the Tuareg and constantly tried to settle them. The fighting upset the ecological balance in the region, with many crops and farmlands suffering in the process. Eventually the French managed to defeat the nomads, disrupting the political system that had existed for so long. The change in political institutions meant a shift in property rights. Clan rulers no longer had control over the wells; thus, the land became open to extreme overgrazing (Wade 1974). French rule eliminated the threat of raids from other groups, allowing farmers to spread to regions that were previously unpopulated. This too intensified land use in the Sahel. The French also divided the Sahel into administrative regions and restricted the movement of nomads across regional borders. Farmers began to use the land more intensively and with less movement.

The French rule altered the agricultural patterns of the Sahel destroying the intricate trade network of the region. The French were interested primarily in export industries; therefore, they emphasized trade from the interior to the coast. Better communication with the coast and the introduction of cash crops led more and more merchants and farmers to abandon trans-Saharan trade. French regulations on currency movements and control over the movement of nomads further hampered north-south trade routes. By 1911 the trans-Saharan trade had collapsed (Lovejoy and Baier 1976). The collapse left the nomads in a precarious position: they were now peripheral to market activity, while at the same time they had begun to use the land more intensively. The previous balance between humans and resources no longer existed. It is at this point that desertification began.

In addition to colonizing West Africa, France was the first nation to attempt development programs in the Sahel. By the 1920s the region had begun to show signs of stagnation, and the French implemented programs to revitalize the area. The French had a three-pronged development scheme: digging more wells, conducting veterinary and medical campaigns, and opening new markets in the south (Swift 1977).

French programs exacerbated the Sahel's economic and ecological problems. The reason was simple: there was no change in the underlying property rights structure. As the French dug new wells, they established no clear ownership rights, leading to overgrazing at the new wells (Sterling 1974). The veterinary and medical campaigns made matters worse, for they led to increased populations of humans and animals, putting further pressure on the land.

With no one to regulate the use of new wells, the larger population intensified the level of overgrazing. The French hoped that nomads would slaughter more cattle for the market, thereby maintaining "proper" herd sizes; opening new markets in the south was meant to facilitate this. Yet for the nomads, cattle were privately owned while the pastures were not. The nomads' incentive was to maintain the largest herds possible, regardless of the impact on the land. It is no wonder that nomads have opposed foreign assistance programs. As Wade (1974, p. 235) stated, "Few Western innovations, when considered over the long term, have worked in the inhabitants' favor."

Neocolonial Policies in Independent Africa

The French remained in power through the first half of the 20th century. Finally in the 1960s amid international pressure and financial difficulties, the French government granted independence to the region. The new nations faced numerous obstacles in their development, many originating in the era of French rule. Trade was difficult in a region that the French had divided into different states. Each state now had its own government with its own bureaucracy, and border restrictions made trade between nations cumbersome. The problem was compounded by self-interested administrators who tended to overproduce regulations, which stifled the market process. Perhaps the most debilitating policy of the new governments was their failure to assign individual property rights.

Consider, for example, the nationalized forests. In addition to the overgrazing that plagued the region, collectively owned land posed another problem: deforestation. Forests were depleted as individuals collected wood for burning. The problem still exists, for more than 90 percent of the population in Sub-Saharan Africa depends on wood as a primary source of energy (Barnes 1990). Trees and ground cover are necessary to help maintain the soil in the farmlands. When the trees are removed, the soil breaks down, gradually turning the area into barren wastelands.

The main reason for deforestation is, again, the lack of private property rights. In the 1930s, in an effort to regulate the use of wood, the French nationalized ground cover. The result was the tragedy of the commons, with the ground cover being overused and no individual having the incentive to plant anything more. James T. Thomson (1977, p. 61) stated in his examination of the Inuwa District of Niger: "The inability to effectively exclude animals and humans from any but garden-sized plots during the dry season means that no one has any incentive to improve the quality of the woodstock on his own fields."

On gaining independence, the African states maintained the system established by the French: nationalized ground cover, with enforcement by forestry officials at the national level. Villagers had no respect for authorities, feeling that the land had been unjustly expropriated. It was possible to purchase permits to cut wood, but permits were often abused or neglected altogether. Enforcement was minimal, and national forestry officials were extremely open to bribes. The regulated common property, in effect, reverted to an unregulated common property: "Daily experience confirms that ground cover—grasses, brush, and trees—is an unregulated common property subject to exploitation by any and all" (Thomson 1977, p. 61).

The result was that the nomads were forced to move further south in search of better lands, and the slash-and-burn methods used by the nomads resulted in more land being destroyed as they moved south. Furthermore, the nomads moved into regions infested with tsetse flies, which posed serious health problems to them and their cattle. The farmers, on the other hand, were forced to search for new farm lands to replace the eroded fields they were using. The encroaching desert led them to use marginal lands, which, in the past, had been allowed to lie fallow, sometimes as long as 20 years (Wade 1974). Poor land management led to desertification, which in turn affected the farmers' ability to grow food. The frequency of crop failures put strains on the urban population, which now had to pay higher prices for food.

In Africa, the urban population uses a high proportion of income for food purchases. Food prices are an extremely volatile issue, and slight price fluctuations may lead to rioting and urban unrest. African governments have their political power bases in the cities. Therefore, agricultural markets are heavily regulated, with state marketing boards controlling the price of crops; prices are held artificially low to benefit urban areas (Bates 1981). There is a clear expropriation of rights from the rural population to the urban population.

Modern governments have laid a heavy hand on the economies of the Sahel. Development programs, regulations, and price controls that hamper growth and development are common, leading to overgrazing, crowding out in the capital markets, disincentives for market activity. The new governments have also divided the nations politically. The multi-ethnic trade of previous empires acted as a limiting factor on the neglect or misuse of one group by another. Today's nomads, however, are not a significant power base and are therefore largely neglected by national governments. The trading empires constrained political opportunism because the market process by its nature dissipated power. As Hayek (1944, p. 145) stated, "To split or decentralize power is necessarily to reduce the absolute amount of power, and the competitive system is the only system designed to minimize by decentralization the power exercised by man over man."

When markets were replaced by a regulated economy, first by the French and later by independent governments, discrimination and separation along ethnic lines became important as groups vied for political power. The nomads suffered the greatest harm from this system. Evidence of discrimination appeared in the refugee camps for drought victims—a study of nutritional intake levels of farmers and nomads revealed that the nomads had a nutritional intake seven to ten percent lower than the farmers; furthermore, disease was more prominent in the nomad camps (Sheets and Morris 1976).

After years of overgrazing and stifled market activity, the system broke down. A drought that began in 1968 forced thousands of nomads to sell their cattle and move to refugee camps or urban areas. The land could no longer support agriculture; crops failed and the farmers were left hopeless. By 1970 the drought reached critical proportions, taking heavy tolls in both human and animal terms. Devastating conditions endured for three more years. Finally in 1973, "normal" rainfall returned to the Sahel.[2]

Foreign Assistance in the Sahel

At this point, Western aid to the region became more prominent; it is therefore necessary to examine the impact of aid in the Sahel. Western nations have provided aid to the Sahel for some time. Before 1950 the aid was French; after independence more nations became involved, with the United States playing a major role. Many of the West's humanitarian projects have caused great harm because the programs neglected the importance of the underlying institutions, especially the ineffective system of property rights. As mentioned in an in-house report at the Agency for International Development (AID), "It must be recognized that assistance agencies have ignored the principles [of effective resource management], and the consequence of indiscriminate support has produced negative results or, on occasion, disaster" (quoted in Wade 1974, p. 234).

Medical aid programs intensified the pressure on the land without providing any monitoring system for land use. Similarly, the practice of digging wells, which was a popular aid project even after the French, increased the size of herds and the problem of overgrazing. Thousands of wells were dug at $200,000 apiece. By permitting an artificially high population in the Sahel, the programs only made the final collapse more resounding.[3] Hundreds of square miles of land were lost from overgrazing and trampling by cattle in search of water and sustenance.

Once the disaster occurred, Western aid shifted to relief programs such as food distribution and emergency medical provision. The disaster programs were equally unsuccessful. Inefficient management and the lack of cooperation between donor and recipient governments led thousands of tons of food to sit idle on docks or in

[2]The use of the word "normal" is misleading. In fact, one of the many problems with disaster relief programs was that they were based on assumptions of a return to normal weather conditions. Yet in the Sahel, drought is an unpredictable part of "normal" weather conditions. For a discussion of the possible misuses of the concept of normal weather, see Katz and Glantz (1977).

[3]In fact, Sinn (1988) suggests that the optimal aid package would allocate more resources for development not of the Sahel, but the countries to its south. This allocation would induce migration and relieve some of the pressures on the Sahel.

distribution stations, only to be eaten by rats (El-Khawas 1976). Aid programs did not gear their distribution toward local capabilities. Although distribution problems have been overcome to some extent, conflicts among the indigenous population still impair the ability to effectively distribute emergency aid (Wiseburg 1976).

Conclusion

Famine and desertification in the Sahel are due primarily to human action. Before government policies stifled market activity, the people of the Sahel developed an intricate system of trade, which allowed them to survive in the harsh climates below the Sahara.

The market is a spontaneous, emerging order that evolves through human interaction. The great trading empires of the Sahel were founded upon such an order. The entrepreneur plays a special role, for any successful innovations move the social order to a more developed stage. The market, not politics, drives development:

> The market modifies completely the nature of social relationships and the personalities of the bargainers. They become anonymous. No obligation deriving from kinship or political position rests on either seller or buyer. . . . Sellers and buyers are free to accept and reject any price. . . . This license contrasts with behavior outside the market and helps to give the domain of the market special character [Hopkins 1973].

Government intervention has all but destroyed the market process in the Sahel; everywhere that entrepreneurs turn they are met with regulations. Dirigiste policies have imposed severe distortions on resource allocations. With the dynamics of the market dampened, the region's rulers began to look for other methods of development. Many felt that if the population was educated, development would ensue. But education was not the problem. Stereotypes of the population as subsistence farmers who were unwilling to change are erroneous. Historically, the population has responded to change positively. In dealing with drought, for example, farmers developed more than 20 different crops to vary the growing cycle and conserve the soil. Nicholas Wade (1974) claimed there was an "impressive record of innovation. . .which is quite at variance with common negative criticism of the African as unduly conservative." Similar evidence existed during the drought:

> To anyone travelling through the Sahel during the drought, most impressive of all, even more impressive than the devastation was the tenacity of the people, their capacity to adapt and change their habits, their diets, their residence, and their very way of life in order to survive [Ware 1976, p. 167].

Change has always been a factor in the life of nomads. There is little evidence to suggest the nomad will not give up his hard way of life (Glantz 1976). In the prosperity of the previous era, nomads invested in the savanna and left nomadism when it was economically feasible.

The problem in the Sahel is not one of an ignorant population. The problem is that all modes of change are thwarted through government control over economic institutions. The governments of the Sahel would like change, but they insist on directing the change, thereby protecting their role. They enact policies too inflexible to provide beneficial, long-run change. Political time horizons are short, with little emphasis on future impact (see Brough and Kimenyi 1986). Western aid allows the governments of the Sahel to continue policies that inhibit development (Bauer 1984). Foreign aid is used to cover losses caused by inefficient policies.

What is needed is an institutional change to enhance the emergence of efficient property rights in accordance with economic efficiency.[4] Properly defined property rights would lead to a more efficient use of available resources, environmental balance, and encouragement of economic growth through production and exchange. Perhaps the most telling example of such an institutional change was discovered by Norman H. McLeod. Examining satellite photos of the Sahel, he discovered a pentagon-shaped region that still held its vegetation at the height of the drought. Upon ground-level examination, the region was found to be a French cattle farm with a mere strand of barbed wire keeping the desert out (McLeod 1976). Development authorities have claimed that private property is too drastic a change for the people of the Sahel; yet as was

[4]Scully (1988) provides empirical analysis suggesting the importance of property rights. He finds that politically open societies subscribing to the rule of law, property rights, and markets grow roughly three times as fast and are two and one-half times as efficient as those societies where such rights are attenuated.

observed, there was a trend toward private property rights long before colonialism.

Government activity in the Sahel destroyed the people's ability to maintain a balance between humans and nature. Poor policymaking and indiscriminate Western aid have laid to waste what could have been a prosperous region. Wade (1974, p. 237) has concurred with this point, remarking that, "A whole vast area which might with appropriate management have become a breadbasket providing beef for half of Africa instead became a basket case needing more than $100m worth of imported food just for survival."

References

Barnes, Douglas F. *Population Growth, Wood Fuels, and Resource Problems in Sub-Saharan Africa.* Industry and Energy Department Working Paper, Energy Series Paper No. 26. Washington, D.C.: World Bank, 1990.

Bates, Robert. *Markets and States in Tropical Africa.* Berkeley: University of California Press, 1981.

Bauer, P. T. *Reality and Rhetoric: Studies in the Economics of Development.* Cambridge, Mass.: Harvard University Press, 1984.

Brough, Wayne T., and Kimenyi, Mwangi S. "On the Inefficient Extraction of Rents by Dictators." *Public Choice* 48 (1986): 37–48.

Cleaver, Kevin M., and Schreiber, Goetz A. *Reversing the Spiral: The Population, Agriculture, and Environment in Sub-Saharan Africa.* Washington, D.C.: World Bank, 1994.

Curtin, Philip D. "Pre-Colonial Trading Networks and Traders: The Diakhanke." In *The Development of Indigenous Trade and Markets in West Africa.* Edited by C. Meillassoux. London: Oxford University Press, 1971.

El-Khawas, Mohamed. "A Reassessment of International Relief Programs." In *The Politics of Natural Disaster*. Edited by Michael Glantz. New York: Praeger Publishers, 1976.

Franke, Richard W., and Chasin, Barbara H. *Seeds of Famine: Ecological Destruction and Development Dilemma in the West African Sahel.* Totowa, N.J.: Allanheld Osmun and Co., 1980.

Glantz, Michael. "Nine Fallacies of Natural Disaster: The Case of the Sahel," In *The Politics of Natural Disaster*. Edited by Michael Glantz. New York: Praeger Publishers, 1976.

Glantz, Michael. "The U.N. and Desertification: Dealing with a Global Problem," In *Desertification*. Edited by Michael Glantz. Boulder, Colo.: Westview Press, 1977.

Hayek, Friedrich A. *The Road to Serfdom*. Chicago: University of Chicago Press, 1944.

Hayek, Friedrich A. *Law, Legislation, and Liberty*. Chicago: University of Chicago Press, 1973.

Hayek, Friedrich A. "Competition as a Discovery Process." In *New Studies in Philosophy, Politics, Economics, and the History of Ideas*. Edited by Friedrich A. Hayek. Chicago: University of Chicago Press, 1978.

Hopkins, Anthony G. *Economic History of West Africa*. New York: Columbia University Press, 1973.

Katz, Richard and Glantz, Michael. "Rainfall Statistics, Droughts, and Desertification in the Sahel." In *Desertification*. Edited by Michael Glantz. Boulder, Colo.: Westview Press, 1977.

Le Houerou, H.N. "The Nature and Causes of Desertification." In *Desertification*. Edited by Michael Glantz. Boulder, Colo.: Westview Press, 1977.

Lovejoy, P.E., and Baier, S. "The Desert-Side Economy of the Sudan." In *The Politics of Natural Disaster*. Edited by Michael Glantz. New York: Praeger Publishers, 1976.

McLeod, Norman H. "Dust in the Sahel: Cause of Drought?" In *The Politics of Natural Disaster*. Edited by Michael Glantz. New York: Praeger Publishers, 1976.

Meillassoux, C., ed. *The Development of Indigenous Trade and Markets in West Africa*. London: Oxford University Press, 1971.

Miracle, Marvin P. "Capitalism, Capital Markets and Competition." In *The Development of Indigenous Trade and Markets in West Africa*. Edited by C. Meillassoux. London: Oxford University Press, 1971.

OECD. Organization for Economic Cooperation and Development. *The Sahel Facing the Future*. Paris: Organization for Economic Cooperation and Development, 1988.

Rabushka, Alvin. *Toward a Theory of Racial Harmony*. Columbia, S.C.: University of South Carolina Press, 1974.

Scully, Gerald W. "The Institutional Framework and Economic Development." *Journal of Political Economy* 96 (June 1988): 652–62.

Sheets, Hal, and Morris, Roger. "Disaster in the Desert." In *The Politics of Natural Disaster*. Edited by Michael Glantz. New York: Praeger Publishers, 1976.

Sinn, Hans-Werner. "The Sahel Problem." *Kyklos* 41 (1988): 187–213.

Sowell, Thomas. *Race and Culture*. New York: Basic Books, 1994.

Sterling, Claire. "The Making of the Sub-Saharan Wasteland." *The Atlantic Monthly* 233 (May 1974): 98–105.

Swift, Jeremy. "Sahelian Pastoralists: Underdevelopment, Desertification, and Famine." *Annual Review of Anthropology* 6 (1977): 457–78.

Thomson, James T. "Ecological Deterioration: Local-Level Rule-Making and Enforcement Problems in Niger." In *Desertification*. Edited by Michael Glantz. Boulder, Colo.: Westview Press, 1977.

Tucker, Compton J.; Dregne, Harold E.; and Newcomb, Wilbur, W. "Expansion and Contraction of the Sahara Desert from 1980 to 1990." *Science* 253 (1991): 299–301.

Wade, Nicholas. "Sahelian Drought: No Victory for Western Aid." *Science* 185 (1974): 234–37.

Ware, Helen. "Desertification and Population: Sub-Saharan Africa." In *The Politics of Natural Disaster*. Edited by Michael Glantz. New York: Praeger Publishers, 1976.

Wiseburg, Laurie. "An International Perspective on the African Famines." In *The Politics of Natural Disaster*. Edited by Michael Glantz. New York: Praeger Publishers, 1976.

World Bank. *World Development Report 1994*. Washington, D.C.: World Bank, 1994.

11. Indigenous African Institutions and Economic Development

Emily Chamlee-Wright

In the attempt to establish institutions which foster economic development in the Third World, economists often look to the West as a model. This indeed has been the case in Ghana, West Africa. In Ghana's urban centers, the large buildings which house Barclay's Bank, Standard Charter Bank, and Ghana Commercial Bank loom over the traditional market stalls and street traders. This sight might be heartening to those who recognize Third World entrepreneurs' limited access to capital as the primary constraint in advancing economic development. Indeed, these institutions play an important role in financing large-scale industry and high-volume import and export exchange. But this is only a small proportion of market activity in Ghana. The majority of business people never enter the doors of such institutions.

The most striking feature of West African markets is the overwhelming proportion of female traders. While a few items will traditionally be sold by men, most of the trading activity is conducted by women. For example, the United Nations Development Fund estimates that 80 percent of all food production, processing, and marketing in West Africa is carried out by women. While limited access to capital is of general concern to development theorists, the limits facing female entrepreneurs are considered to be particularly severe (Simms 1981). The presence of formal Western-style credit institutions has done little to alter the situation.

Emily Chamlee-Wright is Assistant Professor of Economics at Beloit College. She thanks Don Lavoie for his direction and recommendations on earlier drafts of this paper. George Ayittey, Michael Alexeev, John Paden, and Jack High also provided many helpful comments. This chapter is reprinted, with some revisions, from her article in the Spring/Summer 1993 *Cato Journal* (Chamlee 1993).

The observations presented here are three-fold. First, the reasons why Western-type credit institutions have not reached the average West African entrepreneur will be explored. It will be argued that formal banking procedures have evolved to fit a Western cultural context and cannot be expected to fill the same role in the West African context. Second, indigenous credit and mutual assistance institutions which could potentially fulfill this role will be identified. Such institutions will be shown to reflect the cultural context in which they emerged, and how they in turn can accommodate specific credit needs. Third, the obstacles facing such indigenous institutions will be identified, with the purpose of suggesting shifts in policy. The analysis presented here is primarily based on findings from interviews of 49 market women conducted in the central markets of Accra and Kumasi, two prominent trading centers in Ghana, and the smaller market Madina, which is outside of Accra.[1]

Western Credit Institutions and the Local Entrepreneur

Recognizing the inability of Western credit institutions to reach the small entrepreneur is not to suggest a case of market failure or that such institutions were not as important a part of Western economic development as we had thought. Rather, these institutions are quite successful when operating within a specific cultural context. While it is easy to recognize the impact a certain cultural context has in general, the fact that formal Western institutions also emerge out of and reflect a particular culture is often lost, when analyzing Third World institutions.

Western or Western-type financial institutions have emerged in a setting where the entrepreneurs are for the most part educated, literate, and male (so entrepreneurs are not at risk of being locked out of the process simply for the reason of gender). Entrepreneurs demonstrate their credit-worthiness with a documented credit history, and the cultural setting they live in supports this method of accountability with rules of record keeping and documentation. Thus, it is not surprising that institutions that have emerged in this context are not successful in providing financial services to the bulk

[1]In Accra, interviews consisted of 15 street vendors, 12 stall traders, and 9 lock-up shop traders. In Kumasi, interviews consisted of 4 street vendors, 3 stall traders, and 3 lock-up shop traders. In Madina, 3 stall traders were interviewed.

of the population in the West African context, given that small entrepreneurs are for the most part illiterate women, the least educated members of society. It is a matter both of the small business person not accepting the practices of the formal banking institutions as well as the formal banking institutions not having much interest in reaching out to this section of the market. In short, it is simply too costly for the formal institutions to offer lending services to the small entrepreneur.

Market women are not likely to be familiar with complicated bank procedures, particularly the written forms. Many women, even in the urban markets, speak only their local language and not the official language, English. For the banks' part, the only gauge of credit-worthiness of potential borrowers is to require a long term savings account. The majority of market women could scarcely dream of acquiring the sum needed for an initial deposit (Lycette 1985). This is not to say that a credit history does not exist, rather that the formal institutions have no way of acquiring this information, as it is embedded within the kinship and "sororital" alliances. Even if they are able to establish a savings account, any loan amount for which they would be eligible would not be worth the bank's time to process and administer. Having evolved in a Western context, formal banking institutions have developed a corporate culture and a system of rules into which Ghanaian market women simply do not fit.

Indigenous Solutions to Acquiring Credit

Indigenous financial arrangements provide an alternative to the formal banking system. The potential of these alternative arrangements is not widely considered to be promising, however, given that the amount of credit most often extended is no more than a few dollars (Robertson 1984). Yet, there are still reasons not to dismiss the indigenous arrangements out of hand. First, we must recognize that the bulk of investment activity is financed through indigenous arrangements and not the formal banking institutions. Thus, even if the indigenous sector faces strict constraints, they are nevertheless serving a valued function in the market that is not met elsewhere. Second, it is not necessarily the case that larger loans are needed. The relative success of development programs such as the micro-loans project in Bangladesh and other areas indicate that small loans or just a few dollars can make a substantial difference. Third, to the extent that the indigenous arrangements are stunted, it is often the result of state regulation and restrictions on trade. Thus, an investigation into the operations of indigenous financial solutions will help us identify which regulatory practices cause the most disruption to their ability to function.

The size, scope, and function of indigenous credit and mutual assistance societies will first be detailed, indicating the essential features for their proper functioning. Then, the major obstacles attenuating the progress such societies might deliver will be discussed. Lastly, the relevant institutional and policy shifts which ought to be considered if the indigenous solutions are to provide the maximum possible benefits will be addressed.

Women's associations vary in size, scope and function. Such societies are traditionally based in kinship and tribal structures. It might be said that migration both into the city by those from the rural areas, and out of the city to the suburban areas has caused irreparable damage to the kinship and tribal systems such that they can no longer perform the advisory and credit functions to the degree that they once did. But to the extent that these structures provide less support for those in the urban environment, other culturally based support systems are evolving to fill the void.

Christian churches, particularly in Accra, provide another layer of community involvement. Almost all the Christian church organizations provide some form of mutual aid on a regular basis. Many also play an advisory role for traders looking to expand their business.[2] Some even provide an opportunity to acquire credit through church programs specifically designed to start people in business. Thus, to the extent that the ability for kinship and tribal structures to provide these services is faltering in the urban areas, the religious institutions are stepping in with similar services of their own. As Western religious institutions replace traditional forms, they have had to adapt and expand their role in the new context. Specifically,

[2]Of the 25 women who were asked about their religious affiliation, 4 were Muslim, 2 were agnostic, and the rest were Christian. Among the Christians, 14 different churches were presented. Of those, only the Assemblies of God, Central Gospel Church, and Deeper Life Ministries did not offer mutual assistance for funerals, births and marriages. All but the Anglican Church and the Central Gospel Church offered regular opportunities to receive business advice.

they have had to take on at least some of the functions previously performed by traditional structures.

The second important support system that is filling the void left by the decline of tribal and kinship structures in the urban areas is the formation of female societies which cut across tribal and kinship lines. These can range from small clusters of 3 to 5 women who trade near one another on the street to the elaborate trade organizations of several hundred women in the established markets. Inclusion in the clusters or organizations is not solely determined by tribal affiliation or kinship ties (though these are still important when they exist). Successful face to face interaction which is repeated daily engenders the trust necessary for the formation of close bonds. Physical proximity allows traders in a specific area to observe one another's behavior, as well as establish a reputation for themselves. The question arises: can we not then speak of these clusters or organizations of women as a *culturally* based phenomenon? In other words, does gender constitute a cultural structure as, for instance, tribal affiliation does?

The answer is "yes" when we recognize that in the West African context, gender itself provides the basis for cultural specificity. West African women indeed have a culture distinct from that of West African men. The same is the case for children in the West. Deborah Tannen's (1990) work demonstrates that same-sex play groups during childhood lead boys and girls to develop distinct cultures from one another, and this explains many of the systematic differences between the ways in which adult men and women relate to one another. Tannen's argument is that as children establish same-sex peer groups, boys and girls develop separate language patterns. Besides communication, male peer groups use language to establish status, or hierarchical relationships. Female peer groups, on the other hand, use language to establish connection, or more lateral relationships. As these different language patterns develop, so do distinct cultures. As Western children enter into adulthood, the male-female relationship tends to replace the same-sex peer group as the primary relationship. Yet each retains the behavioral and linguistic patterns learned as children. Thus, communication between men and women is essentially cross cultural communication.

Given that this is the case in the West, consider the importance a female specific culture is likely to play in the traditional West African context. The conjugal unit, while not incidental, rarely replaces gender specific groupings as the primary relationship. The mother-daughter relationship, for instance, plays a primary role throughout a woman's life, even as the daughter marries. The strict division of labor across gender perpetuates the importance of same-sex peer groups into adulthood as women work side by side with one another. The traditional role female cooperation plays in production, child rearing and the enforcement of social norms (Sudarkasa 1981, Wipper 1984) also perpetuates the influence of a gender specific culture into adulthood. The most dramatic instance lies in the traditional compound system which separates living quarters for men and women (Robertson 1984).

Most of the market women, particularly those at the more marginal levels of operation exhibit a strong sense of camaraderie with the women who trade in their immediate area. The traders form themselves into close-knit groupings, or clusters, sometimes as small as three to five women. These connections serve a vital economic function of mutual support. Even direct competitors will sell for one another in the case of sickness. Most traders are socially, as well as financially linked with other traders.

Anthony Kronman (1985) describes this method of reciprocal behavior as "union," whereby individuals seek to "reduce divergence (of interests) by promoting a spirit of identification or fellow-feeling between the parties. . ." (Kronman 1985, p. 21). As opposed to other arrangements designed to combat opportunism, "union" does not assume opposition of interests. Rather "[union] seeks to eliminate the condition of separateness that makes the opposition of interests possible in the first place" (Kronman 1985, p. 22). Thus, casual chat, gossip, and in-depth discussions which involve traders in one another's lives serve more than just a social function, but are also an important prerequisite for securing mutually supportive financial relationships.

Robert Axelrod (1981) describes how a high probability of repeated interaction generates cooperation under conditions where (1) there is no sanction for breaking the rules of cooperation, (2) there is no way to gauge the behavior of other players outside of the game, and (3) there is no way to change the other players' utility function. While Axelrod's analysis is internally consistent, it is not as applicable to the specific case of West African market women as

Kronman's "union." First, West African market women do indeed have sanctions for breaking the rules of a credit society. Indigenous arbitration methods (discussed below) and the threat of ostracization are time honored methods of minimizing such opportunistic behavior when it does occur.

Second, the ability of traders to gauge one another's behavior in their day to day trading activities is a vitally important source of information. Simply bumping into another trader day after day is not enough to ensure a successful cooperative link. Trust, of which repeated interaction is only a part, must also be established. Trust involves careful assessment of another's character, not simply calculating the probability of seeing the same person again. A trader may faithfully return to the market day after day, but if she is frequently rude to her customers, is a spendthrift, or is drunk on a regular basis, other graders are not likely to see her as a good risk. The repeated interaction enables this assessment, but by no means constitutes trust in and of itself. Third, Axelrod's condition that the players cannot interact outside of the game, or in other words, cannot influence the feelings one has for the other, is clearly not applicable in this case. The bonds of friendship are paramount in establishing the financial support networks.[3]

Women at the upper end of the scale who have been financed by their husbands, however, often do not show as much interest in joining together with other women. One relatively prosperous batik trader refused to take part in any of the trade or credit associations. In fact, she reported that she did not gossip or go out of her way to be sociable with the neighboring traders. She resented the thought that illiterate women would try to tell her how to run a business. She thought that the associations were more for the illiterate traders, not for someone as well educated as she. This woman's business was financed, however, by her husband who held a prominent civil service position. Further, the fact that her husband was able to buy a large house gave her the opportunity to produce the batik herself

[3]Klein and Leffler's (1981) discussion concerning the role advertising (or investment in one's reputation) plays in the success of contractual performance is also illuminating here. According to Klein and Leffler, such investment is like posting a bond, signaling a credible commitment to fulfilling the contract. Kronman's "union" still seems more applicable, however, in the case of West African market women, given the emphasis placed on shared interests in the "sororital" order.

as the process requires a large protected space. This gives further indication that the female camaraderie plays more than just a social role, but serves a financial function of which relatively wealthy women need less.[4]

Hawkers (Street Vendors)

The smallest forms of indigenous credit and mutual assistance occur among clusters of women who sell in the same area. Such clusters will gather to engage in group "susu." Members of a group susu association make either daily or weekly contributions to a common pot. The pot is then distributed to members in turn, usually on a monthly basis.[5] These arrangements can be on-going or for specific purposes. Engaging in group susu has the advantage over saving with a "susu man" as he charges a commission of one day's savings per month. Further, depending on the rules the group wishes to follow, the women who receive the pot first have a source of free credit.

While the susu arrangement offers a financial resource, credit can also come in the form of goods. Women who have lost their capital will often rely on friends to advance them produce or other goods for which they will pay at the end of the day or the week. One woman who lost her capital through fines levied by the city council helps her friend sell rice in return for a small sum at the end of the day. This amounts to a transfer, as there is no benefit to the rice seller for "hiring" her friend, yet the ethic of mutual support is reinforced so that the rice seller could rely upon similar support if such a situation were to befall her. Besides financial support, this arrangement also affords the opportunity for the woman who has lost her capital to maintain her position in the peer group, so that when she is able to secure her own goods for sale, she will be able to ease back into the market culture.

[4]Fifteen out of the 18 traders interviewed (about 83 percent) belonged to trading associations, whereas only 5 out of 12 (about 42 percent) of the more prosperous lock-up shop operators belonged.

[5]Hawkers who have no fixed trading position tend to save anywhere from C200–C500 ($.47–$1.18) per week. Thus, if there are four members in the group, each will receive C800–C2,000 ($1.88–$4.71) once a month. See Little (1965) and Little (1973) for details of rotating credit associations in other areas.

Generally, among street vendors, there is little opportunity to belong to an on-going mutual assistance society,[6] as they do not have the financial capital necessary to make regular contributions, but the "hat will be passed" as needed to aid friends who have given birth, are getting married, or who must provide funeral arrangements for a family member.

Since trading on the street is officially illegal, a system of *de facto* property rights has emerged on the sidewalk. As the city council guards make their way down the street, the hawkers pass an audible signal to alert each other to the guards' presence. As if choreographed by Busby Berkeley himself, the traders hoist large trays of fruit, vegetables, fish, utensils, and other goods atop their heads. Women who sell goods too heavy to place on their heads need to secure a position close to the entrance of the established market. Once the signal is heard, she can quickly move her goods inside the market and lose the city guards in the maze of the market (a maze far more familiar to women than the male guards). Many women "inherit" these positions in the market from their mother, an aunt, or a sister. When a position is well established, any woman who attempted to encroach upon this space would be harassed out of the spot by the surrounding women with a barrage of insults. This de facto property rights system enables larger groupings, as women can count on their peers returning to the same spot in the market.

Let me point out, however, that de facto property rights are not as efficient as full rights of ownership. Following Armen Alchian and Harold Demsetz's (1973) identification of the essential elements of private ownership, de facto property rights fall short of the mark. Specifically, while de facto private property rights provide some level of stability and exludeability, the element of transferability is significantly stunted. Stability is maintained as long as trader consistently returns to the same location. Further, neighbors will often exclude would-be interlopers from taking over a selling position in the case of the limited absence of another trader. But the efficient allocation of the resource depends on the ability of a trader

[6]Some women will still have such support within their home village. But access to such support would most likely require returning to the village, as much of the assistance is given in-kind rather than in cash. Women are reluctant to take advantage of this source of support if it means they must give up the independence and financial prospects the urban setting offers.

to smoothly transfer it to another. While selling positions can be "handed down" from mother to daughter,[7] for example, generally, traders cannot sell the space to the highest bidder. Among her neighbors, a trader's legitimate claim to a selling position only holds as long as she maintains that position. Thus, while the de facto property rights system works remarkably well, it cannot guarantee the efficient allocation of resources.

Many women are fortunate enough to have established a contact with a store-front shop owner, with the agreement that the owner will allow the street vendor to hide in the shop when the city guards pass by. While there is an opportunity for side payments here, most women who have such a position acquired the favor through personal contacts. The lack of payment, however, should not be seen as a sign that such permission does not represent a valuable resource to the street vendors, as it enables them to engage in more substantial credit relationships, again, because of the decreased flight risk. Further, the stable position enhances profits as the trader is able to establish a regular clientele.

Among the hawkers who secure stable trading positions at the entrance of a store, the group susu societies grow from about 4 to about 12 members. The monthly pot for a four member group where each contributes C200 per week is C3,200 ($7.53) while the monthly pot of a 12 member group with the same contribution is C9,600 ($22.59). The annual return per member does not change as the size of the group grows, but the larger monthly pot will be more helpful in acquiring costly pieces of equipment or a move into selling a more lucrative product. Further, because of the combined effect of the reduced flight risk and the benefits of building a regular clientele, the contributions tend to increase among traders who have established trading positions. Thus, we see that a well established trading position translates into substantial financial gain when we consider the difference between a C9,600 ($22.59) per capita annual return for a susu association with contributions of C200 per week, and a

[7]This process happens over time. The mother, for instance, will begin by bringing her daughter to the market. The daughter will circulate goods on the street, returning to her mother's position for more supplies when needed. Eventually, the daughter may sit with her mother, establishing a rapport with the other traders. By the time the mother quits the market, the daughter has already established her legitimate claim to her mother's selling space.

C28,800 ($67.76) per capita annual return where the contributions increase to C600 per week. Below I will discuss some of the particular obstacles hawkers face in acquiring even more stable trading positions.

Market Stalls

Credit and savings associations and mutual assistance societies taken on a different character once inside the established market stalls. Though the market stalls officially belong to the city council, the de facto property right in the market stall allows for more complex credit and mutual assistance associations to develop. The number of participants in even the informal arrangements often increase to 20 or 30. The amount of contributions also increases, partly because these women have more money to save, but also because a woman is very unlikely to abandon a stall to avoid contributing to a group susu organization. Trust still plays an extremely important role here, as newcomers are not quickly included in such arrangements. A trader's behavior is carefully observed and her character closely assessed before she is given a chance to prove her trustworthiness. If she drinks too much or comes to the market late, her neighboring traders are likely to conclude that she will not last long in the market, and thus she is a risk to the rest of them if she were to be included in any financial arrangements.

Within the established markets, a separate trade association exists for almost every type of good sold. The functions performed generally do not include credit, though informal side arrangements are facilitated by the frequent contact made between members in the associations. They also serve a quasi-political function as grievances to the city council will be made through these organizations. They serve a regulatory function by reinforcing behavioral norms. Consistently rude or dishonest behavior can be met with termination from the association. In turn, the association provides financial security in the form of mutual assistance benefits for funerals, marriages and births. Health benefits are also often provided out of the fund of regular contributions. Membership within the association is not required, though it is particularly advantageous for those far from their home villages and separated from the family support system.

Though sometimes there are attempts made by a particular association to restrict the number of sellers and enforce cartel prices, these efforts have been largely unsuccessful. The general feeling in the market is that such anti-competitive behavior is not a legitimate role of the associations.[8] The hair stylists' association recently tried to prohibit any non-member from practicing inside Makola market in central Accra. The issue was brought before the market queen who ruled in favor of the hair stylists who wished not be a part of the association.

The other major functions these associations fill are giving business advice to those having financial difficulty and providing arbitration services. Disputes between members of the same association can usually be handled internally. If the dispute involves traders of two different associations, the case can then be brought to the market queen.[9] Each major market chooses a market queen. Traditionally, the market queen is chosen by consensus. Through sustained face-to-face interaction in the market, the most trustworthy and experienced traders were easily identifiable. In the larger urban markets, there is the possibility for more than one choice, thus an election process has been implemented. The results are essentially the same, however. As long as a leader maintains the respect of the traders, a market queen is likely to serve many terms.[10]

Lock-Up Shops

The next level of market activity is the lock-up shops, concrete structures in which traders can leave their goods overnight. These

[8]Of the 30 women interviewed inside the established markets, 20 were members of a trading association. The traders who did belong were asked if their association regulated the prices they charged. Virtually all said that their association (16 represented in all) did not. Most traders indicated that they would quit the association if it attempted to put such controls on their business.

[9]Officially, the case could ultimately be appealed to the city council. According to Francis Eshun, the public relations officer of the Accra city council, these disputes are often simply "petty female squabbles" and the council is reluctant to become involved. If the city council must pass down a judgment, they generally support the decision of the market leaders so as to discourage future requests for intervention by the council. Though it is a misconception that these disputes and their resolution have no real economic consequences, it is on the other hand a fortuitous one. By endorsing a policy of staying out of "petty female squabbles," the integrity of the system of conflict resolution is not undermined by bureaucratic tinkering.

[10]There is also a market queen who presides over the collection of all the smaller markets in the urban areas. In Accra, this position has been held by a woman named Manan Lokko since the early 1950s. Since she is too old to come to the market every day, her role is primarily symbolic. However, she is an extremely important symbol, as is demonstrated by her ability to mobilize opposition to city policies. When the

women have all the options open to them for acquiring credit that the stall traders do, but will frequently have further opportunities for acquiring credit. Some cloth manufacturers, for example, put high volume traders in contact with one another, the hope being that by pooling their resources they will be able to purchase even larger quantities. This is also a way for the manufacturer to share the risk, and thereby grant more cloth on credit. If a member of the cluster is short on her share of a payment, the other members will cover it knowing that they may need the favor returned at some future time. These clusters often form the basis for expanded business ventures, and are a trusted source of business advice.

The capital needed by a trader to secure a lock-up shop is considerable. To be assigned use of the space, she must pay the city council C26,000 ($61.18). She is also responsible for the construction of the structure itself (a structure which still officially belongs to the city council even though she pays for its construction). A simple 8′ × 12′ concrete structure costs about C550,000 ($1,294). In addition to this, she pays an annual rent to the city council of C20,000 ($47).[11] If she has this kind of working capital, she is far more likely to be able to secure a loan through one of the official banking institutions. Once she is operating at this level, it is generally not a problem acquiring credit in this way. The problem is in reaching that level. The minimum savings and deposit requirements for starting and maintaining a savings account (the only way to prove one's credit worthiness to the official banking establishment) is a distant possibility for most traders in the market.[12]

---

city council announced they were moving the market women away from the Rex Cinema, a central location in Accra, in order to start construction of new office space, the market queen was able to summon thousands of women to the steps of the city council. The administrators inside the city council reported many staff problems during this time, because all the workers in the office had some tie, either a sister, a mother, an aunt, or wife in the market, who was pressuring them to use their influence in the city council to stop the policy from being implemented.

[11]Note that these figures do not include taxes, the magnitudes of which will depend on the particular good sold and the volume of trade. The operating taxes range from C40 per day (about $.10) for small scale street vendors to C100,000 per year ($235) for larger scale cloth sellers in lock-up shops.

[12]Both Standard Charter and Ghana Commercial Bank require an initial deposit of C10,000 ($23.53) to open a saving account. They will not consider a loan for less than C100,000 ($235). For a first time loan, they require cash collateral of half the amount of the loan, plus property or a guarantor. In addition, the borrower must insure the

Impediments to Indigenous Institutions Fostering Economic Development

What is stopping the evolved indigenous institutions from fostering more economic development? In her study of Ivorian market women, Barbara Lewis (1976) cites the erosion of tight kinship ties and particularly the individualist character of the market as the reasons for the decline of the rotating credit associations and indigenous mutual assistance societies. It seems unlikely, however, that after centuries of competitive markets, individualism is the cause of these relatively recent problems. She does not seriously consider the role government policies have played in stunting the effectiveness of indigenous arrangements of credit and mutual assistance, a line of inquiry essential to understanding the Ghanaian context. More than any other influence, state and municipal control of resources and market mechanisms has inhibited indigenous institutions from providing credit and mutual assistance and thus has retarded the development of the local economy.

Criminalizing Market Activity

In 1979, Flight Lieutenant J. J. Rawlings staged a military coup to oust the corrupt head of state Acheampong. Rawlings promoted his regime with an anti-corruption campaign, ordering the incarceration (and sometimes death) of bureaucratic elites who hoarded consumer goods and dealt in political favors. The rhetoric of the military regime struck a popular chord with the average citizen who had been locked out of the system of privilege yet was spending more and more for basic requirements. Rather than seen as a reflection of perverse incentives introduced by the marketing board structure, the relatively high prices of corn, cassava, yam, and other basic items were unfortunately seen as part of the general graft and corruption.

---

shop and goods such that the loan will be paid off in the event of extensive accidental damage or theft. Barclay's Bank requires a minimum initial deposit of C50,000 ($118) to open a savings account and will not consider lending less than C1,000,000 ($2,353). Again, the first time borrower must provide cash collateral of half the amount of the loan, plus property or a guarantor. Barclay's Bank requires the borrower to purchase life insurance in order to secure the loan. A policy for a healthy 30 year old will cost around C150,000 ($353). Barclay's Bank also requires potential borrowers to carry out the bulk of their transactions in the form of checks. Small entrepreneurs deal only in cash both when purchasing supplies as well as in accepting payments.

In retaliation for selling above the state-controlled prices, the major markets of Accra were destroyed. In central Accra, government soldiers flattened Makola Market Number One with dynamite. Many women were beaten and publicly flogged, their heads shaven, and often imprisoned. This contributed considerably to the general decay of indigenous markets in the early 1980s, where even produce which grows abundantly in the Ghanaian climate could not be found for sale in the urban areas.[13]

For a short period, government control was turned over to civilian rule, but conditions did not improve, as the President Dr. Hilla Limann, retained the policy of stringent price controls. On December 31, 1981, Rawlings staged another coup, this time stepping up his anti-capitalist rhetoric. Drawing on a mixture of dependency theory, anti-Westernism, and Nkrumah's neo-colonialism, Rawlings favored at least a partial withdrawal from the global economic system (Haynes 1989, p. 109). Never did Rawlings blame his own interventionist policies for the continued economic decline. Only in 1983, when he was in considerable danger of losing political control, did he grudgingly release the price controls as a condition of an IMF Economic Recovery Program (ERP). Since the controls were lifted, the local economy has slowly improved, but the experience has left deep scars.

Currently, the illegality of trading on the street is still a major barrier to the most marginal of all traders from accumulating the capital necessary to secure a market stall, cooking equipment, or any other means of expanding a business. While officially, trading on the street is illegal, unofficially it is tolerated. This does not mean, however, that the city council simply turns a blind eye. Rather, the ambiguous status of hawkers places them in the precarious position of being hit from both sides.[14]

[13]Many women abandoned the urban areas to return to their rural villages, as subsistence farming was more lucrative than urban trade under such circumstances.

[14]The ambiguous status of these women is demonstrated by the attitudes of the city council guards. At midday, guards can be seen carrying on polite conversation with and purchasing *kenkey* or small meat pies from the same women to whom they are meant to be issuing a citation. Yet, once or twice a week, guards can also be seen making their way up a street violently smashing the stools and tables upon which women will sit or set their wares. During these demonstrations, no fines are issued, no bribes are solicited. There is no purpose here other than to send a clear message that the street traders are in fact criminals.

The most cautious strategy a street vendor can take is to always keep moving, as the general rule is that city guards will not fine a trader as long as she does not loiter in one spot. This however means that she cannot establish a predictable trading position and therefore cannot build a regular clientele. On the other hand, hawkers who establish a consistent trading position run a greater risk of being fined or at least pressured for a bribe. Evidently, the guards are keen enough to price discriminate. The bribes can be a token C200 (about $.50) or bag of rice or tomatoes every couple of weeks, or can be a more substantial amount of C1,000 to C2,000 ($2.35 to $4.71) a week if the city council guard chooses to target a trader he knows is running a profitable enterprise.

While these kinds of costs are imposed upon hawkers because of their officially illegal status, the fact that it is unofficially tolerated means that the city expects a daily tax from each trader. Thus, the ambiguous status of the street vendor is as much a curse as it is a blessing. The daily tax[15] paid to the city council guards, the fines levied when a trader is caught setting her wares down on the sidewalk,[16] the loss taken when supplies are confiscated by the city council, and the regular tributes paid to the city council guards to avoid citation, when added together represent a substantial burden upon street vendors.

In Accra, about 1,500 traders per month have their goods confiscated and must pay at least C5,000 to the city. A single C5,000 citation can mean the difference between being able to feed a family and economic ruin. Besides the taxes and fines, there are implicit costs as well. Even if the fine is paid and the goods are returned, perishable supplies are often spoiled as it may take several days to borrow the money from friends and family. Further, once confiscated, the goods are in considerable danger of disappearing into the pockets of city council employees. In turn, the trader is likely to lose a valuable source of credit if, because of the financial burden of the

[15]The daily tax is C40 or about $.10. The irony that trading on the street is illegal, yet taxable, is not lost on the street vendors. One such woman proclaimed that if the city guards were all fired, hawkers would then be able to save enough of their money to build their own market stalls and not have to trade on the sidewalk.

[16]Usually the fine is C5,000 (about $12), but if the trader is a repeat offender or if the volume of goods she trades is unusually large, the fine can be doubled or even tripled.

fines and the loss of her goods, she is unable to pay, or is late in paying, her suppliers.

Monthly incomes of street vendors have a wide variance, anywhere from C7,000 ($16) to C28,000 ($66). Thus, the daily tax and two small tributes of C250 translates into 23 percent of a C7,000 monthly income. Nearly 95 percent of a C7,000 monthly income is lost to the city council if the trader is unfortunate enough to be issued a single C5,000 fine. As the city guards tend to extract more from successful traders, those at the upper end of the income scale also lose a considerable amount of their income to the city council and the pockets of the city guards. The daily taxes, regular tributes of C3,000 per month and one C5,000 fine translates into 33 percent of a C28,000 monthly income. This percentage increases if her goods are spoiled or stolen while in the custody of the city council. For instance, if a trader also loses half of a C10,000 stock of goods, the effective rate rises to just over 50 percent. A trader is not likely to be fined every month, yet two to three fines a year can devastate any savings a trader may have accumulated, dashing chances of establishing a stationary selling position, a prerequisite for substantial levels of both formal and indigenous credit.

Fortunately, the city council no longer controls prices. However, a considerable amount of waste and inefficiency is still introduced by other restrictions on market activity. As valuable resources are diverted from the productive market sector to the unproductive bureaucratic sector, the potential of the local economy to enhance the financial prospects of the most marginal entrepreneurs is mitigated.

Unintended Consequences of Bureaucratic Intervention

While legal sanctions against street vending have the obvious and intended consequence of frustrating this sort of market activity, bureaucratic maneuvering often erects systematic, though unintended barriers to successful market interaction. Finally recognizing the deleterious effects of price controls, all was to be remedied as the city council began to rebuild the markets after 1983 when the ERP was under way. Yet, all was not remedied. The market traders were compensated with new stalls, but the city council could not rebuild the trust relationships which had developed over decades of face-to-face interaction among neighboring traders. Market women were given new stalls, but not the same neighbors. The potential benefits from forging new relationships have been dampened given the general atmosphere of uncertainty. No trader is sure when another similar occurrence will happen.

Since the inception of the ERP, other reasons have been found to relocate traders, either to make room for a parking lot (the result of a successful lobbying campaign by the taxi companies), or to thin out the market to help the flow of traffic. No matter what the motivation, the result is the same: the destruction of the credit and mutual assistance societies that had emerged over years of interaction with the same people. Further, such disruptions particularly frustrate elderly traders, such that they do not return to the new locations. This is a devastating blow to the indigenous credit institutions, as a vacuum of experience and trust is left, rather than a gradual transition of authority.[17]

Currently, the Accra city council is planning to spread the markets out to alleviate traffic problems in the most central part of the city. The criterion by which the city council decides who gets moved to the new location will be according to the size of the delivery trucks involved. For example, yams are delivered in large vehicles which block traffic, thus yam sellers will be removed to the new more distant location. Tomatoes, on the other hand, are delivered in smaller vehicles, so tomato vendors would be allowed to remain in the central markets. This proposal demonstrates the inherent danger of allowing market decisions to be made solely on the basis of bureaucratic concerns.

This is not to say that traffic congestion is not a problem in central Accra, but overriding market considerations is not the solution. If the campaign is successful, the move will once again wrench traders from their network of trust and support, and thereby undermine the evolved system of indigenous credit. If entrepreneurs anticipate the move and shift their behavior in response to such a policy measure (e.g., yam sellers may switch to selling tomatoes), this will in turn increase the costs and risks associated with buying and selling

[17]The effects of these policies can be seen in the differences between the markets in Accra and Kumasi and other areas more distant from such political upheaval. The described indigenous institutions in Kumasi are more stable and offer more substantial opportunities for support than in Accra, where most of the political and bureaucratic maneuvering has taken place.

yam, an important dietary staple.[18] The solution lies not in overriding the market process, but rather, in allowing it to work. The congestion problem will be best addressed by a system of market, not state set prices for selling space. Below, I will return to the issue of privatization.

Lack of Scarcity-Indicating Prices for Selling Space

On any given day, a market trader could walk into the city council offices and acquire selling space within the market. According to the city council, many spaces are currently vacant. For C25,000 ($59), a trader can secure an assignment to a market stall. Yet, many street vendors will tell you that there are no available spaces in the market. Others will say that there are spaces available, but the prices are too high. When asked how much they would have to pay to acquire space in the market, they quote prices two to sometimes three times higher than the price quoted by the city council. This is particularly puzzling, given that during the previous year, the city council provided new market stalls at no cost to which street traders could move. However, the women stubbornly refused to stay and returned to trading on the street.

Was this a case of the hawkers acting irrationally or at the very least belligerently? Are city council officials simply lying when they say that spaces are available? Or are the market traders simply confused, not realizing that the stalls are available and less expensive than they think? The answer is "none of the above." The fact is that spaces are available in the market. Further, the city council did (unsuccessfully) attempt to move traders from the street by providing free selling space. Yet, the traders are not confused, nor was their response to the offer of free selling space irrational or simply belligerent. The confusion stems solely from the fact that the stall prices do not reflect relative scarcity or desirability.

As the state officially owns the market stalls, it is incapable of reflecting their true value in the price structure. The fact that some spaces are available at the prevailing rate, should not lead to conclude that the rent charged by the city council comes close to

[18]This proposed "solution" also reflects the male bias at the bureaucratic level. Only someone who has never done the shopping for the family at the end of a long day of selling in the market would see separating the items needed for the traditional daily meals across distant ends of the city as a solution.

reflecting scarcity conditions. In charging a single rate, the city council assumes that a homogeneous good, "market stall space," is being offered. But not all market stalls are created equal. The market stalls span a wide heterogeneous array in terms of location, access to facilities, sanitary conditions, and customer appeal.

Some stalls are near the openings of the market and attract a significant amount of traffic. Yet, the same price will be charged for a stall which is tucked away in an obscure part of the market which sees little traffic. Some stalls are on a dirt surface, yet it will cost as much as another stall on concrete, which will attract customers even during the rainy season and will not ruin a trader's goods with mud stains. The case mentioned above, when hawkers were offered stall space at no cost only to return to the street, was again a situation where the selling space was inappropriately priced. In fact, the "free" selling space was placed in an obscure corner of the city and attracted little traffic. Thus, the zero price charged was simply too high, as the opportunities for profit were more abundant on the street.

Likewise, the differences between the accounts as to the prices and availability of selling space reflect, not confusion on the part of the traders, but the city council's inability to appropriately price heterogeneous resources. Most street traders know that some stalls are available at the set price of C25,000. But they are quick to point out that the only stalls available at this price are in a poor location and will not attract customers. The prices that they quote which are two to three times higher than the official price are the prices in the secondary market. As a trader leaves the market, she will pass on the stall space at a price which reflects the true value of the resource.[19] However, the secondary market is officially illegal, and therefore ownership cannot be guaranteed if a stall is acquired through a black market transaction.

It is not being argued that the city council officials are simply too simple-minded to see the obvious. In fact, on the surface, the market

[19]Note that stall space in a good location is a valuable resource which is often passed from one generation to the next. A well placed market stall acts as both a source of venture capital for a daughter or niece expanding a business (or perhaps a granddaughter starting out), as well as a source of social security for the retiring trader. As an older women makes a gift of the space to a daughter, niece, or granddaughter, she can expect some form of support (either financial or in-kind) from the recipient.

stalls do seem to all look alike. If we only look at their structure and design, they are more alike than different. Their heterogeneity is only manifest as the market process unfolds. In other words, it is only through market activity that one can discover what the true value of such resources are. Thus, merely encouraging greater attentiveness on the part of the city council will not produce a price structure which appropriately reflects relative scarcity. As it is absent a mechanism for discovering what the value of these resources are, the bureaucratic process has no means of acquiring this sort of particularized knowledge. Prices which reflect the relative scarcity and desirability of a resource can only be discovered through a market process.

Policy Implications

Full scale privatization of the marketplace stalls and shops would solve or at least mitigate the most debilitating obstacles facing indigenous trade. By affording the occupants of market stalls private ownership rights, the pricing and allocation of stall space would fully reflect market conditions rather than arbitrary state set prices. Private ownership would also afford the opportunity to un-bundle the resource by allowing owners of stalls to rent to more than one occupant. Traders could then either divide the space, split the selling day or week or involve a combination of the two. This would reduce the per person cost of acquiring space in the market and thus reduce the crowding on the street.

Privatization would also open the way for private developers to erect new structures which would likewise reduce the level of crowding. A private developer would price the spaces in a new structure according to market conditions and not need to rely on a rigid set price structure as is the case under municipal management. Further, by allowing private developers the opportunity to erect new markets, they will have to compete for occupants, not only by pricing the stall space according to market conditions, but through services as well. Once entrepreneurs have a choice as to who they rent or buy from, as opposed to having to rent from the state, the market will reward those developers who provide services seen as essential to the marketplace, such as toilet and locker facilities, security, or shelter from the rain; all cited as serious drawbacks to the current marketplace environment.

This is not to say that all developments will necessarily provide these services. Some may offer only the barest elements of a marketplace structure. But the prices of such stalls would then reflect the lack of services and would allow the opportunity for those on the lower end of the income scale to establish a fixed location in order to trade. This is an essential move for the most marginal of the traders, as this is a clear indication of a person's credit worthiness to a potential lender (either to formal banking institution or indigenous sources of credit). Thus, an array of quality will allow for an array of prices, such that the move from street vending to a fixed location is not such a cataclysmic jump.

Private rather than municipal management of the marketplace is likely to result in fewer cases of full scale upheaval, and the resulting loss of valuable credit and mutual support networks. The allocation of stall space and location will be based on market conditions, not political or bureaucratic considerations. If a marketplace is the most profitable venture, political maneuvering will not override market conditions as they do in the case of municipal management. If market conditions were to shift dramatically, however, at least in the private context, the traders would have the option of establishing themselves in a new space as a block, by renting a row of stalls, for instance. This option is a virtual impossibility under current municipal management. Further, in the private context, there is the opportunity for long term leasing and purchasing arrangements to emerge, such that traders would have to be compensated if they are to be enticed to move; again, an option which is clearly not available under municipal management.

Thus, privatization efforts will have both the expected benefits of rational market pricing and allocation of resources, but it will also have some not so obvious benefits as well. Private development would supply new market space at prices which reflect scarcity conditions. The array of rental rates or prices likely to emerge would provide opportunities for the most marginal traders to establish a fixed location and therefore access to greater sources of credit. The private context would allow the un-bundling of resources, providing even further opportunities for the small scale entrepreneur. Perhaps most importantly, by fostering stable property rights, privatization efforts would support and enhance the performance of indigenous credit and mutual assistance networks.

Clearly the economics profession is aware of the advantages market coordination affords over bureaucratic control, yet sound policy conclusions seem to consistently elude us in Third World contexts. The arguments made here suggest that we have missed opportunities for promoting economic development because we have ignored the cultural specificity in which institutions emerge. Specifically, we have tended to assume that one model, the Western model, of a credit is the only path towards development. Rather than forcing West African culture into the mold of Western institutions, we are likely to meet with more success if we advocate policies which allow indigenous institutions to work to their full potential.

References

Alchian, Armen, and Demsetz, Harold. "The Property Rights Paradigm." *Journal of Economic History* 33 (1) (1973): 17–25.

Axelrod, Robert. "The Emergence of Cooperation among Egoists." *American Political Science Review* 75 (2) (1981): 306–18.

Chamlee, Emily. "Indigenous African Institutions and Economic Development." *Cato Journal* 13 (Spring/Summer 1993): 79–99.

Haynes, Jeffrey. "Ghana: Indebtedness, Recovery, and the IMF, 1977–87." In *The African Debt Crisis*, pp. 99–125. Edited by T. Parfitt and S. Riley. New York: Routledge, 1989.

Klein, Benjamin, and Leffler, Keith. "The Role of Market Forces in Assuring Contractual Performance." *Journal of Political Economy* 89 (4) (1981): 615–41.

Kronman, Anthony. "Contract Law and the State of Nature." *Journal of Law, Economics, and Organization* 1 (1) (1985): 5–32.

Lewis, Barbara. "The Limitations of Group Action Among Entrepreneurs: The Market Women of Abidjan, Ivory Coast." In *Women in Africa: Studies in Social and Economic Change*, pp. 135–56. Edited by N. Hafkin and E. Bay. Stanford: Stanford University Press, 1976.

Little, Kenneth. *West African Urbanization: A Study of Voluntary Associations in Social Change.* Cambridge: Cambridge University Press, 1965.

Little, Kenneth. *African Women in Towns.* Cambridge: Cambridge University Press, 1973.

Lycette, Margaret. "Financing Women in the Third World." ICRW Occasional Paper No. 1. Washington, D.C.: International Center for Research on Women, 1985.

Robertson, Claire. *Sharing the Same Bowl: A Socioeconomic History of Women and Class in Accra, Ghana*. Bloomington: Indiana University Press, 1984.

Simms, Ruth. "The African Woman as Entrepreneur." In *The Black Woman Cross Culturally*, pp. 141–68. Edited by C. Steady. Cambridge: Schenkman, 1981.

Sudarkasa, Niara. "Female Employment and Family Organization in West Africa." In *The Black Woman Cross Culturally,* pp. 49–63. Edited by C. Steady. Cambridge: Shenkman, 1981.

Tannen, Deborah. *You Just Don't Understand.* New York: Ballantine Books, 1990.

Wipper, Audrey. "Women's Voluntary Associations." In *African Women South of the Sahara,* pp. 69–86. Edited by J. Hay and S. Stichter. New York: Longman, 1984.

Part III

The Failure of State-Led Development Policy

12. The First World's Misbegotten Economic Legacy to the Third World

Doug Bandow

Famine has claimed tens or hundreds of thousands of lives in Africa; a $2.0 trillion dollar debt burdens poorer states and threatens to bury some nations. Annual growth rates and food production in the Third World have fallen throughout the 1980s and 1990s. While a few countries appear to be breaking free from the cycle of poverty and debt, many others—Zaire, Sudan, and the like—are imploding. At the same time, formerly communist nations are facing increasing political and economic difficulties, as the euphoria of 1989 has given way to the ugly reality of the 1990s. Unless governments of poorer nations, particularly those in Sub-Saharan Africa, the Transcaucasus, and Eastern Europe, are willing to make tough political choices, their international economic and debt situations will continue to deteriorate, with potentially catastrophic consequences.

The main sign of hope is that today there is a growing consensus across political ideologies and geographic boundaries that bare economic survival and eventual prosperity require an increased reliance on market mechanisms. Disagreements remain over a multitude of specific issues—the proper role of the state, the importance of income redistribution, the need for debt relief, and so on—but doubt about the importance of a vibrant private sector has all but disappeared. Indeed, even the few nations that remain committed to draconian state economic control, economic basket cases such as Cuba and North Korea, are now loosening ever so slightly their own economic regulations in a desperate attempt to solve the problems resulting from their sclerotic economies.

Doug Bandow is a Senior Fellow of the Cato Institute. This chapter is adapted from the author's article in the *Journal of Economic Growth* (Bandow 1986).

While this intellectual revolution is obviously welcome, a number of developing nations have long and successfully avoided the dominant socialist development model. In East Asia, for instance, Japan, Taiwan, South Korea, Singapore, and Hong Kong have achieved phenomenal levels of growth through general, though varying, reliance on the free market. Such pairings as Taiwan and China, South and North Korea, and West and East Germany have provided powerful evidence of the superiority of market-oriented domestic policies.

Similar conclusions have also been statistically verified. In 1983, for instance, the World Bank surveyed developing nations and their economic policies; it found that growth rates consistently fell as market distortions increased. A decade later a special World Bank report on Africa reached the same conclusion (World Bank 1983, 1994). Similar studies by private researchers have found the rate of economic progress to be correlated with such factors as low trade barriers and a positive investment climate. Finally, the slow growers tend to have overvalued currencies and high ratios of taxes to gross national product (GNP). Report economists E. Dwight Phaup and Bradley Lewis (1985, p. 90): "Resource endowment, lucky circumstances, former colonial status, and other similar factors make little difference in the speed with which countries grow economically. But the results of domestic policy choices pervade every economic area."

Despite this record, extensive state economic intervention has long existed around the world, including the West, for political and philosophical reasons. Unfortunately, as decolonization quickened after World War II, most Third World states traveled the socialist path. The decision was in part nationalistic: African states, in particular, believed that true independence required indigenous control of economic resources. Ghana's Kwame Nkrumah explained that his nation's "socialist transformation would eradicate completely the colonial structure" of the economy (Ayittey 1986, p. 9).

The Rise of Statism in Developing Countries

Statism also tended to work to the advantage of the elites who initially gained power in newly independent nations. While Western political institutions had grown up over decades and centuries, gaining some resilience against powerful political interests, democratic systems in the former colonies were far more fragile. Thus, control of the economic system helped assure continued political domination for ruling groups.

But there was also a belief that the state had to guide the development process. Said Nkrumah: "only a socialist form of society can assure Ghana of a rapid rate of economic progress without destroying that social justice, that freedom and equality, which are a central feature of our traditional way of life" (Ayittey 1986, p. 9). This dirigiste philosophy was not based on historical experience: rapid economic and social progress was primarily a phenomenon of Western classical liberal regimes, not of their mercantilist predecessors.

Indeed, in many traditional societies, the concept of development was profoundly alien. Robert Rothstein (1977, p. 179) has stated: "Imported doctrines of rapid growth and industrialization, and simplistic exhortations about the ease with which the conditions of underdevelopment could be overcome, also ensured that the developing countries would become increasingly involved with a complex international environment—and for this, the Western governments and Western experts must share some part of the responsibilities." In short, Western officials encouraged ambitious leaders of small countries to drag their peoples into the industrial age as quickly as possible.

Having helped ordain the goal of rapid industrialization, Western politicians and economists also played a major role in developing the statist strategies that Nkrumah and other Third World nationalists espoused. "African socialism," for instance, was more a Western than an indigenous concept. Burkina Faso's external relations minister, Leandre Bassole, captured the essence of the issue during a 1986 special session of the United Nations: "Africa's development has almost always been the brainchild of persons who have had and still have a very questionable understanding of our profound being" (United Nations 1986, p. 46).

That Western thought has had such a profound influence on developing nations in Africa and elsewhere is ironic, for many influential Western intellectuals and politicians have had patronizing and even hostile attitudes toward "backward" peoples struggling to bridge the chasm between traditional and modern societies. Complains Deepak Lal (1983, p. 204), an Indian economist who has consulted with numerous international agencies, "at its bluntest, behind at least part of the [statist development strategy] is a paternalistic attitude born of a distrust of, if not contempt for, the ordinary, poor, uneducated masses of the Third World." Leading Westerners simply believed nonwhite non-Westerners to be incapable of organizing their lives and economies as had people of European extraction.

Only somewhat less offensive are the "professional humanitarians" who, in the words of Peter Bauer (1978, p. 143), view citizens of the Third World "as helpless victims of Western misdeeds in need of their ministrations." While private development groups and charitable organizations generally have not advocated a specific development strategy, many have erroneously blamed global poverty on Western exploitation and an unfair international economic system.

Nevertheless, much of the statist development program popularized by the West and adopted by developing countries stemmed from intellectually honest, if terribly misguided, economic schools that arose in opposition to the classical liberal tradition. After all, newly independent nations have not been alone in adopting socialist policies; virtually every industrialized state greatly increased state economic intervention over the last century. The fundamental difference is that the industrialized states are more developed and their economies are therefore more resilient; the "dirigiste dogma," as Lal calls it, was far more destructive for developing countries.

Western Socialist Influences on Developing Countries

Many Westerners have acted as the Sirens in Homer's *Odyssey*, luring Third World economies onto the rocks. One of the most important was Lenin, who is responsible for death and destruction in lands far beyond his own nation's borders. While Marx, ironically, viewed the colonial experience as a progressive force in the undeveloped world (lauding the potential of capitalism to transform such societies in the *Communist Manifesto*), it was Lenin, in *Imperialism: The Highest Stage of Capitalism*, who specifically applied socialist principles to the Third World. His thesis was essentially that the proletariat in underdeveloped states would continually become more impoverished by the exploitation of the capitalist colonial powers. Naturally, following decolonization, the communist solution was the same economic prescription as that proposed for the developed world, i.e., state control of the means of production, central planning, and forced industrialization.

Until their demise, the USSR and its allies continued to advance this position. In 1962 Soviet spokesman I. Potekhin (1962, p. 14) argued that "the economic essence of colonialism, whatever form it takes, consists in exporting a part of a colony's national income to the metropolitan country without return imports of an equivalent value. This explains why metropolitan countries made such big strides in their economic development during the last century while colonies lagged behind." In fact, the Soviet Union refused to provide foreign aid because, in its view, world poverty was the fault of exploitative colonialists.

Of course, the Leninist analysis of underdevelopment is demonstrably false. While colonialism was morally offensive, it did not generally impoverish Third World peoples. Indeed, the European powers introduced the concept of economic growth to their subjects; the developing countries with the least historical contact with the West, such as Ethiopia, Afghanistan, and Nepal, are also among the globe's poorest countries.

Nevertheless, Lenin's arguments have had enormous influence on the Third World, providing ruling elites with a program for political action and an excuse for economic failure. The Marxist-Leninist critique also gained influence because it had ardent advocates in the West. For instance, the late Paul Baran (1957, pp. 249–50), a well-known development economist from Stanford, wrote that "it is in the underdeveloped world that the central, overriding fact of our epoch becomes manifest to the naked eye: the capitalist system, once a mighty engine of economic development, has turned into a no less formidable hurdle to human advancement." Therefore, a "socialist transformation of the advanced West would . . . enable the peoples of the underdeveloped countries to overcome rapidly their present condition of poverty and stagnation."

Naturally, in Baran's view, developing states, too, needed to assert public control over their economies. He said, "the establishment of a socialist planned economy is an essential, indeed indispensable, condition for the attainment of economic and social progress in underdeveloped countries" (Baran 1957, p. 261). Even economists who did not consider themselves Marxist-Leninists often offered remarkably similar policy prescriptions. Sweden's Gunnar Myrdal, a Nobel Prize winner, once wrote of upper and lower "classes" of nations and an increased "class consciousness" in the Third World;

he consistently promoted large-scale aid transfers and state-led development programs (Myrdal 1956a, p. 201).

There was a time when Third World leaders could perhaps be forgiven for harboring Marxist delusions. For example, Indian Prime Minister India Jawaharlal Nehru declared in 1936 that "there was a progressive deterioration, everywhere except in the wide-flung Soviet territories or the USSR, where, in marked contrast with the rest of the world, astonishing progress was made in every direction" (Singh 1977). At that time there was great American interest in the Soviet experiment as well. Today the entire Marxist-Leninist paradigm has been thoroughly discredited.

A related if somewhat less pernicious philosophy was provided by the British Fabian socialists. They argued for a gradual collectivist transformation, an approach that, according to Indian economist Jagdish Bhagwati (1985, p. 60), exercised "a powerful impact through the large numbers of the Indian elite that were processed through the English educational institutions prior to Indian independence in 1947." Other developing countries, too—especially other former British colonies—looked to Fabian principles to organize their economies.

The London School of Economics, which promoted the socialist development model, was perhaps the most important educational institution for English-speaking colonial subjects. The British Fabian Beatrice Webb explained in her autobiography that she and her husband Sidney felt "assured that with the School as the teaching body, the Fabian Society as a propagandist organization, the LCC [London County Council] as object lesson in electoral success, our books as the only elaborate original work in economic fact and theory, no young man or woman who is anxious to study or to work in public affairs can fail to come under our influence" (Moynihan 1978, p. 11). As a result, leaders throughout the underdeveloped world adopted Fabian socialism.

The Colonial Legacy of Interventionism

But officials in many newly independent nations did not have to struggle to turn statist ideologies into policy, because European administrators had earlier created the necessary government controls. The policies promoted by the London School of Economics eventually suffused the British Colonial Office. Many officials in

London and colonial governors "took for granted the case for the most diverse forms of state economic intervention" (Bauer 1984, p. 94).

Intervention took many forms: restrictive licensing of businesses, such as cotton ginneries; tight import regulations; and state monopolies in key exports. The best-known export controls involved cocoa, but trade in cotton, palm oil and groundnuts was similarly controlled. Agricultural marketing boards, which invariably offered farmers below-market prices for their crops, were a related Western creation. These disruptive measures, which benefited powerful interest groups while impoverishing the great mass of people, were part of the administrative apparatus handed to incoming governments upon independence. The impact of this Western "gift" to the Third World was enormous: "the incoming African rulers welcomed the various controls, because they gave them a close grip over their subjects, and enabled them to pursue more effectively their personal and political purposes. They extended these controls whenever they could" (Bauer 1984, pp. 94–95).

At the same time, the colonial powers created the wasteful framework that governed much public spending by the post-independence regimes. While at the time increased "investment" in social projects was viewed as evidence of progressive rule, most of the funds were generated locally, through distorted economic policies such as export monopolies. It was this growth in the size and power of the public sector that initiated the disastrous politicization of African life, where state spending was used to enrich friends and political allies. In short, it was the Europeans who taught educated colonial elites both how to use economic controls to extract vast wealth from their countrymen and how to spend the funds for their own political advantage.

Even where money was not misappropriated, the spending foreshadowed the wasteful prestige investments seen today: capital cities rising out of the hinterland, state airlines to nowhere, and money-losing government enterprises and cooperatives. In Sierra Leone and Ghana, the marketing boards in pre- and post-colonial times amassed huge surpluses that they then dissipated on projects that did not contribute to economic development. Massive amounts of indigenous capital were wasted, leaving the nations in a deteriorating economic position.

Indeed, the creation of a dirigiste economic structure, hand-made for the authoritarian leaders who took control in developing countries, may be the most important and destructive legacy of colonialism. New regimes would have sought to extend their control over the economy, but, according to Bauer (1981, p. 183):

> Without the policies of the closing years of colonial rule the incoming governments would not have inherited the effective and comprehensive state controls established in the 1950s, especially the state export monopolies and the large reserves accumulated by them. They would not have inherited the methods, potentialities and wherewithal for establishing quasi-totalitarian policies, nor the same inducement for attempting to do so. Without these controls, and especially the state export monopolies, the prizes of political power would have been far less and there might have been less scope for large-scale organized oppression and brutality.

Development Economists as Promoters of Interventionism

With an economic regulatory system established by Western colonial powers, Third World elites could turn to any number of development economists to justify state-led development programs. For years the so-called structuralist school was dominant. It considered developing economies inflexible and unresponsive to market forces. Changes in factors such as prices, taxes, and regulations were thought to have little effect on economic progress. Leading proponents of this view included Gunnar Myrdal, Albert Hirschman, Hans Singer, Ragnar Nurkse, and Paul Rosenstein-Rodan.

In fact, so pervasive was the anti-capitalist bias in terms of Third World development that even economists who recognized an important role for the private sector in advanced economies viewed developing states differently. Wrote Robert Heilbroner "in the great transformation of the underdeveloped areas, the market mechanism is apt to play a much smaller role than in the comparable transformation of the West during the industrial revolution." Heilbroner saw the need for more than just active public sector management: "powerful, even ruthless, government may be needed." He even saw communism "as a technique for attempting to bring about the deep-seated changes required for rapid modernization" (Heilbroner 1968, pp. 15, 616).

Moreover, as noted earlier, this attitude was shared, for different reasons, by many non-academics. Much of the cultural and religious intelligentsia with whom Third World diplomats, U.N. delegates, and government officials had contact were inclined toward the socialist model. Such Western opinion leaders may have known little about economics or the Third World, but their opinions gave important moral support to the romantic notions of "African socialism" promoted by the likes of Tanzania's Julius Nyerere.

The structuralist/antimarket world view promoted by the West and adopted by the developing states has had two related impacts. The first has been to reinforce the notion, akin to biological or environmental determinism, that global poverty and underdevelopment can be solved only by readjusting outside economic factors, such as trading relations, aid flows, technology transfers, and so on.

The much-ballyhooed Independent Commission on International Development Issues, chaired by the late West German Chancellor Willy Brandt, exhibited this attitude. The panel included American luminaries Katharine Graham and Peter G. Peterson, former British Prime Minister Edward Heath, and the late Swedish Prime Minister Olaf Palme. The commission's two reports—*North-South: A Programme for Survival* (1980) and *Common Crisis North-South: Co-operation for World Recovery* (1983)—did not even mention the domestic policies of developing countries. Instead, they advocated massive international resource transfers as the panacea for global poverty.

Such pronouncements from Western elites reinforced the popularity of so-called "dependency theory." Advanced by development economists including Myrdal, H. W. Singer, and Thomas Balogh, dependency theory holds that Western investment and trade harm poorer nations. Some Third World academics, especially in Latin America, pressed its ideas further. The capitalist "center," they argued, continued to exploit the underdeveloped "periphery" through its dominant economic position. And while "the main doctrines of the dependency school have found little acceptance, the influence of the school has been considerable," writes Oxford University's Ian M. D. Little (1982, p. 220), politicians, political theorists, and sociologists have been particularly attracted to a theory that blames outside people and institutions for domestic failures.

Unfortunately, however, the writing of many Western development economists and leaders has done more than divert attention from the domestic causes of Third World poverty. The same people have prescribed many of the policies that have most harmed poorer states in their struggle to develop.

The second effect of the structuralist/antimarket worldview has been to promote central planning. Indeed, for years the only question was how extensive the state control should be. Some Westerners, for instance, saw a role for the private sector even though they advocated government-led development programs. Robert Heilbroner (1968, p. 617) wrote: "The guiding force of development is apt to be tilted in the direction of central planning. Regardless of the importance of private enterprise in carrying out the individual projects of development, the driving and organizing force of economic growth will be principally lodged with the government." Similarly, in a generally sensible book that details the politicization of economic life in the Third World, Robert Rothstein (1977, p. 296) argues that a market economy is unlikely to work well in underdeveloped states, so "it might make sense to consider creating a policy-making system that attempts to combine less elaborate forms of national planning . . . with a more extensive effort at local planning," along with "a more modified and limited market system." Even Little, despite his devastating critique of the structuralist and socialist development schools, sees a need for extensive state involvement.

Many development economists advocated a much greater role for the public sector. Wrote Myrdal (1956a, p. 201), "the special advisers to underdeveloped countries who have taken the time and trouble to acquaint themselves with the problem, no matter who they are . . . all recommend central planning as the first condition of progress." And not just a little government control; "one of the most serious shortcomings of policy in the countries in which comprehensive planning has been undertaken is the failure to plan more ambitiously and on a larger scale." Tokyo University's H. Kitamura, a development economist then with the United Nations Commission for Asia and the Far East, contended that "only planned economic development can hope to achieve a rate of growth that is politically acceptable and capable of commanding popular enthusiasm and support" (Kitamura 1963, p. 202).

The failure of central planning in the Eastern European states is obvious to all; the resulting economic disaster throughout the Third World has been documented by Bauer and others. Yet it seems that no experience was sufficient to dissuade the Western enthusiasts of state control. Myrdal (1956b, p. 65), for instance, appeared to believe that the lack of success of economic intervention in the industrialized states made it more imperative to apply the same policies to the Third World: "Central economic planning is always a difficult thing and, where it has been tried, it has not been much of a success in the advanced countries. Now, what amounts to a sort of super planning has to be staged by underdeveloped countries with weak political and administrative systems, and a largely illiterate and apathetic citizenry."

The strategies generally suggested by Myrdal and others for central governments to enforce were equally misguided. One of the most harmful strategies was "import substitution," the use of import tariffs, quotas, and subsidies to protect and promote domestic industries. Myrdal was a leading advocate of this approach, though he was not alone; experts across the globe, including Hirschman, Rosenstein-Rodan, Nurkse, and Raul Prebisch all "converged from different directions onto import-substitution strategy" (Bhagwati 1985, p. 292). Today most development economists admit that this policy stifles growth. The world's most rapidly growing economies, the East Asian states, have eschewed import substitution and have instead concentrated on producing inexpensive exports. Nevertheless, the claims of advocates of import substitution—that it would, for instance, promote economic independence and creation of domestic enterprises—made it politically popular for years.

Once governments began to plan, their focus quickly shifted to forced industrialization, with emphasis on steel, petrochemicals, and other heavy industries. Indeed, writes Lal (1983, p. 80), "among Marxists and others on the Left, industrial self-reliance through the promotion of heavy industry has become a sine qua non of development." Soviet and later Indian economists advocated forced industrialization, and while most development economists did not recommend the specific industries to be favored, the result was certainly foreseeable: governments are concerned with prestige and politics, and the most symbolically important projects tend to be the least competitive. Moreover, this wasteful form of autarky was practiced by what many Third World leaders believed for years to be the most successful, publicly planned model of national development ever—the Soviet Union.

A by-product of the drive to industrialize, one condoned and even promoted by Western observers, was the calculated impoverishment of rural populations. Through marketing boards of the sort first created by the British colonial authorities, Third World governments routinely expropriated the crops of their farmers in order to support their growing urban populations. The result was steadily declining per capita food production, which has forced many developing states to reverse course and increase returns to their farmers. But two decades ago Heilbroner (1968, p. 621) was writing that development would require "measures that will transfer the food surplus from the peasant cultivator to workers on capital projects."

The most effective exponents of this rather antiseptic injunction for official theft were the USSR and China, which ruthlessly collectivized their peasant populations. At least two African nations—Tanzania and Ethiopia, both fervent believers in an independent Third World course—adopted similar policies, with disastrous results.

Some Western economists who did not advocate large-scale government economic planning nevertheless endorsed forms of intervention that have been increasingly recognized as failures in the industrialized nations. Expansive fiscal and monetary policies, for instance, were a Keynesian norm. Equally counterproductive was consistent pressure on developing countries to increase taxes.

The "orthodox" position of development economists, explained Professors Richard Bird and Oliver Oldman, is that "most developing countries tax little, and should tax more, particularly through progressive taxes and land taxes" (Bird and Oldman 1975). Walter Heller (1975, p. 27), a former adviser to President John F. Kennedy, termed high income tax rates "a suitable instrument for achieving some of the ends of economic policy and distributive justice." Richard Goode (1975, p. 273) said that "most underdeveloped countries need to raise more revenue, many of them, much more."

Throughout the Third World governments collect a small share of their total revenues from income taxes. In the mid-1980s the highest share taken by a Latin American nation was 17.5 percent; just three African countries were collecting more than 20 percent, but not for want of trying. The shortage of revenue was in large part due to the steepness of the tax rates and the low thresholds at which high rates applied. For instance, Brazil applied a tax rate of 60 percent starting at the $28,000 income level. Far worse was Chile, where anyone earning over $3,000 a year paid 55 percent of their income in taxes, and Ghana, where annual earnings exceeding $450 were subject to a 60 percent tax.

Effects of Aid from International Organizations

As culpable as are the menagerie of Western economic advisers who developed the statist philosophies adopted by developing nations, the governments of the industrialized nations have done something even worse. They have paid Third World leaders to adopt the dirigiste model. The activities of international agencies, such as the World Bank, the International Monetary Fund, regional development banks, and U.N. Development Program, as well as programs initiated by the U.S. Agency for International Development (AID) and philanthropic foundations, have all helped Third World officials put into effect the collectivist nostrums advanced by Lenin, Myrdal, and others.

One reason for this phenomenon is the political tensions involved in recipient/donor relationships, and the interest of public bureaucracies in perpetuating their role. Argues Gerald Helleiner (1981, p. 29), an economics professor at the University of Toronto, "the recipient governments or government departments ally themselves with external donors for their pursuit of their own domestic interests against other domestic (and foreign) actors."

Also, Western development institutions could not help but be swayed by the same intellectual currents affecting academia and government more generally. That is particularly true of Western nations' development assistance agencies, whose staff, according to Karl Borgin and Kathleen Corbett (1982, p. 30) "are socialists and have been recruited under the social democratic governments in the Scandinavian and Continental countries and the Labour government in England. All are obsessed with the idea of transferring resources from the industrialized countries to Africa."

Even the World Bank felt these influences. In 1983 Stanley Please, a senior adviser to the World Bank's Senior Operations Vice President, reflected that when he joined the institution two decades before, "as a committed socialist. . . I was surprised and shocked by the emphasis which the Bank at the time gave to the public sector in general and to the government in particular. Here was an institution which had the reputation of being ultra free enterprise and market-oriented, yet had more confidence in the rationality, morality and competence of governments than I ever had" (Please 1983, p. 7).

Support for the public sector is reflected in the Bank's lending policies. Though in its early years the Bank focused on infrastructure projects thought necessary to encourage private investment and would not underwrite industrial projects that were not expected to be privatized, those policies were abandoned even before Robert McNamara became president of the World Bank in 1968. By 1981, when McNamara left office, total lending had increased from $954 million to $12.3 billion. It rose to $23.7 billion in 1993 before dipping slightly.

In the 1980s the Bank committed roughly 80 percent of its funds to government enterprises, or parastatals, fueling the disastrous public sector explosion in such countries as Mexico and Brazil. Even now, much of the lending still goes for purposes that could be handled privately. And some Bank loans were truly atrocious: In 1975, for instance, under the rubric of "rural development," the Bank lent Tanzania $10 million to finance the *ujamaa* village resettlements—the Soviet-style collectivization program that brutalized peasants and destroyed the nation's agricultural economy. The Bank has since placed greater rhetorical emphasis on encouraging market-oriented economic reforms in recipient nations. But the money continues to flow even to the most inefficient economic systems (Bandow 1994a, pp. 149–74).

The problem with the IMF has been somewhat different. All IMF loans are conditioned on policy changes, but the IMF has frequently required counterproductive reforms. Morris Goldman (1985, p. 106), a former congressional staffer, has argued that "in some cases, in fact, the IMF has set back development in LDCs by supporting a larger government sector, increased taxes, reduced trade, and slow or no growth."

While the overall goal of IMF programs is sound economic growth, they have often allowed countries to comply by tightening economic controls. The IMF's insistence on improving the balance of payments and reducing public deficits has often caused debtor countries to restrict imports and raise taxes. The IMF is not interested in whether a country is capitalist or socialist so long as it does not run a large current-account deficit.

Examples of questionable loan programs include the 1981 agreement with India, which authorized India to increase the public sector's economic role even though the government already owned three-fourths of all industry. In contrast to short-term international payments balances, successful long-term development requires more emphasis on private firms, yet IMF funds were lent to state enterprises in oil, petrochemical, steel, fertilizer, and engineering. The IMF also pressed for higher tax rates, particularly for farmers. In Jamaica, the IMF has been concerned only with the final budget deficit number, rather than the means of achieving a balance. The 1981 agreement between Jamaica and the IMF resulted in sharp increases in taxes and business license fees. Goldman (1985, p. 220) complained, "so long as the government is able to meet its commitments over the short term, the IMF seems almost indifferent as to how the loan recipient does so—even if it is from destructively high domestic taxes."

It should come as no surprise, then, that there are no success stories of countries graduating from IMF programs to self-sustaining economic growth. Rather, nations have remained on the Fund dole for one, two, three, and even four decades (see Bandow 1994b).

The U.N. Development Program (UNDP) has also had a pernicious influence in foisting alien economic philosophies on Third World nations. During the 1970s and early 1980s it joined the rest of the U.N. system in promoting the idea of a New International Economic Order to redistribute the world's resources (Bandow 1985). The UNDP is supposed to encourage economic growth in developing states, but it has relied almost exclusively on state-led economic strategies.

All UNDP funds go to governments; the agency consciously avoids projects without close public sector involvement. The agency places enormous emphasis on "planning" and "preinvestment" studies, reinforcing the inclination of Third World governments to direct economic activities. Money was given to Senegal, for instance, to draft a national development plan, which was, essentially, the sort of "super" economic planning advocated by Myrdal. "While the specific goals of these efforts are for the most part laudable," write economists Edward Erickson and Daniel Sumner (1984, p. 13), "the presumption upon which such aid is based is that planning, rather than market forces and private incentives, is the key to economic growth."

Other organs of the United Nations have also advocated the dirigiste development model, though they have done so as a political lobby for the Third World rather than as representatives of Western nations. The General Assembly has ritualistically joined the call for a New International Economic Order, but many of the votes have involved a split between First World and Third World countries. Even more persistent has been the United Nations Conference on Trade and Development (UNCTAD). UNCTAD, which spent years pressing for measures to prop up commodity prices, has also pressed for increased foreign aid and extensive international economic regulation. The organization was long headed by Argentine Raul Prebisch, one of the leading structuralist economists. Prebisch's ideas were particularly influential in Latin America, where they gave added respectability to similar ideas proposed by economists from developed countries. Under Prebisch's intellectual influence many countries adopted harmful strategies of import substitution and fixing of commodity prices. However, at least within UNCTAD and other UN organizations developed states cannot be blamed for originating the worst proposals. They long opposed the program of the Group of 77 developing nations, and have agreed only to compromise measures such as the Common Fund, which failed in its stated goal of stabilizing commodity prices.

Effects of Aid from Western Governmental and Non-Governmental Agencies

National development agencies such as AID are also not free of blame. While AID did not quite so consciously promote the socialist model, its programs have effectively underwritten the statist development approach. Some assistance programs have been wasteful failures, though not otherwise harmful. For instance, the agency poured millions into the African Sahel but, reported AID's inspector general, "food production projects in the Sahel have accomplished little, if any, desired results" (AID 1984). Funds for warehouse production, water sanitation, irrigation, and milleries have yielded virtually no long-term effects.

Unfortunately, however, some "successful" AID projects have had a decidedly negative impact. Public Law 480, the Food for Peace program, has created well-documented, pervasive disincentives for indigenous farmers. Other grants have strengthened state control of the economy. In the 1970s AID began Operation Mils Mopti in Mali to increase food production and marketing, yet the government marketing board continued its practice of de facto crop expropriation, driving down production. AID also spent roughly $200 million to help Egypt create a domestic cement industry, essentially as part of a counterproductive import-substitution economic strategy.

In Indonesia the government seized farmers' property for an AID-financed irrigation project. And El Salvador in the 1980s conducted large-scale land reform at American expense, an effort frequently cited by AID as a major achievement. Unfortunately, agricultural production fell because most land titles were vested not in small farmers but in state cooperatives. AID promoted a benign version of communist farm collectivization.

The Reagan Administration attempted to promote free enterprise and policy reform in recipient nations, but little changed. Spending by the Private Enterprise Bureau of AID was a minuscule portion of total foreign aid outlays; moreover, much of its activities consisted of subsidies to American businesses. And though AID's policy advice often makes sense, it has also pressed for tax hikes in several Latin American and African countries, including dirt-poor Niger. Indeed, former AID administrator Peter McPherson said that "governments we help have all taken major fiscal steps to reduce expenditures and increase revenues"—that is, to raise already prohibitively high tax rates or to tighten collection practices (Bethell 1986).

All told, the AID record has been one of gross waste and mismanagement (Bovard 1986, Johnson 1995). So bad has it been that even AID itself acknowledged in a detailed review of its programs released in 1989 that "only a handful of countries that started receiving U.S. assistance in the 1950s and 1960s has ever graduated from dependent status" (AID 1989, p. 112). And the Clinton administration, though more favorably disposed towards foreign aid, also has had to recognize reality. Yet another task force concluded that "despite decades of foreign assistance, most of Africa and parts of Latin America, Asia and the Middle East are economically worse off today than they were 20 years ago" (Kamen and Lippman 1993). The point is simple: "Money—or the lack thereof—is not a significant constraint on development," reports the Development Group for Alternative Policies. "All too often, Third World agencies are overloaded with funds that they cannot effectively absorb and utilize" (Hellinger et al. 1988, p. 5). But the money, though unable to generate economic growth, has proved to be a powerful lure for borrowers to adopt state-led development strategies.

Nongovernmental organizations, too, have promoted dirigiste development. Throughout the post-war period the Ford Foundation, the Harvard Institute for International Development, and the MIT Center for International Studies all supported the local and central planning bureaucracies of India and Pakistan. Although American economists provided by them generally proposed modest market incentives, such as higher prices for farmers, all three organizations endorsed state planning. One Harvard economist, for instance, argued that the "government of Pakistan needs far more than a five-year Plan . . . [it needs] a continuing organization capable of advising on current economic policies and on the long-run development program. . . . [The] opportunity provided by the Five-year Plan could be used to move . . . a few steps in [that] direction" (Rosen 1985, p. 40).

Most Western advisers presumably believed in such a statist approach, though conformity was also enforced by the indigenous governments' willingness to work only with those who supported dirigisme. Observed John Lewis, former director of AID for India, "it has been decided in India that it is the duty of the government—and it cannot be delegated—to create and maintain the 'growth perspective,'" so "outside supporters of the Indian development process who refuse to accept this proposition well-nigh disqualify themselves from the outset" (Lewis 1962, p. 28). Unfortunately, only recently has New Delhi taken serious steps to loosen hopelessly overbearing state control; India's economy remains hopelessly over-planned. Not surprisingly, the country remains among the poorest on earth, number 18 on the World Bank's list in 1994, despite decades of often massive foreign aid transfers.

Conclusion

That there are lots of Western people and institutions to blame for bad economic advice does not absolve the ruling elites of developing nations for their decisions. Both theory and practice have always favored a market-oriented development approach; the comparative advantages of free economies have long been obvious from even the most cursory review of the relative economic progress of the neighboring Chinas, Koreas, and Germanies, for example. Thus, while the Third World may not have consciously desired the economic disaster that has overtaken so many of its members, that result was predictable, even inevitable, given the development path chosen by most newly independent states. Writes the African economist George Ayittey (1986, p. 3): "The root cause of black Africa's crisis lies . . . in [its] political leadership. Even without using western, eastern or some other foreign criteria, that leadership is a failure by our own indigenous African standards." It is a point Ayittey has driven home in subsequent articles and books (Ayittey 1992, 1994).

To fix ultimate responsibility on that leadership, however, still does not excuse Western institutions for their role in perpetuating poverty in the Third World. From Marxist-Leninists to statist colonial powers to socialist economists to supposedly free-market international and national aid organizations, all have played a role in fostering the destructive dirigiste philosophy that still holds sway throughout much of the developing world. That Western nations and multilateral institutions like the World Bank are now emphasizing the market approach is an important, if long overdue, act of repentance, and Third World nations should not view such advice as yet another example of Western economic imperialism. Instead, the West's push for policy conditionality of aid is, if anything, an unstated attempt to counteract the flood of bad advice of past years. It is development economists in industrialized states, rather than policymakers in developing states, who really have the most to be embarrassed about.

Of course, even the rapid turn to market economics being undertaken now by some developing states will not spare poor countries the enormous pain and hardship that has accompanied all peoples as they have tried to jump from the agrarian to the industrial age. The process is often unexpectedly complex and frustratingly slow; the development experience also varies from country to country, depending on people's culture, religious tradition, legal structure, and economic heritage. Unfortunately, one of the worst Western values assimilated by Third World leaders is impatience, particularly the determination to meet development goals immediately, irrespective of the human cost of doing so.

The industrialized North can and should help its lesser developed neighbors. But it can best do so by opening up its markets, encouraging the flow of trade, investment, and technology, and assisting Third World countries in creating the sort of stable legal, democratic political, and free economic institutions necessary for growth to occur. What poorer states do not need is more detailed advice on how to best plan and manage their economies. For if the postwar experience proves anything, it is that the dirigiste model—promoted by the West and implemented by the South—is bust.

References

AID. U.S. Agency for International Development. "Inadequate Design and Monitoring Impede Results in Sahel Food Production Projects." Washington, D.C.: U.S. Agency for International Development, 31 January 1984.

AID. U.S. Agency for International Development. *Development and the National Interest: U.S. Economic Assistance into the 21st Century.* Washington, D.C.: U.S. Agency for International Development, 1989.

Ayittey, George B.N. "Misguided Development Policies: The Experience of Black Africa." Paper presented at a Cato Institute conference, 1 May 1986.

Ayittey, George B.N. *Africa Betrayed.* New York: St. Martin's Press, 1992.

Ayittey, George B.N. "Aid for Black Elephants: How Foreign Assistance Has Failed Africa." In *Perpetuating Poverty: The World Bank, the IMF, and the Developing World,* pp. 126–45. Edited by Doug Bandow and Ian Vásquez. Washington, D.C.: Cato Institute, 1994.

Bandow, Doug, ed. *U.S. Aid to the Developing World: A Free Market Agenda.* Washington, D.C.: Heritage Foundation, 1985.

Bandow, Doug. "The First World's Misbegotten Economic Legacy to the Third World." *Journal of Economic Growth* 1 (4) (1986).

Bandow, Doug. *The Politics of Envy: Statism as Theology.* New Brunswick, N.J.: Transaction Publishers, 1994a.

Bandow, Doug. "The IMF: A Record of Addiction and Failure." In *Perpetuating Poverty: The World Bank, the IMF, and the Developing World,* pp. 15–36. Edited by Doug Bandow and Ian Vásquez. Washington, D.C.: Cato Institute, 1994b.

Baran, Paul. *The Political Economy of Growth.* New York: Monthly Review Press, 1957.

Bassole, Leandre. "African Leaders at United Nations." *Africa Report,* 12 November 1986.

Bauer, Peter T. "Letter to Commentary on Moynihan Article." In *The First World and the Third World,* pp. 139–47. Edited by Karl Brunner. Rochester, New York: Center for Research in Government Policy and Business, Graduate School of Management, University of Rochester, 1978.

Bauer, Peter T. *Equality, the Third World, and Economic Delusion.* Cambridge, Mass.: Harvard University Press, 1981.

Bauer, Peter T. *Reality and Rhetoric: Studies in the Economics of Development.* Cambridge, Mass.: Harvard University Press, 1984.

Bethell, Tom. "Searching for the Next Marcos." *National Review,* 25 April 1986, p. 42.

Bhagwati, Jagdish. *Wealth and Poverty.* Oxford: Basil Blackwell, 1985.

Bird, Richard, and Oldman, Oliver, eds. *Readings on Taxation in Developing Countries.* Baltimore: Johns Hopkins University Press, 1975.

Borgin, Karl, and Corbett, Kathleen. *The Destruction of a Continent: Africa and International Aid.* San Diego: Harcourt Brace Jovanovich, 1982.

Bovard, James. "The Continuing Failure of Foreign Aid." Cato Institute Policy Analysis No. 65, January 31. Washington, D.C.: Cato Institute, 1986.

Erickson, Edward, and Sumner, Daniel. "The U.N. and Economic Development." In *The World Without a U.N.* Edited by Burt Pines. Washington, D.C.: Heritage Foundation, 1984.

Goldman, Morris B. "Multilateral Institutions and Economic Development." In *U.S. Aid to the Developing World: A Free Market Agenda,* pp. 93–115. Edited by Doug Bandow. Washington, D.C.: Heritage Foundation, 1985.

Goode, Richard. "Taxation of Savings and Consumption in Underdeveloped Countries." In Bird and Oliver (1975, p. 273).

Heilbroner, Robert. *The Economic Problem.* Englewood Cliffs, N.J.: Prentice-Hall, 1968.

Helleiner, Gerald. *International Economic Disorder.* Toronto: University of Toronto Press, 1981.

Heller, Walter. "Fiscal Policies for Underdeveloped Countries." In Bird and Oliver (1975, p. 27).

Hellinger, Stephen, et al. *Aid for Just Development: Report on the Future of Foreign Assistance.* Boulder, Colo.: Lynn Reinner Publishers, 1988.

Independent Commission on International Development Issues. *North-South: A Programme for Survival.* Cambridge, Mass: MIT Press, 1980.

Independent Commission on International Development Issues. *Common Crisis North-South: Co-Operation for World Recovery.* Cambridge, Mass.: MIT Press, 1983.

Johnson, Bryan. "Inspector General Finds Fraud and Waste at AID." *Heritage Foundation F.Y.I.,* 11 January 11 1995.

Kamen, Al, and Lippman, Thomas W. "Task Force Favors Restructuring and Refocusing Troubled AID." *Washington Post,* 3 July 1993.

Kitamura, H. "Foreign Trade Problems in Planned Economic Development." In *Economic Development with Special Reference to East Asia.* Edited by Kenneth Berrill, p. 202. London: Macmillan, 1963.

Lal, Deepak. *The Poverty of Development Economics.* London: Institute of Economic Affairs, 1983.

Lewis, John. *Quiet Crisis in India.* Washington, D.C.: Brookings Institution, 1962.

Little, Ian M.D. *Economic Development: Theory, Policy, and International Relations.* New York: Basic Books, 1982.

Moynihan, Daniel Patrick. "The United States in Opposition." In *The First World and the Third World,* pp. 105–37. Edited by Karl Brunner. Rochester, New York: Center for Research in Government Policy and Business, Graduate School of Management, University of Rochester, 1978.

Myrdal, Gunnar. *An International Economy.* London: Routledge and Kegan Paul, 1956a.

Myrdal, Gunnar. *Development and Underdevelopment.* Cairo: National Bank of Egypt, 1956b.

Phaup, E. Dwight, and Lewis, Bradley. "Winners and Losers: Differentiating Between High-Growth and Low-Growth LDCs." In Bandow (1985, p. 90).

Please, Stanley. "A Candid Look at Yesterday." *The Bank's World* (World Bank), September 1983, p. 7.

Potekhin, I. *Problems of Economic Development of African Countries.* Moscow: Progress Publishers, 1962.

Rosen, George. *Western Economists and Eastern Societies.* Baltimore: Johns Hopkins University Press, 1985.

Rothstein, Robert. *The Weak in the World of the Strong.* New York: Columbia University Press, 1977.

Singh, V.B., ed. *Nehru on Socialism.* Delhi: Government of India, 1977.

World Bank. *World Development Report 1983.* New York: Oxford University Press, 1983.

World Bank. *Adjustment in Africa: Reforms, Results, and the Road Ahead.* New York: Oxford University Press, 1994.

13. Shut Down the Architects of a Failed Policy

Paul Craig Roberts

The 19th century was an era of capitalism, but the 20th century has been an era of planning. Everywhere it took root, planning, whether in communist or noncommunist countries, subverted markets and made political connections the route to riches.

Historically, Latin America has been a mercantilist society. Since colonial times, the politically connected have lobbied the government for privileges and protection. A system of perverse property rights has traditionally existed, with government jobs bought and sold like commodities but severe restrictions placed on the production and sale of goods and services. Public property became the private property of the purchasers of government jobs, and private property was fettered with so many taxes and regulations that it has been essentially public. Economists have a term for the use of government to attain a favorable business position. They call it "rent seeking."

Development planning strengthened the rent-seeking tradition. Many decades of lending by multilateral institutions such as the World Bank, augmented during the 1970s by commercial banks, put hundreds of billions of dollars into the hands of corrupt Latin American governments that allocated the money politically and stole the rest. Real development experts would have realized that the task was to break up the mercantilist or rent-seeking system, not to entrench it with hard currency from the West.

By 1980, such an amalgam of taxes and controls so blocked people's opportunities in Latin America that economies were beholden

---

Paul Craig Roberts is Chairman of the Institute for Political Economy in Washington, D.C., and a columnist for *Business Week*. He is coauthor of *The Capitalist Revolution in Latin America*.

to politically connected elites. With government tentacles reaching farther than they ever had, rent seeking completely dominated the economy, stimulating the redistribution of existing resources rather than the production of new ones. As economies became dominated by state monopolies, costs soared and corruption exploded, while the real entrepreneurs were sidelined to the black market.

Forty years of development planning financed by $400 billion in development assistance and $136 billion in commercial bank loans lowered no transactions costs and brought no new ideas. Instead, it raised barriers to development that were as high as the Andes. Pre-Adam Smithian mercantilist policies were implanted that reflected the ancient mentality of colonial Spanish and Portuguese rule.

The Planning Mantra

The international development institutions became the conduit for spreading planning and government control throughout Latin America. Founded in 1945, the World Bank was supposed to be a lender of last resort to economically sound projects in underdeveloped countries. Almost at once, however, influential academics, World Bank employees, and interest groups lobbied for more aid. Yet, there were few well-designed projects that merited support. To remedy this problem, the World Bank, the largest lender to Latin American countries, advocated the adoption of national development plans in the hopes of improving the quality and quantity of projects. The quality of projects never improved, but the bureaucratic imperative to lend resulted in falling lending standards.

The International Monetary Fund (IMF) was established in 1945 with the aim of helping countries to maintain currency par values under the Bretton Woods system of fixed exchange rates. When that system was abandoned, the IMF was left without a mission. Like bureaucracies everywhere, it refused to die and found its new calling in bailing out countries with balance of payments problems.

The Inter-American Development Bank (IDB), the Alliance for Progress, and the U.S. Agency for International Development (USAID), were all created when faith in planning was high. Opened in 1960, the IDB is the second largest lender to Latin America. Planning is prominent in the IDB's charter (Art. III, sec. 7(a)(vi)), which provides that the "loans made or guaranteed by the Bank shall be principally for financing specific projects, including those forming part of a national or regional development program."

Created by President Kennedy in 1961, the Alliance for Progress was essentially a cooperative effort between the Organization of American States (OAS), the USAID, the IDB, the World Bank, and the United Nations (Inter-American Economic and Social Council 1963). The United States pledged to provide $24 billion in aid for countries that adopted development plans, and countries opened planning ministries and wrote development plans that were reviewed by the OAS.

USAID was created in 1961, and in Latin America it became the U.S. arm of the Alliance for Progress. Early USAID assistance concentrated on developing infrastructure and institutions in less-developed countries (LDCs), in accordance with "the original and main purpose of program credits. . .to help finance national development programs" (Organization of American States 1971, p. 145).

Professors, licking their chops at lucrative consulting contracts, hailed the founding and expansion of the international development institutions as the greatest hope for progress for the peoples of the Third World. In 1963, Robert Heilbroner enthused about the "Great Ascent" of man in the LDCs that would have no parallel in history as countries embarked upon the development planning course. The only ascent was that of international bureaucrats and their millions of cohorts in the governments of LDCs.

Protectionism reigned as countries closed markets and raised tariff barriers to try to stimulate subsidized domestic industries under the guise of "import substitution." Capital controls were instituted, multiple foreign exchange rates were used to privilege favored importers, and the law was used to favor special interest groups at the expense of the general public. Latin American countries followed foreign advisers' recipes for high tax rates, currency devaluations, and a plethora of regulations with the assurance that putting more resources into the hands of government would stimulate development. None of those policies promoted economic progress. Instead, they resulted in high inflation, high interest rates, political instability, poverty, and the flight of capital and people from the region.

An economy based on subsidies is not self-financing, and when oil prices fell (adversely affecting Mexico and other oil producers in the region) and foreign loans dried up, countries found themselves mired in systemic crisis. The "lost decade" of the 1980s was ushered in, as IMF-imposed austerity programs squeezed hard-hit populations in order to bail out government failures, and living standards plummeted. The debt crisis of the 1980s was a bonanza for the IMF and World Bank because it gave them a rationale for expanded lending.

Foreign advisers were the last to admit that the system they had helped to build lay in ruins. They argued that the debt crisis was only a temporary liquidity problem. Thus, the IMF and the World Bank designed adjustment programs that aimed to facilitate debt repayment in the short run, but left the bloated state sector substantially intact. IMF agreements between borrower countries are not made public. Yet those agreements typically have entailed raising taxes to balance the budget, freezing wages and prices to slow inflation, and devaluing the currency to cut imports. This mishmash of policies was designed to create a trade surplus in order to make interest payments on the debt.

Latin America's failures were a monument to misguided economic ideas. Marxist and Keynesian economics, British and French socialism, the New Deal in the United States, and the postwar Marshall Plan for Europe all played a role in convincing the West to tie aid to planning. But above all, development economists buttressed their hopes on the alleged success of the Soviet economy.

Many plaudits to the Soviet Union are found in the development literature. For example, Gunnar Myrdal (1956, p. 144) viewed the Soviet model "*as fundamentally a system for the development of underdeveloped countries*. An undiscerning bunch, development economists found inspiration in fraudulent Soviet bloc GNP growth statistics. The delusion lasted until Gorbachev-era scholars deflated the conceits. For example, in *The Turning Point*, Soviet economists Nikolai Shmelev and Vladimir Popov (1989) explained "why it is impossible to use official statistics." They reported that "for three decades, from the end of the 1920s through the end of the 1950s, statistical distortions were so great that even the ordinal numbers were altered."

Flight from Mercantilism

Latin America reached its own turning point in the 1980s, when the leaders of countries such as Mexico and Argentina began to dismantle the mercantilist, government-run, system that their own parties had built. Chile began the free-market revolution in the 1970s, but the rest of the region did not take notice until the Mexican Institutional Revolutionary Party (PRI) began to back away from the rent-seeking economy it had cultivated to serve its power. From Mexico to Argentina, many countries are opening their economies to international competition and cutting back bloated state sectors to allow the private sector to take over development. They have privatized, deregulated, cut taxes, and stimulated competition in their business sectors. They have allowed the formerly disparaged Yankee and his capital to come in. "Trade, not aid" became the slogan in the region, as Mexico, Chile, and Argentina sought free-trade agreements with the United States. This is a stunning reversal of the old protectionist mentality.

Profit seeking is displacing rent seeking as the basis of economic life, but reforms need more time to take root. Countries have divested thousands of state enterprises, but getting rid of grasping elites trying to get their hooks back into the economy is more problematic. In the region, only Chile has completely broken free of the past and cemented a capitalist society based on private property and free enterprise. Today Chile's democracy is the most secure, and the benefits are the most widespread.

Mexico still has a few large enterprises, such as Pemex, the national oil company, and CFE, the public railroads corporation, in state hands. Its ability to attract foreign capital has been set back by a currency crisis stemming from monetary mismanagement and a confidence-shattering peso devaluation in December 1994. Argentina needs to reform labor laws to give firms more flexibility to adjust to international competition. A new class of wealthy entrepreneurs is forming in Argentina and Mexico, as it did in South Korea and Japan in the early years of their transformation, and a middle class is rising, but many others have yet to see the benefits of marketization.

Multilateral development institutions continue to lend to state-owned enterprises while preaching privatization. On balance the record of multilateral lenders is negative. Yet the World Bank, IMF, and other international development agencies continue to lend to governments and state-owned companies that mismanage their affairs. The 1995 Mexico peso crisis is an example. Devaluationists in the IMF colluded with consultants to the international agencies,

Clinton Administration officials, and Mexican exporters to recommend that Mexico devalue. The decision to devalue was a gratuitous political act that destroyed investors' confidence in Mexico. The devaluation caused capital flight and a substantial reduction in Mexicans' incomes. Fears were aroused that the loss of confidence would spread to Argentina and other emerging market economies. Once again, crisis proved to be a bonanza for the IMF, which seized the opportunity to dictate economic policy to Mexico in exchange for bailout loans. To qualify for $17.8 billion in IMF loans, Mexico promised to raise taxes and interest rates in order to suppress consumer demand, and to freeze prices and wages to offset the inflationary impact of higher prices for imported goods.

The Mexican peso devaluation created more problems than it solved. It saddled Mexico with austerity when it needed growth and with political unrest when it needed cohesion. It threatened the solvency of the newly privatized banking system. Moreover, the $50 billion peso rescue package slapped together by the Clinton Administration had risks of its own. If Mexico had failed to restore investors' confidence in its currency and its future, the $50 billion would have been siphoned off in speculators' profits as hedge funds shorted the peso, leaving the country with massive new debts and a destroyed currency.

Shaky Loan Portfolios

Sooner or later, the development policies that failed for Latin America will fail for the region's multilateral creditors. Two recent World Bank reports show that World-Bank financed projects are failing at a rate that would quickly lead to bankruptcy if the institution were a private company. The February 1992 report (World Bank 1992, pp. 1–3) evaluated 359 projects, representing investments of some $43 billion. The report found that 36 percent of the projects had failed by the time their funding was completed and only half of the remaining 64 percent would survive over time. In other words, the World Bank projected a success rate of only 32 percent.

The following year, project performance was even worse. A March 1993 report (World Bank 1993, pp. xv–xvi) evaluated 278 projects involving total investments of more than $32.8 billion and concluded that 37 percent of the projects had failed by the time funding was completed. The report estimated that only 42 percent of the remaining 63 percent would survive over time. Thus, only 26 percent of the projects were deemed successful.

The March 1993 report noted that the 1991 results were part of an "overall downward trend in project performance" that had been observed over the previous two years. It also pointed out that lending to the World Bank's best customers in Asia is declining, while lending to Africa, the poorest performer overall, has been increasing.

The two pessimistic reports may be optimistic themselves. The World Bank freely admits that its project monitoring capability is poor. Moreover, the bank's evaluation techniques would never survive scrutiny in a commercial operation.

The IMF's portfolio is in no better shape, although that institution is more reticent about publishing studies that reveal this to be the case. Sizeable arrears have appeared on the IMF's books in the past few years, and there is a constant scramble in the IMF to reschedule loans in all but name.

The IDB's portfolio is also shaky. In 1994, the IDB received an expansion of taxpayer guarantees to boost its capital by two-thirds (to $101 billion) to continue lending $6 billion per year.

Development bank portfolios are in bad shape, because the projects financed were never expected to earn a market rate of return. It has been taken for granted that project loans will be repaid out of general government revenues. A March 1993 World Bank memorandum that assessed the reasons for failure of so many of their projects concluded that one of the reasons was "There is no accountability for failure." It was followed by a report that stressed the need for "more accountability for performance" (World Bank Group 1994).

It has occurred to officials in the international agencies that privatization is crowding out development planning and undermining their role. At a December 1993 IDB seminar that assessed the IBD's lending program during 1979–92, panelists were openly downcast at the fact that Latin American economies were improving. They were worried that there would be no more need for IDB loans and technical assistance if countries continued to privatize and attract private investment capital. One panelist cheered up the crowd, however, by pointing out that there is such a long record of crisis in the region and that eventually countries would get into trouble again and need IDB help.

It is not useful to maintain at taxpayer expense institutions that have vested interests in the failure of market reforms. It is inimical to economic development to impose austerity on the private sector while encouraging rent seeking by pouring more loans into the government's coffers.

All of the international development institutions are themselves rent-seeking organizations that attempt to use loans and advice to expand the influence and budgets of the officials who run them. Such organizations are ill-suited to spread market-based development.

In the 1990s the World Bank and IDB have produced numerous studies on the inefficiency and mismanagement endemic in government-owned companies and the need for privatization of many activities. In June 1992 the World Bank hosted a landmark conference in which it lauded the benefits of privatization in developing countries. Panelists discussed a forthcoming study, "Welfare Consequences of Selling Public Enterprises," by World Bank economists (Galal et al. 1994). The study examined privatizations in each of four countries: Britain, Chile, Malaysia, and Mexico. The sale of four airlines, three telecommunications firms, two electricity utilities, a road-freight transporter, a container port, and a lottery business were examined. Overall, the World Bank economists concluded that privatization does add to national wealth, as according to their results 11 of the 12 sales resulted in net increases in wealth.

The study was a turning point. It exploded the myth long prevalent in the World Bank that a unit of capital in the hands of the state is as efficient as in the hands of the private sector. It stripped the World Bank of its justification for lending to government agencies.

The acceptance of private property and markets by some international bureaucrats is a welcome development. However, the inefficiency of government and the benefits of privatization apply to the development institutions themselves. Indeed, the World Bank only installed a cost accounting system in the 1990s—almost 50 years after its founding. Where there is no bottom line and no accountability there can be no real development. At a May 1994 Society for International Development seminar, economist Norman Nicholls of the World Bank's private-sector arm concluded that "government failure is worse than market failure to date." Now that poor countries have learned, at great expense, that markets are far more effective than governments at delivering the goods at reasonable cost, the international development institutions have outlived the statist era.

Shut Down the Purveyors of Failure

The development banks should be privatized or closed. The World Bank Articles of Agreement provide for the suspension of operations and the settlement of obligations. The provisions state, however, that a majority of the World Bank governors, meaning shareholding governments, would have to exercise a majority of the vote to "permanently suspend its operations in respect of new loans and guarantees." This is not likely to happen.

A more feasible alternative is the unilateral pullout of a major donor country such as the United States. This step could provide the stimulus to set in motion the closure of the World Bank. The Bank's Articles of Agreement state that "any member may withdraw from the Bank at any time by transmitting a notice in writing to the Bank." Withdrawal would become effective on the date that such a notice was received.

Upon withdrawal, according to the Articles of Agreement, a country is liable for its share of outstanding loans and loan guarantees so long as any part of the obligations contracted before it ceased to be a member is outstanding. But it ceases to contract new obligations or share in the expenses and income of the Bank. As of the last quarter of 1994, the United States was liable for about $30 billion in loans and loan guarantees of the World Bank.

If one major donor were to pull out, other countries would face greater burdens. If unwilling to expose their taxpayers to greater risks, other countries might also withdraw. Remaining countries would have an incentive to demand a realistic asset evaluation in order to settle the departing countries' accounts with the World Bank. This tactic would put an end to the World Bank's accounting fictions, and the process of deciding how to close it could begin.

The World Bank's Articles of Agreement do not specify how best to close down the institution, leaving room for flexibility. The pertinent provision states that after suspension of operations, "the Bank shall forthwith cease all activities, except those incident to the orderly realization, conservation, and preservation of its assets and settlement of its obligations." The IMF and IDB charters have similar provisions regarding suspension of operations and unilateral pullout of a donor country, and the United States could withdraw from all of them simultaneously, thereby setting in motion a consideration of alternatives to liquidating these institutions.

One option would be to sell the portfolios of the World Bank and IDB in the secondary market and redeem whatever percentage of their own outstanding bonds the proceeds would allow. The governments that provide guarantees of World Bank bonds would make up the difference.

Alternatively, the development banks could swap their loans for equity in state companies slated for privatization in the borrowing countries and turn themselves into private investment companies owned by their former bond holders. Normally, privatization raises the value of assets. Thus, with successful debt-equity swaps, the development banks might be able to avoid falling back on taxpayer guarantees.

Either alternative is superior to continuing at taxpayer risk institutions whose strategy has failed.

If we have learned the lessons of public-sector failure in the 20th century, no one will any longer speak of economic development as something that happens apart from the private sector. From now on, economic development must be based on the proven success of free enterprise, sound money, and private property.

References

Galal, Ahmed; Jones, Leroy; Tandon, Pankaj; and Vegelsang, Ingo. *Welfare Consequences of Selling Public Enterprises.* New York: Oxford University Press, 1994.

Inter-American Economic and Social Council. *The Alliance for Progress: Its First Year: 1961–1962.* Washington, D.C.: Pan American Union, General Secretariat, Organization of American States, 1963.

Myrdal, Gunnar. *An International Economy: Problems and Prospects.* New York: Harper and Brothers, 1956.

Organization of American States. *External Financing for Latin American Development.* Baltimore: Johns Hopkins University Press, 1971.

Shmelev, Nikolai, and Popov, Vladimir. *The Turning Point: Revitalizing the Soviet Economy.* New York: Doubleday, 1989.

World Bank. *Evaluation Results for 1990.* Washington, D.C.: World Bank, 1992.

World Bank. *Evaluation Results for 1991.* Washington, D.C.: World Bank, 1993.

World Bank Group. "Learning from the Past, Embracing the Future." Washington, D.C.: World Bank, July 1994.

14. Western Subsidies and Eastern Reform

Peter Bauer

Western subsidies to reformist governments in Eastern Europe are not generally necessary for the prosperity of these countries and the survival of their governments. The contribution of such subsidies is at best very limited. They are more likely to be damaging. In certain clearly defined exceptional circumstances, reflecting not poverty as such but other legacies of communist rule, modest support preferably as bilateral grants, might be helpful. But reduction in the trade barriers against exports from these countries would be far more effective.

Conventional Arguments for Subsidies

Official subsidies to governments of poor countries are widely seen in the West as a moral, political, and economic imperative. Their progress is said to be of vital importance to the West and it is regarded as impossible without external subsidies. The core argument, popularized as the vicious circle of poverty, has been the central theme of post-war development economics. It was concisely formulated by Nobel Laureate Paul Samuelson (1951, p. 49): "They [the backward nations] cannot get their heads above water because their production is so low that they can spare nothing for capital formation by which the standard of living could be raised."

This argument is refuted by every individual, family, group, community, and country that has emerged from poverty without subsidies. If the argument were valid, we should still be in the Old Stone Age.

Peter Bauer is Emeritus Professor of Economics at the London School of Economics, University of London, and a Fellow of the British Academy. This chapter is reprinted, with some revisions, from his article in the Winter 1992 *Cato Journal* (Bauer 1992).

Provided they are motivated to improve their lot and are not inhibited by government policy or lack of public security, poor people can and do generate or secure sufficient funds for economic advancement. They can save enough even from small incomes for direct investment in agriculture, trading, and many other purposes. They can also work harder or longer or redeploy their resources more productively.

Governments and enterprises of poor countries have access to commercial external funds. Ability to borrow abroad does not depend on the level of income but on responsible financial conduct and productive use of funds.

If property rights are clearly defined and reasonably protected, external commercial funds are available even in the face both of poverty and political risk. Since World War II much foreign investment has taken place in Asia and Africa amid acute political uncertainty. Substantial investment trusts targeted to Eastern Europe have already been established in the West. And Western corporations have set up thousands of joint ventures and subsidiaries in Eastern Europe, including the former Soviet Union—that is, in countries where political risk is compounded by an incompletely developed legal system. The skills and attributes that accompany the inflow of equity capital can play the same role in Eastern Europe in transforming methods and habits as they did in many less developed countries (LDCs).

Thus subsidies are not necessary for emergence from poverty. It is indeed an unwarranted and distasteful condescension to argue that while the peoples of poor countries crave material progress, they cannot achieve it without subsidies from the West.

Nor are subsidies sufficient for advance. The many billions of official aid both from the West and the Communist bloc to Ethiopia, Sudan, and other African countries have not secured their progress. To have money is the result of economic achievement, not its precondition.

The Politicization of Life

Although subsidies are demonstrably neither necessary nor sufficient for economic advance, it may seem self-evident that they must promote it because they are an inflow of resources. However, this does not follow. This inflow sets up adverse repercussions that can far outweigh any benefit. Some arise whether the subsidies go either to the public or to the private sector; others arise because they go to or through recipient governments.

An inflow of capital raises the real rate of exchange and thereby impairs foreign trade competitiveness. With equity capital this is usually offset by increased productivity of resources, but that is unlikely with official subsidies.

External subventions promote or reinforce the belief that economic improvement depends on outside forces other than domestic effort. Subsidies encourage governments to seek foreign assistance through beggary or blackmail instead of looking to change at home. Such attitudes often spread from the government or other groups.

Unlike manna from heaven, which descends on the whole population, these subsidies go to the government. They therefore increase its resources, patronage, and power, compared to the rest of society. External subsidies have also helped to sustain governments especially in Africa, whose policies have proved so damaging that only the subsidies have enabled them to remain in power and continue with such destructive policies. Altogether, the subsidies have contributed significantly to the politicization of life in recipient countries.

When life is extensively politicized, people's fortunes come to depend on government policy and administrative decisions. The stakes, both gains and losses in the struggle for power, increase greatly. This encourages or even forces people to divert attention, energy, and resources from productive activity to concern with the outcome of political and administrative decisions.

Politicization of life provokes tension and conflict, especially in countries with different ethnic and cultural groups as in much of the Third World and Eastern Europe. Groups and communities that have lived together peaceably for generations have been set against each other by the politicization promoted by these official subsidies.

Subsidies also make it easier for governments to restrict the inflow of foreign capital, especially equity capital. Aid-recipient governments commend inward foreign equity investment but in practice restrict it because this suits their political purposes and the commercial interests of their supporters.

These restrictions are plainly anomalous when the argument for external subsidies is a shortage of capital. Inflow of equity capital—

together with the commercial, administrative, and technical skills that accompany it—have been the prime instrument of the economic advance the world over.

Reformist governments in Eastern Europe are less likely to restrict the inflow of equity investment than LDC governments. But cushioned, by external subsidies, they could still be tempted to do so for political reasons.

A Double Asymmetry in the Effects of Official Subsidies

Economic advance depends on personal, cultural, and social factors and political arrangements; it does not depend on the cost and volume of investable funds. And because commercial capital from abroad is available to people who can use it productively, it follows that the maximum contribution external subsidies make to economic advance cannot exceed the avoided cost of borrowing, that is, the interest and amortization charges that would have been payable to the creditors as a proportion of GNP.

Thus the most subsidies can do is to reduce the cost of a resource that is not a major factor in economic advance. Any possible benefit would be too small to register in GNP statistics. And as we have seen, the inflow of subsidies sets up adverse repercussions that affect critical political and social factors.

There is a double asymmetry in the effects of official subsidies. First, any favorable effect through the reduction in the cost of investable resources affects a factor not critical for economic advance, while major adverse effects operate on critical determinants. Second, a volume of subsidies too small to benefit economic performance appreciably is nevertheless amply sufficient to set up the adverse effects. It is the relationship of the subsidies to GNP that is relevant to the favorable effect, namely, a reduction in the cost of investable funds. And because the subsidies go to governments, it is the relationship of the subsidies to government receipts and foreign exchange earnings (themselves readily subject to government control) that is relevant to major adverse repercussions. Because GNP is necessarily a large multiple both of tax receipts and foreign exchange earnings, the subsidies must be far larger relative to these magnitudes than to GNP.

It is unequivocal that external subsidies are neither necessary nor sufficient for economic advance. Whether they promote or retard it cannot be established so conclusively. But this uncertainty in no way affects the conclusion that the subsidies can do no more for development than the avoided cost of borrowing and that this modest contribution tends to be offset by adverse repercussions.

It is crucial to recognize that the subsidies entail major adverse consequences. Belief that an inflow of resources must benefit the population at large, and certainly cannot harm it, has promoted the uncritical acceptance of foreign subsidies. Once the damaging repercussions are recognized, a less questioning stance might come to be adopted.

Subsidies as a Device to Maintain Government Power

Although government-to-government subsidies can do little or nothing for economic achievement and advance, they can alleviate acute shortages, especially of imports. By maintaining a minimum level of consumption, the subsidies avert total collapse and conceal from the population, at least temporarily, the worst effects of destructive policies. This result, in turn, helps the government to remain in power and to persist with these policies without provoking popular revolt.

The same process can also apply in reverse. If a shortage of necessities develops for reasons outside the control of the government, and for which no provision could have been made, subsidies might help the government to survive. As we shall see, this possibility bears on Western assistance to the reformists.

Government Policy and Economic Advance

Multiparty democracy is widely seen as a necessary condition of a market system and of economic improvement. Multiparty democracy may well be desirable. But what matters for economic advance, especially improved living standards, is not how the government is established but what is envisaged as its tasks. Whatever its origins, a government is most likely to promote the economic advance and well-being of the people by the effective performance of a specific range of tasks while refraining from extensive control of economic life.

The list of tasks is familiar: public security, which means protection of life and property, including the definition of property rights;

maintenance of the value of money; management of external relations in the interests of the population; provision or oversight of basic education, public health, and transport; assistance to those in need who cannot help themselves and are not helped by others. It is by combining these functions with restriction on state economic control that a government can most effectively promote personal freedom and economic welfare.[1]

Obstacles to Liberalization

In the West, in public discourse on reform in Eastern Europe, introduction of multiparty democracy and establishment of a market system are usually linked or even identified. This practice is misleading. Multiparty democracy may well be thought beneficial for various reasons, such as conferring legitimacy on a government reducing the dependency of people on a single ruler or party. But the two types of reform are quite distinct. Establishment of a market system from scratch is far more difficult than introducing multiparty democracy.

Reformists in the former Soviet Union and elsewhere in the East recognize that replacement of the command economy by a market system is indispensable for economic reform or even for averting economic collapse. Accordingly, they try with differing degrees of commitment to dismantle the command economy. In doing so they attempt an unprecedented task. In the course of history, ruling groups have often introduced a new constitution or established and extended the suffrage. But there is no recorded instance of a government introducing a market system where there was none before. In the West the institutions, attitudes, and modes of conduct of a market order have emerged in the course of centuries of sustained social and economic evolution. People in the Soviet Union never knew a functioning market system and its arrangements. To take a simple example, job search was practically unknown to people in the Soviet Union. They were directed into jobs from the time they left school. This is also true, to a lesser extent, in Eastern Europe. The attempt to establish a market system from scratch is therefore inevitably a leap in the dark.

[1]In some instances the subsidies go through the government for subsequent allocation to other entities. In the present context the distinction is immaterial as the distribution and use of the funds require official sanction.

In the post-communist countries, the hazards and difficulties of this leap are much exacerbated by major legacies of the command economies. In particular, two distinct but interacting obstacles stand in the way of market-oriented reform: unpreparedness of the people and hostility of the bureaucracies and other established interests.

People who have spent their entire adult lives under a comprehensive command economy are necessarily unfamiliar with a market economy. They face severe difficulties of adaptation that they do not relish. Under the command economy, people's economic fortunes depended on the government. People were not looking for jobs and activities but were directed into them. People were engaged in activities in which production was divorced from the supply of valuable commodities and where output was measured by the cost of inputs, which was unrelated to economic cost. Such people are bewildered by the market system. They find it difficult to accept the opportunities, risks, and rewards of the market. They attribute any economic reverse to malice or exploitation.

Many people in these countries are most apprehensive about the effects of extensive reform on their own fortunes. They fear the steep rises in prices and housing costs following the removal of subsidies and controls and the withdrawal of state-provided health services.

Reformist governments inevitably have to rely extensively on existing personnel in the public services, including the military, the police, the civil service, the public utilities, and the state enterprises. On grounds both of self-interest and ideology, much of this personnel is opposed to the dismantling of the command economy. They try to frustrate reform by stirring up popular discontent and apprehension and by denying supplies to the private sector or to areas of activity controlled by the reformists. They cannot be expected to surrender, without resistance, the power, positions, and privileges they enjoy. As U.S. Senator Strom Thurmond said, "You can't get a hog to butcher itself." Altogether there is much latent and open opposition to the market system. More international trade and investment could help to overcome some of this hostility, especially through acquainting people with the market order.

Gradual versus Radical Reform

Faced with these daunting difficulties, two distinct schools of thought have emerged among committed reformists in Eastern

Europe: gradualists and radicals. The former argue that the population is not ready for far-reaching change and would respond by resistance, even revolt, or by lethargy and listlessness. They recognize that people, whether as individuals, families, or entire societies, cannot readily absorb abrupt changes. The radicals argue that slow, gradual change enables opponents to marshall their forces and that delay extends the period of unpopularity aroused by reform. They urge that half measures are more likely to discredit the market system than to make it more acceptable.

Strangers to a country and to its political culture are poorly qualified to judge between gradual and rapid change. Two observations favoring the radicals may be in order.

In the West, proposals for economic reform have often elicited dire predictions about the outcome. These predictions have usually been disproved by the results. Examples include the German currency reform of 1948 and Thatcherite policies of the 1980s.

Comprehensive reform need not be shock therapy causing widespread acute hardship. If the measures for reform are carefully thought out, especially the sequence of different measures, the reforms need not involve extensive hardship. Moreover, some of the changes such as decontrol of prices and rents that harm some groups benefit others. Compensation paid to the former could be financed at least in part by taxation of the beneficiaries.

What Can the West Do?

There are several things the West can do to promote economic advance in Eastern Europe. First and foremost, Western countries should reduce their trade barriers. Eastern Europe would benefit because international trade acquaints people with the market system; helps to allay suspicions about its operation; and promotes market-oriented attitudes, habits, and conduct, which would emerge only from direct experience.

Although reduction of Western trade barriers can be a potent instrument for economic advance in the circumstances of Eastern Europe, more may be needed to assist the reformists. Hostility to the market by the bureaucracies and popular fears could inhibit economic advance and could also create shortages long before the government can accumulate reserves against such contingencies. Foreign loans may then also be very expensive. To service them may absorb much of the benefits of reform, which would be sufficiently unpopular politically to endanger the government. Even large inflows of commercial capital may not avert such dangers. Such investment benefits the economy as a whole and enlarges the tax base, but does not promptly make funds available to the government. Under these circumstances, subsidies might secure the survival of market-oriented reformist governments by alleviating acute shortages, notably of imports.

This argument for external subsidies hinges on the legacies of communist rule and is altogether different from that based on poverty. This difference is important for the timing and method of the subsidies. These subsidies should be provided only to governments irrevocably committed to promotion of the market economy. Such reform is both difficult and unpopular. It will be pursued only if without it economic collapse would endanger the government. If subsidies are provided ahead of far-reaching reforms, the reforms will be postponed or abandoned—perhaps forever. Meanwhile, subsidies facilitate the maintenance of military establishments.

Subsidies should be grants, not soft loans. Soft loans or government guaranteed loans compose a substantial grant element. They also confuse investment with handouts, and they provoke tensions between donors and recipients: donors see them as assistance; recipients see them as a burden.

The grants should be for a strictly limited period, say three years. This period would be long enough to overcome the obstacles of bureaucratic hostility and popular apprehension. If those obstacles cannot be overcome in a few years, then the support should be withdrawn. Equally if they are overcome, no further support is necessary.

Bilateral grants (going directly from donor to recipient government) are far preferable to multilateral grants (going through the international organizations). The bilateral method permits a vestige of control by the taxpayers, the real donors; termination of bilateral subsidies in the face of wasteful or destructive policies is far easier; a measure of conduct between supplier and user of funds also makes for greater effectiveness; and self-perpetuation and self-aggrandizement can be somewhat more readily restrained.

Another advantage of bilateral subsidies is of special importance in our context. They need to be administered by people wholly in sympathy with the dismantling of the command economy. Such people are even less likely to be found in the international organizations than in the national bureaucracies. The international organizations attract people with a dirigiste or socialist outlook, perhaps because of the distance of these organizations from grassroots politics.

The international organizations do not command expertise not available otherwise. Any specialized knowledge can be readily purchased by the national government departments.

The oft-heard claim is unfounded that the international organizations are disinterested and objective and that, therefore, subsidies allocated by them are more likely to be effective. In fact, the delegates and staffs of these organizations have distinct personal and political interests, which the more energetic and ambitious among them pursue vigorously.

It is often said that the reformists need technical assistance rather than financial support, especially for the development of the human and financial substructure, such as accountants, lawyers, tax inspectors, and computer personnel. But the reformists can purchase these resources. They know best which experts they require and how many of each kind.

Subsidies for general purposes seem preferable to project subsidies. It is easier to secure commercial funds for the latter. And after decades of command economies, it is necessary that people should understand that projects ought to cover their economic costs; specific subsidies obscure this.

Altogether, the recipients ought to be free to spend the subsidies in whatever direction they think will suit their purposes. If they are thought to deserve financial support, they should be given wide latitude in spending the money. They may even use some funds to pay off redundant personnel to mitigate opposition to reform, or to use it to service debt if they think this would help the credit worthiness of their countries.

It is widely urged that the sovereign debt of Eastern countries should be scaled down or even forgiven altogether as a form of support. Such suggestions raise awkward problems. In general, blanket debt reduction or cancellation specifically rewards the incompetent, profligate, and dishonest compared to those ready to meet their obligations. But the reformists can plausibly argue that they should not be saddled with debts contracted by the rulers of command economies when they themselves are trying to replace the command economy by market order. They can, and do, argue that their predecessors dissipated the loans in directions that have not yielded productive assets. This contention is in no way affected by the fact that much or most of the indebtedness was incurred through subsidized loans from the West.

On the other hand, wholesale default on sovereign debt, however contracted, goes counter to attempts to establish and maintain property rights, a measure that is crucial to the operation of a market system. Perhaps the least of the evils would be if reformist governments were to make sustained, modest payments on the debts contracted by their predecessors. Similarly, some compensation for confiscated property, where its owners or their legitimate heirs are identifiable, would promote confidence in the maintenance of property rights.

The effect of subsidies in raising the real exchange rate and thereby impairing international competitiveness could be minimized by paying the funds into special accounts in the West on which the recipients could draw for buying imports.

Such subsidies involve costs and risks. But these need not be heavy if support goes to committed reformists for a strictly limited period, and if donors are prepared to cut off funds when they recognize failure in the course of that limited period.

There are also risks in refusing support. If the reformists go under and this can be plausibly attributed to lack of external assistance, this failure would undoubtedly lead to demands for much increased subsidies to LDCs. Demise of the reformists would threaten the West with a flood of refugees and might also pose a real or fictitious security risk.

Conclusion

The thrust of public discussion, as well as the measures already taken, differ radically from the arguments outlined here. It is the low level of incomes in the former Soviet Union and Eastern Europe, rather than the specific legacy of communist command economies, that is envisaged as the ground for support. Financial assistance, rather than freer trade, is in the foreground. The international organizations, notably the World Bank, the IMF, the European Commission, and the Bank for European Reconstruction and Development, are envisaged as the sources, arbiters, and channels of subsidies. Substantial subsidies have already been provided without any assurance of commitment to reform.

The currently adopted and envisaged methods of assistance to the Eastern governments do not reflect the merits of the case, but rather the climate of opinion, the play of political forces, and above all the influence of the aid lobbies, especially the international organizations, in politics, the media, and the academies.

References

Bauer, Peter. "Western Subsidies and Eastern Reform." *Cato Journal* 11 (Winter 1992): 343–53.

Samuelson, Paul A. *Economics: An Introductory Analysis*. 2d ed. New York: McGraw-Hill, 1951.

15. The Mischief of Moving Average Pricing

Alan A. Walters

Averaging in Marginal Cost Pricing

One of the strangest paradoxes is the ubiquity of instructions to fix prices at long-run marginal cost in spite of the clear implication from the theory of welfare economics that one should price at short-run marginal cost. The temptation, apparently common to all bureaucracies, seems to be to use some sort of long-run marginal cost so as to avoid the oscillations (that is, the reality) of short-run marginal costs. In practical terms this implies some averaging or spreading of the fixed costs over the projected outputs to produce some mutant of average costs, and calling it long-run marginal cost. Fixing price according to this bastard concept is theoretically absurd and, in practice, has lead to considerable waste.[1]

There is, however, some vestigial rationalization for such antics. After all, it is difficult to measure short-run marginal costs, and in most industries the short-run marginal cost does tend to move in greater amplitude than average costs. The task of tracking short-run marginal cost may be so expensive that it is best not to try, since the gains would not exceed the cost. (I have yet to see this "burden of proof" type of argument demonstrated. But no matter.)

Such a defense, however flimsy, cannot be deployed to defend other types of averaging of marginal opportunity costs which, apparently, are becoming common in the pricing policies for agriculture. In many countries in the Third World, the government fixes the prices offered to domestic producers of some important agricultural

---

Alan A. Walters is Vice Chairman and Director of AIG Trading Groups, Inc., Director of IDEA Ltd., and Chairman of CounterCyclical Investment Fund. He served as Chief Economic Advisor to Margaret Thatcher. This chapter is reprinted from his article in the Spring/Summer 1987 *Cato Journal* (Walters 1987).

[1]See, for example, Walters (1968).

commodities. Such government price fixing often ostensibly reflects politically motivated favored treatment for certain groups. In other cases, however, reforming governments have embraced the principle that domestic prices should be fixed to reflect the opportunity cost as reflected in world market prices. The ostensible objective is to bring farm-gate domestic prices into line with world market prices—allowing for the cost of transportation of wheat from, say, Kansas, and adding on a supposed "compensating tariff" (of 25 percent, as an example) so as to treat agriculture the same as the proposed protected industry. Note, however, that the price in Kansas does *not* reflect any additional special export promotion subsidies that would nowadays undoubtedly accompany an export of grain from either the United States or the European Economic Community (EEC). In that sense the Kansas price basis is above the marginal opportunity cost. One might argue that this is explicit dumping and so should be shunned in pricing policy; in order to avoid red herrings, this view, although in my opinion fatally flawed, is assumed to be correct for the remainder of this paper.

Smoothing Policies and Moving Averages

The mechanism by which the price in any year is determined, however, typically involves taking a *moving average* of the past three years, the current year, and the futures market quotations of the next year. It is therefore a five-year moving average of market prices.[2] As with all such processes, the effect of taking a five-year moving average will depend critically on the time pattern of oscillations in the underlying series. One would normally choose a five-year moving average to smooth out an underlying five-year cyclical component of the series, as well as the presumed random elements entering into the price in any given year (due to weather, civil unrest, and so on). In order to discuss the effects in a sensible way I shall assume that the average period of cyclical oscillation is exactly five years. This gives an air of verisimilitude since the *average* period of oscillation of the business cycle over the last century is probably in the region of four to five years.

[2]In practical application there are many problems of valuation, such as the appropriate exchange rate to translate Kansas dollar prices into local currency. These are irrelevant to the main point that is being made in the text.

Even more important is the issue of the underlying *trend.* Granted the period of cyclical movement, then the moving average will reveal the trend in prices. Since the middle of five years is mid-year for year three, and since year four is the current year, the moving average will locate the trend of prices *one year before.* Thus, with all the components being well behaved, the procedure will fix government prices this year at *last* year's trend value. Unless the world market prices exhibit stationarity, that is to say the trend is neither increasing nor decreasing, this procedure will give an additional bias against adjusting to the trend. In order to avoid confusing this effect with all the others, I shall *provisionally assume stationarity* of the underlying price series.

An Idealized Illustration

A numerical illustration not too far from actual experience may illustrate the process. Suppose the annual price goes through the following sequence:

Year:	1	2	3	4	5	6	7	8	9	10
Price:	80	40	70	90	100	80	40	70	90	100

The five-year moving average is constant at 76. For two years of the cycle where the price is 80 and 70, the moving average is within less than 10 percent of the actual price. But for the boom years it is only three quarters of the market price, whereas in the depths of the recession the moving average is 90 percent above the market price.

Does it make sense to isolate or insulate or "protect" the farmer from the realities of world markets? Perhaps political realities, whatever that may be taken to mean, may dictate no other course. But, whatever the politics may be, it is worth examining the *economic* consequences of such a policy. It is as well to examine the policy consequences first in the case where the moving average has exactly the right periodicity and where it nicely finds the true trend. Next we can examine the consequences of confounded cyclicalities and shifting trends and other unfortunate characteristics of real world price series. Finally we review briefly the historical examples of such smoothing schemes, such as the marketing boards in British West Africa, and the political temptations of such world market insulations.

Giving the "Right Signals"

The usual ostensible argument for MAS (moving average smoothing) is that the price will reflect the long-run trend and so will not give rise to oscillations in gross farm incomes that are thought to be not in the farmers' interest. Further, the steady price of 76 would be the appropriate signal for long-run investment decisions, whereas, were the farmers subjected to the fluctuating prices in the real world, they would probably make the wrong decisions. (In this stylized case, this amounts to the assertion that the farmer cannot do simple addition and carry out his own averaging. One's credulity is much strained; even illiterate peasants tend to be numerically rather sharp at least where their own interests are concerned.)

In our previous example, the farmer with the same production costs in each year and the same quantity of output annually would have precisely the same net and gross income over the five-year period—whether there is a MAS of prices or not. The only gain is that of a constant rather than a variable income flow. In many countries this is thought to be a significant improvement since it avoids the farmer borrowing and lending in order to finance a stable consumption pattern. If there are distortions in credit markets this may be a considerable gain. (Although the policy implication surely is to tackle such distortions directly, rather than limit the supply of and demand for credit.) Assuming that administration of such a scheme is costless, and that other things are equal, the proposed smoothing will be a good thing.

Other things, however, will never be equal. Earlier we assumed that, with oscillating world prices for the farmer's outputs, he would not be able to adapt his production to take advantage of high prices or to avoid the price troughs. Even in the short run, and a fortiori if the cycle is predictable, the farmer will adjust his outputs and the amount he produces, stores, or sends to market. Only if the output/market response is near zero or negatively related to price (that is, the supply curve is backward bending for that rather wide price range) are there no gains to be made from allowing world prices to rule. I suspect there is now sufficient accumulated evidence to dismiss such a perverse form of response. Supply curves slope upwards and, even in the short run of a year or so, there is considerable flexibility of supply. The farmer will be able to *increase* his income and welfare by adapting to world market prices. Isomorphically, the consumer will be better off with the variable world market prices than the MAS controlled price, since he will adjust his purchases—substituting into the commodity during the price slump, and economizing, by switching to substitutes, during the price boom. And it follows that if *all* or a sizable number of countries follow this policy of open markets, this will mitigate the oscillation in world prices. In other words this is truly a boost, rather than beggar, thy neighbor policy.

Imperfect Credit Markets

The main rationalization for MAS is that credit markets are "imperfect" or more positively involve large "distortions." Better, it is said, to smooth away the need for credit. Of course, by so doing one smooths away a corresponding supply of credit from the private sector. But in any case the *demand* for total credit is not diminished; it is simply transferred to the government. Indeed since the MAS policy precludes the adjustments referred to above, the demand for credit will be *greater* with the MAS than with the open policy. So the argument boils down to a preference for more government borrowing and lending rather than giving the private sector a choice in this process.

Even if one accepted the fact of great distortions in private credit, one should also examine the existence of large distortions in the alternative government credit markets. The issue of government paper, including currency, is associated with obvious distortionary effects—inflation, compulsory government bond and note holdings by banks and other institutions at below-market yields, government credit allocations according to political preference rather than market performance, and so on. Nor can government produce anything comparable to the vast informal private credit market within extended families and other groups which provides for the majority of private credit needs.[3]

It is not at all clear that on balance the distortions are more with the private than the public sector. But even if this be accepted, then it does not follow that the appropriate policy is to shelter producers

[3]Although I concede that in some countries, where fraudulent conversion of public funds to private uses is on a massive scale, it is possible that the fraudulent funds are channeled into productive uses, albeit in the form of capital flight.

and consumers of the chosen commodities from the exigencies of credit markets. Surely as a matter of efficiency, if not equity, *all* those who use such distorted credit markets should have somewhat similar treatment to the farmers and consumers of the specific commodities under the MAS arrangement. In the face of ubiquitous distortions the obvious policy is to try to eliminate or modify them; if one cannot do so then consider a ubiquitous subsidy (or tax relief) to all distorted credit markets and calculate the cost/benefit involved. In any case, there is no rational argument for MAS for a certain limited number of commodities.

Shocks and Bends in Trends

We conclude, therefore, that with the simple stylized model of MAS there is little to be gained and much to be lost from such smoothing of prices. We now need to examine rather more complex cases to see whether this conclusion is likely to be modified. First, it is clear that much of the variation in prices is due to "shocks" or random effects due to weather, wars, pests, disease, and tastes. The arguments deployed above for the cyclical case carry over, mutatis mutandis, to the shock effects. The only important distinction, on which fortunately little hinges, is that the cyclical pattern could be foreseen, whereas the random effects cannot.

The second complication—a shifting trend—is much more important in practice and in its implications. By the nature of MAS, it will pick up a new trend value only gradually over the five-year period of the process. By the end of the five years, the centered value will track the new trend. It may strike one that five years is a long time for such an adjustment process, since there will be waste, which might be very considerable, over that period. In many cases it is obvious quite quickly that there has been a change in the level or the trend of a price. For example, it was perfectly clear in 1974 that the real oil price was not going to resume its downward trend of the past two or three decades; 1974 was no one-off outlying deviation. A moving average process applied to oil would have delayed the full adjustment until 1979. From the research that has been purused by Bela Balassa on the adjustment to the oil shocks, we know that the quicker the countries allowed the oil price to increase the less costly the adjustment and the fewer the distortions caused.[4] It seems at least

[4]See, for example, Belassa (1985).

likely that such a conclusion would apply to most other important commodities.

Empirical Experience with "Smoothing"

Briefly, we may refer to practical examples of such smoothing operations. Perhaps the best researched examples are the West African marketing boards set up by the British colonial administrations in 1946–48. The authorities stated that the export monopolies would be used to stabilize producer prices to shield producers from short-term and cyclical price fluctuations, and that they would on no account be used for taxing producers and withholding money from them. The outcome was very different and the boards have, for more than four decades, been a major discouragement to wealth creation in the constituent countries.[5] Of course a MAS type of system should in principle prevent any such taxation (or subsidy); but the intention in setting up the marketing boards was exactly the same. Guarantees that the boards would not be used for taxation were reiterated formally to the parliament of the United Kingdom by ministers of the crown. One may therefore doubt whether the MAS would be resolutely pursued during the high-price boom stage of the cycle. The "ideal" of the MAS is alternating (albeit implicit) taxes and subsidies to equalize the price level. But so far as I am aware, there is no working example of such a nicely balanced system. The political and institutional pressures are such that subsidies or taxes persist for long periods, usually many decades.

Other examples of smoothing operations, usually aligned with buffer stock schemes, are to be found in the recently collapsed tin cartel. The precise reasons for the demise of the buffer stock scheme will have to await the unraveling of their most complicated affairs, but it would not be premature to state that one of the main reasons was to misidentify a *secular* shift in price as a mere *cyclical* oscillation. The cost of servicing the large credit needed to finance excess supply and stocks of tin at the support price proved too much for the resources of the cartel members and their bankers.

With its support levels well above world market prices and the promise of adjustment toward world market prices, the MAS as applied to Third World agriculture recalls the Common Agricultural

[5]See especially Bauer (1984).

Policy (CAP) of the EEC. Again the intention was to smooth the prices and supposedly the incomes of European farmers in an adjustment so that eventually agriculture, like industry, could compete more or less freely on world markets. The outcome over the last 29 years has been rather different from this plan.[6]

One of the most poignant aspects of such smoothing schemes is that they are very easy to get into, but very difficult to get out of. Whether they support prices below world market values, as in the case of the West African marketing boards, or above, as in the case of the CAP and United States, the system generates its rents to parties and cliques who find it in their interest to block change, however rational and equitable that reform may be. While informed opinion accepts MAS as an appropriate policy, so will the interested parties deploy such principles to reap the rewards of protectionism (as in the EEC) or confiscation (as in West Africa). MAS provides a veil of legitimacy and intellectual respectability for exploitation and inefficiency.

Conclusion

The thrust of my argument is that, while the instinct of introducing world market prices into LDC pricing policies is entirely laudable, the practice of smoothing by moving average (or indeed any other such technique) negates and even distorts the benefits to be derived from opening economies to the reality of opportunity cost. Moving average smoothing is not merely a less painful way of getting countries to adjust to opportunity cost on world market prices; it is almost precisely the antithesis. It isolates the farmer from the realities of supply and demand, and gives him and the consumer the wrong signals year in year out. Thus it distorts both production and consumption. MAS is easy to get into, and the longer it goes on, the more difficult it is to change. Moreover, the process lends itself to political manipulation. There is no inherent reason why the moving average process should be five years; equally good arguments can be made for two or ten years. And politicians will adjust the time frame when it serves their purposes.

[6]The United States has also indulged in similar policies for certain commodities, for example, cotton and sugar, in "smoothing" adjustment to world market realities, with effects similar to those of the EEC.

While the objective should be to allow the reality of opportunity cost to be reflected in prices, there is also good reason to enable anyone to insure himself against the oscillation of prices. This can be done by government eliminating restrictions on forward and options markets—or perhaps by government deliberately promoting such contractual arrangements. There are myriads of possible structures that would enable a farmer to buy degrees of stability in both his output and input prices. Under the MAS, even when operating "perfectly," the farmer has no choice; he has to "buy" the stability of the MAS scheme of prices. World market prices, together with such futures and options that are mutually agreed, will much expand his choice as well as that of many others.

References

Balassa, Bela. *Change and Challenge in the World Economy.* London: Macmillan, 1985.

Bauer, Peter T. *Reality and Rhetoric: Studies in the Economics of Development.* Cambridge, Mass.: Harvard University Press, 1984.

Walters, Alan A. *The Economics of Road User Charges.* Baltimore: Johns Hopkins University Press, 1968.

Walters, Alan A. "The Mischief of Moving Average Pricing." *Cato Journal* 7 (Spring/Summer 1987): 241–48.

16. The State and the Peasant: Agricultural Policy on Trial

John P. Powelson

When development economics was invented in the aftermath of the Second World War, one of its leading ideas was that industry needed to be promoted before agriculture. Not everyone agreed. Some pointed out that the idea was ahistorical, in that agricultural revolutions preceded industrial revolutions in developed countries. Yet the thesis was attractive to most economic planners. Besides, many Third World leaders were saying that their countries need not develop according to the European model. They would do it their own way.

Development requires both labor and capital, and in agrarian societies the farm is where these are. Planners impatient for industrialization were not willing to wait until agricultural productivity had increased sufficiently to release capital and labor to the city.

Development with an Unlimited Supply of Labor

The planners' case was strengthened by Arthur Lewis's (1954) model of development based on unlimited supplies of labor, which was refined and amplified by other economists such as John Fei and Gustav Ranis (1964). The crux of this model was that less developed countries (LDCs) possessed redundant farm labor. The model assumed that agricultural employment was not determined by the usual laws of supply and demand, but by how many people were in a farm family. Farm families spread work to accommodate the number of family members available. Many farm workers were "underemployed," and development economists generally assumed that the marginal productivity of farm labor was zero. Therefore,

John P. Powelson is Professor of Economics at the University of Colorado, Boulder.

they argued, it was possible to transfer workers from farm to city with no loss of output.

A few economists objected, among them Gottfried Haberler (1957) and Jacob Viner (1957). Zero marginal productivity, they argued, would imply that farm families preferred work over leisure. The concept of zero marginal productivity is valid only if one assumes that the production function of agriculture (the combination of labor and other inputs for making outputs) is fixed. Removing some workers would imply a different production function, Haberler said, because those remaining would be deployed differently.

But the model of development based on unlimited supplies of labor was so attractive that objections to it had little effect. The next question, when farmers moved to cities, was how to make the food follow them. The model implied food consumption would not increase, since the number of people had not increased. There would just be more food in cities and less on farms.

Several methods were suggested to increase the supply of food to cities. Productivity in agriculture would have increased (fewer farmers would be producing the same amount of food). Hence there would be some leftover food on the farm, which became known as the agricultural surplus. In a free economy, farm owners would sell it on the market and might invest the proceeds in stocks or bonds of the new urban industry, which would thereby have the funds to pay its workers.

But most governments of LDCs would not take the chance that farmers would voluntarily direct their savings to cities. They preferred to rely on more coercive methods. Among these, the most acceptable to economists would have been to increase taxes on farm land. That at least would not distort relative prices. To many governments of LDCs, however, the easier way was through state trading and price controls.

If farmers were required to sell their output to state marketing boards at prices lower than market, or were required to buy their seed, fertilizer, and other inputs from state agencies at greater than market prices, then the profits would be squeezed out of the farmers and turned over to the state. This suited the governments—by far the majority among LDCs—that believed industrialization would occur only at the initiative of the state. Squeezing the farmers through state trading and price controls would channel the capital into government coffers where it was needed for state investment in industry.

Many African governments achieving independence needed only to adopt the state marketing systems that their colonial masters had devised to arrogate foodstuffs in the Second World War. Peter Bauer (1954) was among the first to point out the insidious effects of these systems on agricultural production.

At this point, the thinking of economists and the behavior of governments began to diverge. Some development economists began to write in terms of low rather than zero marginal productivity. To them, the problem was to increase productivity, and whether it occurred on the farm or the city depended not on some preconceived model but on where the opportunities and the markets lay. An increase in productivity on the farm would yield profits to invest in improved agriculture or in industry. Free-market economists favored free choice, on the supposition that the farmer would opt for whichever yielded the greater return: reinvesting his own farm, lending to neighboring farmers, or buying stocks or bonds of urban industry. Some economists suggested promoting rural industry, so that it would not be necessary for unemployed farm workers to move to the cities.

The International Labor Organization promoted this shift in thinking through its monumental studies on unemployment in many LDCs. Studies by the World Bank and the Food and Agriculture Organization also played a role, and foreign aid programs and private agencies such as the Ford Foundation (Edwards 1974) also influenced the new direction.

Advocates of state planning, however, argued that financial institutions were not sufficiently well developed, financial opportunities were insufficiently well known, and farmers in LDCs were often too ignorant to make intelligently the choices that free-market economists described. Advocates of state planning were suggesting that market imperfections and high transaction costs were pervasive, although they did not generally use those terms.

On the other hand, economists such as U Tun Wai (1962), having studied rural credit, concluded that farmers were both flexible and astute in setting up the financial institutions most suited to their needs. Later on, Grace Goodell (1986, 1987) reported similar results from her anthropological observations in Iran and the Philippines, and J. D. von Pischke (1991) concurred in a World Bank study on finance that included consideration of the role of credit in the private economy. If there was any problem, these authors proposed, it lay in the mistrust of farmers, even disdain for them, by urban financial institutions, both public and private. In my own, more inclusive work on historical causes of economic development (Powelson 1994), I introduce the term "sectioned society" to indicate a situation in which mistrust between elites and lower classes (such as small farmers) so exaggerates the perceived cost of doing business between these two sections that it is unmanageable. In such cases, the solution lies in greater communication between the two sections and in educating officials of financial institutions, not in educating farmers.

Land Reform

Complementing the belief that the agricultural surplus should finance urban industry was the movement for land reform. Especially in India and Pakistan, the Middle East, and Latin America, land was held in large quantities—hundreds or thousands of hectares—by owners who had obtained it from conquering powers, rented it to peasant farmers in feudal (serf-like) conditions, and farmed it inefficiently. Even in regions with small tenant farms, such as Japan, China, and Egypt, tenancy was considered unjust, and powerful political forces demanded redistribution of land to the tiller.

The economic case for land reform was made by a number of studies showing that yields on large, land-extensive farms were less than on small, labor-intensive farms. The Inter-American Committee for Agricultural Development found this to be so for seven Latin American countries (Barraclough 1973). Uma Lele (1972) wrote that "evidence is overwhelming that under traditional technology, where input of labor is much more important than input of capital, small farms have a higher yield than large farms." Bhagwati and Chakravarty (1969), Khusro (1964), Mazumdar (1965), Rao (1968), Reynolds (1975), and Rudra (1968) reached similar conclusions by reference to other studies. The implication was that a transfer of labor from large farms to small would improve productivity. The same effect might be accomplished by land reform, if large farms were cut up into small ones, which would presumably hire more labor, as other small farms had done.

Postwar land reforms in free-market countries of East Asia were successful. The Japanese reform increased the number of owner-cultivators from 31.2 percent to 61.85 percent of all farm units between 1941 and 1960, while part-tenant, part-owner cultivators decreased from 20.7 percent to 6.7 percent and tenants from 27.7 percent to 5.0 percent (Doré 1959, p. 176). In the 30 years after reform in Japan, agricultural output increased 3 percent to 4 per cent a year (King 1977, p. 199). In South Korea, owners increased from 13.8 percent of the total to 69.5 percent between 1945 and 1965, while tenants decreased from 48.9 percent to 7.0 percent (Ban et al. 1980, p. 284), and agricultural output per person increased by 1.46 percent per year in the 1960s and 1970s (Powelson and Stock 1987, p. 285). Several authors (Ladejinski 1964, Jacoby 1966, and Manzhuber 1970) reported a similar success for the land reform in Taiwan.

As land reform became a prominent plank in the development platforms of most LDCs, planners argued that small farmers needed the organizations of the reform, which brought them government help, because they did not have experience obtaining farm credit, buying their inputs, and marketing their output. That had all been done for them, so it was said, by the erstwhile landowner. Often the erstwhile owner had engaged in these transactions through "connections," such as foreign banks, not available to the new, humbler farmer. President Kennedy's Alliance for Progress with Latin America in 1960 included programs not only for land reform but for farm credit and extension services.

The Beginning of Doubt

From the 1950s through the 1970s, land reform and government assistance remained among the most sacred shibboleths of development economics. Only during the 1980s did some doubts begin to creep in. The doubts affected agriculture and industry. Economists and some planners had already suspected that the special emphasis on industry was misplaced, and that agriculture had been neglected. Import-substituting industrialization was creating the wrong industries—those in which foreigners, not nationals, had comparative advantage—and state-operated mines and factories were unprofitable. Governments operating centralized economic plans were running heavy deficits. Most seriously, agricultural output per person and productivity were lagging in LDCs with controlled economies, in contrast to developed countries and free-market LDCs (Powelson and Stock 1990, p. 383).

Indeed, in many LDCs with controlled economies—more so in Africa than elsewhere—agricultural output per person actually declined for 25 years. Residents of those countries were worse off, foodwise, than they had been a quarter of a century earlier. Journalists and economists became alert to these troubles about the same time, and they quickly grasped that the problems were man-made, not attributable to God. While some journalists and economists included population growth, overgrazing, deforestation, and soil erosion among the man-made effects, others grasped that government policies were among the prime causes.

For over 40 years the drain from agriculture in LDCs continued in much the way it had been envisaged by proponents of the model for development with unlimited supplies of labor. Governments required farmers to sell crops to state agencies at low prices and to buy inputs—seed and fertilizer—from state agencies at high prices. Many governments also required farmers to use technology, fertilizer, and seeds as directed by government agents who knew less about farming than farmers did, and to leave the crops on the vine until inspection, even though they would rot in the meantime. Such policies discouraged farmers and diminished agricultural output. The stream of migration from farm to city, and the number of formerly self-sufficient countries that now have to import food, is testimony of their effects.

In 1980, I began to study the history of land tenure systems all over the world, a work that took eight years to complete (Powelson 1988). I distinguished between historic land reforms by grace, offered to peasants by a "gracious" monarch interested in the welfare of his people, and land reforms by leverage, undertaken because peasants bargained with landlords on the basis of their power to grow and market food. The decline in the feudal systems in Europe and Japan were land reforms by leverage, while the reforms offered by Chinese emperors and governments of ancient Greece and Rome and Middle Eastern societies were principally land reforms by grace. Reforms by leverage lasted over the centuries, whereas those by grace would usually be reversed with the next conquest or dynastic overthrow.

Since land reforms by LDCs from 1945 on were primarily by grace, I wondered whether the same lesson of history—that they would be reversed—would apply to our own century. To find out, a coauthor and I examined 26 land reforms since the Second World War

(Powelson and Stock 1990). To our dismay, we discovered that with few exceptions, the sad lessons of history were being repeated. For the most part, Third World reforms have expropriated land from an already-dying (and therefore politically impotent) aristocracy, and the benefits, instead of being distributed among the peasantry, are primarily co-opted by the state. The 20th century is not unique.

The tactics governments used in co-opting land reforms were the same as those described earlier: as a condition for receiving access to land, in many countries peasants had to buy their fertilizer and seed and obtain their credit from government agencies, and they had to sell their produce to the government through marketing boards or other official organizations. The rationale was that only these agencies could supply the necessary services to validate the reform.

These tactics applied much more to export crops than to food for local consumption, although governments targeted both. The emphasis on export crops seems to have had two reasons. First, export crops are easier to control: they have to exit by one or only a few ports, where they can be counted. Second, governments in LDCs are often more concerned to obtain foreign exchange than their own currency, since regulations they impose frequently make their own currency overvalued.

In many countries, including Algeria, El Salvador, Nicaragua, Peru, and Tanzania, governments required beneficiaries of land reform to join "cooperatives" to obtain the benefits. Sometimes, as in Peru and Tanzania, joining was compulsory. Sometimes, as in Nicaragua under the Sandinista government, it was not legally required, but farm credit would cost more and fertilizer might not be available for farmers who did not join.

I write "cooperatives" in quotation marks because they differ greatly from organizations of the same name in developed countries. In developed countries cooperatives are voluntary organizations of producers or consumers who work together toward results beneficial to themselves. In LDCs, on the other hand, "cooperatives" that farmers *must* join are often vehicles through which governments expropriate the agricultural surplus for themselves or their favorite constituencies.

In Tanzania, farmers were forced into "cooperative" villages at the point of a gun. When they escaped and returned to their traditional homelands they were again forced out, and this time their huts were burned. One genuine cooperative in Tanzania was destroyed by the same government that was forcing farmers into state-organized "cooperatives" (Powelson and Stock 1990, p. 68).

Power and Institutions

If land reforms failed because of state authority, might it not be that excessive power—control over the lives of others—is responsible for many other inefficiencies and injustices in LDCs? Furthermore, is power perhaps enjoyed for its own sake, whether it is successful or not in achieving its stated objectives? In Japan and northwestern Europe, the progenitors of economic development, there was a diffusion of power over the centuries that did not extend to other areas, except for the cultural descendants of Europe (North America, Australia, and New Zealand). In Japan and northwestern Europe from the Middle Ages on, power was gradually traded for goods. The societies became relatively more material-minded and less power-minded, and plural groups developed checks and balances on each other to prevent the extravagant waste of resources (Powelson 1994).

Checks and balances became institutionalized through constitutions, laws and the legal process, property rights, division of the monetary system into public and private spheres, and parliamentary democracy. The free market in goods and services—not yet perfect anywhere in the world—resulted from the bargaining that gave rise to these institutions. Each group wanted a monopoly for its own product, but when it became clearly impossible for all, they settled on the free market as the second-best arrangement for all groups.

Because power has not become adequately diffuse in the Third World, however, governing groups are still able to defy the free market and arrogate goods and services, still able to waste them on pet projects, and still able to have the joy of feeling themselves in control. The Minister of Agriculture may believe that because of his power and position, he knows more about farming than the farmer who has spent his life in the fields. Likewise, the Minister of Education may believe he knows more about teaching than the experienced teacher in an elementary school, and the Minister of Industry more about industry than the private industrialist. Agriculture and agrarian reform are therefore but one illustration of a wider phenomenon, in which elites with little practical experience in a wide variety of fields force their views on the prime actors in those fields, and enjoy doing so. In the concentration of power, we have what I suspect is a prime reason for the underdevelopment of most of the world.

A Ray of Hope?

The failure of central planning and the collapse of communism in Eastern Europe and the Soviet Union have made market liberalization an attractive alternative to state development planning in the Third World. In the early 1980s, for example, China dismantled its communes and divided the land among peasant farmers, allowing them to sell a portion of their crops in the free market. Agricultural output soared as a result, and rural workers used their profits to create thousands of township and village enterprises.

Market-oriented agricultural policies are also taking root in the former Soviet Union and in Eastern Europe. The pace of privatization, however, is slow, because entrenched interests left over from communism and political instability have made free-market reforms difficult to implement.

Some LDCs elsewhere have taken steps toward liberalizing agriculture. In the mid-1980s Algeria began renting its 3,500 collectivized farms to private farmers. With the incentives of the private market, output began to increase. Unfortunately, the civil war between the government and Islamic militants has put a damper on all economic activity, not just agriculture. In 1987, pushed by the International Monetary Fund, the Tanzanian government allowed farmers to market their products more freely and to charge higher prices (Davidson 1993). Output immediately increased. Toward the end of the 1980s, the Peruvian government annulled its previous land reform and forced "cooperatives." Instead of returning the land to former owners, the government parceled out farms to peasants as private property. Additional economic reforms in 1994 increased agricultural output and other types of economic activity.

In 1980, Cuba started an experiment in free peasant markets. But when Fidel Castro discovered a garlic farmer earning $50,000 a year and an entrepreneurial farmer, who had bought two trucks, earning $150,000 a year, he abolished the experiment in 1986, denouncing "middlemen who bought the product of farmers in the countryside, then brought them into the cities and sold them at a profit" (*New York Times*, 20 April 1986). Late in 1994, forced by shortages of meat, chickens, most vegetables, and other food, the Cuban government again permitted farmers to sell crops on the open market, but only after meeting their quotas for the state (*New York Times*, 18 and 26 September 1994).

While these changes and others constitute a ray of hope, caution is in order. Little has happened to mitigate concentration of power in most of Eastern Europe and in the LDCs. Leaders—the same or subsequent ones—may reverse the reforms when reforms threaten their power. That has happened many times earlier in history (Powelson 1994), and there is no reason why it may not happen again. Virtually all the reforms of the past several years have been reforms by grace, which do not redistribute political power to peasants and others of lesser rank.

Conclusion

At the end of the Second World War, development economists and economic planners saw agriculture as a means of financing urban industrial development. "Surplus" labor on farms would migrate to cities, presumably with no reduction in farm output. The crops that had been feeding farmers would somehow be transferred to the city, to feed the same people. Because they had little confidence in the free market, economists and planners in LDCs found ways to effect the transfer, mainly through price controls (forced purchases of farm inputs at high prices from the government and forced sales of farm output at low prices to the government).

Governments in countries that instituted land reforms often gave land only to farmers who cooperated with government marketing boards and supply agencies. But the land governments distributed in land reforms often had a capitalized value of zero or less, since governments skimmed the profits. Doubts about forcing agriculture to subsidize industrial development became widespread in the 1980s, spurred by declining agricultural output per person in many LDCs, by drought, and by inefficiencies and deficits in the government industries that the agricultural surplus financed.

Because of the fall of communism and growing shortages of food, governments in Eastern European and LDCs are now changing policies. Where the new liberalization has been in effect for some years, as in China, Egypt, and Tanzania, agricultural output has greatly increased. But these governments have liberalized their policies only in the face of extreme economic necessity or political pressure from the outside. Since political power remains concentrated, even in East Asia, the miracle states of economic liberalism, there is no assurance that future rulers will stay the course. Institutionalized liberalism depends on diffusion of power and democratic governments, truly representative of all constituents, which are subject to defeat if they do not conduct economic policy to the benefit of the wide body of constituents. There is indeed a revolution in development economics, but whether it will translate into durable policies remains to be seen.

References

Bauer, Peter T. *Dissent on Development.* Cambridge Mass.: Harvard University Press, 1954.

Ban, Sung Hwan; Moon, Pal Young; and Perkins, Dwight. *Rural Development Studies in the Modernization of the Republic of Korea, 1945–1975.* Cambridge Mass.: Harvard University Council on East Asia Studies, 1980.

Barraclough, Solon, ed. *Agrarian Structure in Latin America.* Lexington, Mass.: Lexington Books/D.C. Heath, 1973.

Bhagwati, J.N., and Chakravarty, S. "Contributions to Indian Economic Analysis." Supplement to *American Economic Review,* 59 (4) (September 1969).

Cohen, Roger. *Wall Street Journal,* 10 September 1988.

Davidson, Basil. *The Black Man's Burden: Africa and the Curse of the Nation State.* New York: Times Books, Random House, 1993.

Doré, R.P. *Land Reform in Japan.* New York: Oxford University Press, 1959.

Edwards, Edgar O., ed. *Employment in Developing Nations.* New York: Columbia University Press, 1974.

Fei, John C.H., and Ranis, Gustav. *Development in the Labor Surplus Economy.* Homewood, Ill.: Richard D. Irwin, 1964.

Goodell, Grace E. *The Elementary Structures of Political Life.* New York: Oxford University Press, 1986.

Goodell, Grace E. "The Philippines." In *The Peasant Betrayed: Agriculture and Land Reform in the Third World,* rev. ed. Edited by John P. Powelson and Richard Stock. Washington, D.C.: Cato Institute, 1990.

Haberler, Gottfried. "Critical Observations on Some Notions in the Theory of Economic Development." *L'Industria* 2 (November 1957): 3–5.

Jacoby, Neil. *U.S. Aid to Taiwan.* New York: Praeger, 1966.

Khurso, A.M. "Returns to Scale in Indian Agriculture." *Indian Journal of Agricultural Economics* 19 (October–December 1964).

King, Russell. *Land Reform: A World Survey.* Boulder, Colo.: Westview Press, 1977.

Ladejinsky, Wolf. "Agrarian Reform in Asia." *Foreign Affairs* (April 1964).

Lele, Uma. "Role of Credit and Marketing Functions in Agricultural Development." Paper presented at International Economic Association Conference on "Agriculture in the Development of Low Income Countries." Bad Gotesburg, Germany, 4 September 1972.

Lewis, W. Arthur. "Economic Development with Unlimited Supplies of Labour." *The Manchester School* (May 1954).

Manzhuber, Albert. "The Economic Development of Taiwan." *Industry of Free China* 33 (4) (May 1970).

Mazumdar, C. "Farm Size and Productivity." *Economica* (May 1965).

Powelson, John P. *The Story of Land.* Cambridge, Mass.: Lincoln Institute of Land Policy, 1988.

Powelson, John P., and Stock, Richard. *The Peasant Betrayed: Agriculture and Land Reform in the Third World,* rev. ed. Washington, D.C.: Cato Institute, 1990.

Powelson, John P. *Centuries of Economic Endeavor: Parallel Paths in Japan and Europe, and Their Contrast with the Third World.* Ann Arbor, Mich.: University of Michigan Press, 1994.

Rao, A.P. "Size of Holding and Productivity." *Economic and Political Weekly* (11 November 1968).

Reynolds, Lloyd, ed. *Agriculture in Development Theory.* New Haven, Conn.: Yale University Press, 1975.

Rudra, A. "Farm Size and Yield per Acre." *Economic and Political Weekly* (19 July 1968).

U Tun Wai. "Taxation Problems and Policies of Underdeveloped Countries." *IMF Staff Papers* 9 (3) (November 1962).

Viner, Jacob. "Some Reflections on the Concept of Disguised Unemployment," *Contribuiçoes a Analise do Desenvolvimento Economico.* Rio de Janeiro: Libraria Agit Editorial, 1957.

Von Pischke, J.D. *Finance at the Frontier: Debt Capacity and the Role of Credit in the Private Economy.* Washington, D.C.: World Bank, 1991.

Part IV

Economic Liberalism, Trade, and Growth

17. Subsistence, Trade, and Exchange: Understanding Developing Economies

Peter Bauer

When economists discuss contemporary growth in advanced Western countries, they do not think of internal trade (i.e., wholesale and retail trade) as one of the engines of growth. And they are right. It would be misplaced to associate current economic growth in the West specifically with the distributive sector. Instead, when economists discuss wholesaling and retailing in advanced Western economies they focus on such subjects as the organization of these activities, the nature and extent of competition, concentration, economies of scale, vertical integration, and restrictive practices. The emphasis is on efficiency in the provision of distributive services: in broad terms, efficiency in the link between production and consumption. It is unusual to examine the possibility of any relationship between the activities of traders and the growth of the economy, except to the extent that efficiency in the provision of their services releases resources for other purposes. In short, the emphasis is on the allocation of given resources. In this respect, trading activity is treated very much like any other branch of economic activity.

This orientation is justified. It focuses on the main issues of interest to both economists and policymakers. But this orientation, though appropriate now, would be misleading if it were applied to the Western economies as they were two or more centuries ago. Yet in that earlier period those economies were in many ways far more advanced than those of most less developed countries (LDCs) today.

Peter Bauer is Professor Emeritus of Economics at the London School of Economics and a Fellow of the British Academy. This chapter is a revised and expanded version of the author's lecture presented at the Cato Institute, October 14, 1992, as part of its Distinguished Lecturer Series. The Cato Institute and Lord Bauer wish to thank the Earhart Foundation for financial assistance that made the lecture and its publication possible.

In particular, they were already very largely exchange economies in which subsistence or near-subsistence production was relatively unimportant.

Internal Trade as an Engine of Growth

Historians have recognized that the economic repercussions of trading activities in say, 17th- and 18th-century England went well beyond efficiency in the use of resources in the trading activities themselves. For example, in their recent book on shopkeeping in 18th-century England, Hoh-cheung Mui and Lorna Mui (1989, pp. 291–92) conclude:

> If the major purpose of all these activities by shopkeepers was to drum up business, by so doing they eased the flow of goods and at the same time helped to stimulate as well as satisfy an increasingly widespread demand, a demand that encouraged expansion in industry and overseas trade. It was not an unimportant contributor to the overall economic development of the country—industry, overseas trading and inland distribution moved in tandem, each fructifying the other.

Jacob Price (1989, p. 283) has observed that in 17th- and 18th-century Britain the activities of merchants "left behind" much more than "specific markets for specific products." Their activities helped to create commercial institutions and practices and to raise the level of human capital, which proved to be "of great utility to the entire economy in the ensuing era of rapid industrialization and attendant export growth" (p. 283). Richard Grassby (1970, p. 106) wrote that it was "merchant capital which created markets, financed manufactures, floated the American colonial economies and launched banking and insurance."

In emerging economies the activities of traders promote not only the more efficient deployment of available resources, but also the growth of resources. Trading activities are productive in both static and dynamic senses.[1]

[1]For a further discussion of the role of traders in the development process, see Bauer (1991, chap. 1).

Neglect of Trading Activity

One would therefore expect to find that trading activities feature prominently in modern development economics. Instead, in spite of the economic history of the now developed world, which should have been familiar to development economists, trading activities are barely mentioned in the mainstream literature. It is as if postwar development economics had to begin from scratch, its exponents faced with a tabula rasa.

A charitable interpretation is that exponents of the new development economics thought that early Western experience could not apply to the so-called Third World. This attitude would have been mistaken, since it is evident that all developed countries at one time had the characteristics and levels of income and capital of the postwar Third World.

However, even if it were correct to disregard the economic history of the West, the neglect in development economics of the role of trading activity in the Third World is both unwarranted and surprising. First-hand observation of economic activity in many less developed regions would have shown that trading activity was ubiquitous and that large numbers of people were engaged in it on a full-time, part-time, or casual basis.[2] Moreover, even a cursory reading of the last hundred years' history of some of these regions would have drawn attention to the role of traders in helping to transform them from largely subsistence economies to largely exchange economies. For example, the historian Sir Keith Hancock (1977), after analyzing the major changes in that region, referred to West Africa as the "traders' frontier." Another historian, Allan McPhee, entitled his book, published in London in 1926, *The Economic Revolution in British*

[2]The large numbers involved in trading activities have usually not been reflected in official occupational statistics and official reports. This understatement, or even omission, lends plausibility to the proposition that tertiary activities (which include trading) in poor countries involved a smaller proportion of the labor force than in richer countries; and that the proportion increased with economic growth. I examined this proposition, put forward in the 1930s by Colin Clark and Allan G. B. Fisher, in various publications since 1951. There it has been explained why official statistics are misleading, and why the empirical and theoretical bases for the Clark-Fisher hypothesis are insubstantial. My views are summarized in my recent book, *The Development Frontier* (Bauer 1991).

West Africa. The book makes clear both that West Africa was transformed in a period of about two generations and also that traders were major agents of that transformation.

The neglect of internal trading activity still persists in mainstream development economics. That this is so is clear from Gerald M. Meier's book *Emerging from Poverty* published in 1984. Professor Meier is a very distinguished exponent of development economics. His book sets out the main concerns of the subject. Trading activity (as distinct from international trade) is not mentioned.

Had trading activity and its effects been properly appreciated, mainstream development economics would have been radically different. For example, the influential proposition in development economics known as the international demonstration effect portrayed the availability of Western goods as encouraging consumption at the expense of saving and investment, and hence as inhibiting economic growth. However, in reality, trading activity and the availability of imported incentive goods served to initiate and sustain a process in which increases in consumption and investment (for example, in establishing and improving capacity in agriculture) were able to go hand in hand. It is no accident that throughout the Third World the most advanced regions are those with most Western commercial contacts; and, conversely, the most backward and poorest are those with few such contacts. Interestingly, Karl Marx was emphatic in the *Communist Manifesto* about the positive role of cheap consumer goods in the advance from primitive agriculture to more sophisticated and productive economic activity. The concept of incentive goods and the term itself have dropped out of the development literature.

Similarly, the central notion in this literature until quite recently has been the vicious circle of poverty. According to this proposition poor countries cannot emerge from their poverty because incomes are too low for the saving and investment necessary to raise income. It is difficult to see how development economists could have entertained this notion if they had recognized how millions of poor producers in the Third World had in the aggregate made massive investments in agriculture. These investments were made in the context of their decisions, encouraged by the activities of traders, to replace subsistence production by production for the market. If there had been a vicious circle of poverty, these poor people had failed to notice it. Millions of acres of cultivated land under cash crops such as rubber, cocoa, and coffee, as well as foodstuffs for domestic markets, testify not only to Third World peoples' economic responsiveness and readiness to take a long view but also to the vacuousness of the idea of the vicious circle of poverty.

The notion of the vicious circle of poverty as promoted in the mainstream development literature from the 1940s to at least the 1970s is evidently insubstantial. To have money is the result of economic achievement, not its precondition. That this is so is plain from the very existence of developed countries, all of which originally must have been underdeveloped and yet progressed without external donations. The world was not created in two parts, one with ready-made infrastructure and stock of capital and the other without such facilities. Moreover, many poor countries progressed rapidly in the hundred years or so before the emergence of modern development economics and the canvassing of the vicious circle. Indeed, if the notion of the vicious circle of poverty were valid, mankind would still be living in the Old Stone Age.

The idea of the vicious circle of poverty has been a major lapse in modern development economics. It has influenced policy considerably. It was a major element in the advocacy of massive state economic controls on the ground that only drastic policies of "resource mobilization" would enable an economy to break the vicious circle. It was also a major strand in the successful advocacy of government-to-government subsidies known as foreign aid.

Lapses in economic thinking are not of course confined to modern development economics. One may recall the celebrated near-consensus of economists in the 1950s that the persistent scarcity of the United States dollar would be a continuing problem besetting the world economy. This conclusion could only be reached by a now inexplicable disregard of the rate of exchange (i.e., the price of the dollar). This particular lapse had a short life: the dollar shortage was in fact soon replaced by an international glut of dollars. Lapses in modern development economics have proven to be much more impervious to inconvenient evidence. Thus, the notion of the vicious circle of poverty and the disregard of price on quantities supplied and demanded (supply and demand for short) both of which engulfed much mainstream development economics from the late 1940s persisted for more than two decades. And as I have just noted disregard of trading has persisted much longer.

One should perhaps say that modern development economics has not neglected traders and trading activity completely. To the very limited extent that these subjects have been considered, the emphasis has been on the so-called imperfections of the market. When not ignored, trade has usually been deplored. Thus, real or alleged monopolistic elements in trade have attracted some attention. For instance, the trader who has penetrated an outlying area is apt to be scrutinized as an individual with market power because he is, after all, the only trader on the spot. The fact that his presence adds to the opportunities available to the local people tends to be ignored.

Winston Churchill, who did not claim economic expertise, saw the point. Writing about East Africa, he said:

> It is the Indian trader who, penetrating and maintaining himself in all sorts of places to which no white man would go or in which no white man could earn a living, has more than anyone else developed the beginning of early trade and opened up the first slender means of communication.[3]

From Misfortune to Disaster

Market-oriented economists and advocates of extensive state economic control are agreed on one matter, namely that advance from subsistence production to wider exchange is indispensable for a society's escape from extreme poverty. In the absence of opportunities for exchange, there is little scope for the division of labor and so for the emergence of different crafts or skills. The lack of commercial links with a wider society obstructs or precludes the inflow or emergence of new ideas, methods, crops, and wants. Indeed, unquestioning acceptance of prevailing conditions and the sway of habit and custom are familiar in such economies.

The low level of attainment is accompanied by major hazards. The absence of trading links with the outside world and lack of reserve stocks turn misfortune, such as bad weather, into disaster; belt-tightening becomes starvation. It is not accidental that large-scale famine in the less developed world occurs in subsistence and near-subsistence economies and not in economies already reasonably well integrated into wider regions through exchange relationships. The advance of an economy to wider exchange does not

[3]Quoted in Mangat (1969, p. 61).

involve greater insecurity as part of the cost of material progress; in other words, there is here no conflict between progress and security.

The misery in Ethiopia, Sudan, and elsewhere in Africa is not the result simply of unfavorable weather, external causes, or population pressure. It is the result of enforced reversion to subsistence conditions under the impact of the breakdown of public security, suppression of private trade, or forced collectivization. There is a core of truth in the jibe that the weather tends to be bad in centrally controlled economies. But although the hazards of a subsistence economy are far more acute than those of an exchange economy, they tend to be politically and psychologically more acceptable as being part of the nature of things and in any case not attributable to human agency. But this greater acceptability of the hazards and hardships of a subsistence economy does not diminish their reality.

Advance from subsistence production involves trading activity. This is obvious at a simple level. There can be no production for sale without an outlet and an accessible conduit to it. Producers also need to buy inputs, such as simple tools and equipment. And they will not produce for sale unless they can use the proceeds to buy goods and services they want. The purchase of inputs and of incentive goods and production for sale are in turn closely linked with credit. This is required for the purchase of inputs used in the production of the crops, whether seasonal crops or slow-maturing trees, and also in many cases for sustaining producers until their crops are harvested. Traders are an effective and convenient source and channel of such finance. In these circumstances production of cash crops, whether for domestic or external markets, trade, and credit is intertwined.

But the significance of trade extends far beyond these pipeline services. Contacts through traders and trade are prime agents in the spread of new ideas, modes of behavior, and methods of production. External commercial contacts often first suggest the very possibility of change, including economic improvement.

Small-Scale Operations

Conditions in the Third World tend to ensure the need for a substantial volume of trading and closely related activities. These activities are more labor intensive than in the West because capital is scarcer relative to labor in poor countries than in rich.

A large proportion of producers and consumers operate on a small scale and far from the major commercial centers, including the ports. Individual transactions are small. Individual farmers produce on a small scale and sell in even smaller quantities at frequent intervals because they lack storage facilities and substantial cash reserves. Conversely, because of their low incomes, consumers find it convenient or necessary to buy in small, often very small, amounts, again at frequent intervals. In these conditions the collection of produce and the physical distribution of consumer goods and of farm inputs are necessarily expensive in real terms. Storage, assembly, bulking, transport, breaking of bulk, and distribution absorb a significant proportion of available resources.

In Nigeria, for example, individual groundnut farmers may sell a few pounds of groundnuts at a time and operate 500–700 miles from the ports whence the groundnuts are shipped in consignments of thousands of tons. Imported consumer goods arrive in large consignments and are often bought in minute quantities. In Nigeria matches arrive in consignments of several hundred cases, each case containing hundreds or thousands of boxes. The ultimate consumer may buy only part of a box. The sale of one box is at times a wholesale transaction; the buyer resells the contents in little bundles of ten matches, together with part of the striking surface of a box. Cheap imported scent arrives in large consignments: the ultimate consumer often does not buy even a small bottle but only two or three drops at a time, perhaps a dab on each shoulder of the garment. In some African countries smokers buy single cigarettes, or even a single inhaled drag of a cigarette.

To a Western audience it may seem as if sales of produce and purchases of consumer goods in such small quantities must be wasteful. This is not so. If consumers could not buy in these small quantities, they would either have to tie up their very limited capital in larger purchases or, more likely, would not be able to consume the products at all.[4] The same considerations apply to a farmer's sales of produce to an intermediary.

[4]As Adam Smith observed, "Unless a capital was employed in breaking and dividing certain portions either of the crude or manufactured produce, into such small parcels as suit the occasional demands of those who want them, every man would be obliged to purchase a greater quantity of the goods he wanted, than his immediate occasions required." *Wealth of Nations*, Book II, chap. 5.

It is evident that in these conditions the task of collecting and bulking produce and of breaking bulk and physical distribution of merchandise involves much labor. What may be somewhat surprising is that a large part of this labor is self-employed. This is so because entry into small-scale trading is easy. In the absence of officially imposed obstacles such as restrictive licensing or official monopsonies, there are few if any institutional barriers, few administrative skills are needed, and little initial capital is required. The supply price of self-employed labor is low in the absence of more profitable opportunities. For these reasons small-scale operations are economic in many parts of the distribution system: Large firms are at a disadvantage because their operations require more administrative and supervisory personnel, and these tend to be relatively expensive or ineffective in many poor countries. A multiplicity of small-scale traders in part represents the substitution of cheaper labor for more expensive labor.[5]

A colorful illustration of labor-intensive trade is provided by the extensive business in used containers. Petty traders purchase, collect, store, clean, repair, and resell containers such as tins, boxes, bottles, and sacks. They thereby extend the effective life and use of these products. Labor is used and capital is conserved.

The small-scale trader often does not supply simply marketing services to his customers. In many cases he provides credit, usually in modest sums. This credit is used for such purposes as the purchase of seeds, fertilizers, pesticides, building materials, implements, and consumer goods. The advancing of this credit generally is the final stage in a flow of funds emanating from financial institutions and large trading firms which have direct access to international financial markets. These enterprises advance credit to the larger indigenous traders; the latter advance credit to smaller traders; and so on until the farmer gets his loan. There is, in short, a process of bulk-breaking in the financial market; and the farmer in the hinterland has access indirectly to the world capital market.

[5]The numbers attracted to trade in LDCs may be increased as a result of rigidities in money wages for hired labor. It was Simon Rottenberg (1953) who first pointed out this necessary qualification. But even if these wages were at market-clearing levels the numbers who would find trading attractive would still be very large as long as the underlying economic factors remain the same.

A Western audience may be surprised at the relatively large number of successive independent trading intermediaries who typically are involved in the movement of a farmer's output from the first collection to the final shipment from the port. Again, this succession of intermediaries may seem wasteful and suggest that it would be more economic for the flow of goods to pass through fewer successive intermediaries. But this opinion overlooks two considerations already noted: first, the supply price of the services of small traders is very low, and second, a larger vertically integrated trading firm spanning several successive stages would require relatively expensive personnel for coordination and supervision. In the circumstances, the vertical subdivision of trading activities among successive intermediaries is economic. That this is so is ensured by the option to by-pass a redundant intermediary. No producer, consumer, or intermediary is forced to use the services of any intermediary if he can perform that intermediary's services at lower cost: a redundant bulking or bulk-breaking intermediary will be side-stepped. The same is true of any other trading service such as the provision of credit.

It may be helpful if I anticipate a doubt in some readers' minds. It is often contended that farmers in poor countries are not free to choose among intermediaries in selling their produce because they are indebted to particular traders to whom they have to sell their output at a depressed price. However, where the producer can choose among a number of would-be lenders and trader-lenders, he will choose to borrow where the terms are most advantageous to him. The terms of loans from trader-lenders are a combination of interest payments and the obligation to sell the produce to the lender; what in isolation may seem to be a forced sale at a low price may simply represent an indirect part of interest on the loan. And, of course, many producers are not in debt.

In much of the less developed world, especially in Africa, there is no clear-cut distinction between farmers and traders or moneylenders. The small trader is often the more enterprising farmer who collects produce from neighbors or relatives and takes it to the market. After a while, he may come to trade more nearly full time. And even without such progression, the trader or moneylender in rural areas in LDCs, conspicuously so in Africa, is usually very much anchored in the rural community with farming relatives.

In the same way as many Third World farmers have become part-time or full-time traders, so many traders have become manufacturers. Successful traders accumulate capital and develop business skills that are helpful for the conduct of industrial operations. In the words of Adam Smith, "The habits besides of order, economy and attention to which mercantile business naturally forms a merchant render him much fitter to execute, with profit and success any project of improvement" (*Wealth of Nations*, Book III, chap. 4). Throughout the Third World many viable industrial enterprises have been pioneered and developed by traders.

Nonmonetary Investment

Farmers in poor countries producing for wider exchange have to make investments of various kinds. These investments include the clearing and improvement of land, and the acquisition of livestock and equipment. Such investments constitute capital formation. A part of this capital formation is financed from personal savings and borrowing from traders and others. But much of it is nonmonetized. For example, the clearing or improvement of land is the result of additional effort on the part of the farmer and his family. Very little monetary expenditure is involved.

These forms of investment, when made by small farmers, are generally omitted from official statistics, and are still largely ignored in both the academic and the official development literature.

In many poor countries these overlooked categories of investment are in the aggregate highly important both quantitatively and qualitatively. They are quantitatively significant because agriculture and the activities closely related to it account for much of economic activity. They are qualitatively significant because these categories of investment are critical in the advance from subsistence to exchange. Moreover, such investments are especially likely to be productive, because they are made by people who have a direct interest in the returns.

Besides presenting a misleading picture of economic activity in the Third World, the neglect of this capital formation has had adverse practical consequences. Taxation and other policies have often retarded the expansion of the exchange sector by reducing the farmer's proceeds or by increasing his costs. I believe that these policies would not have been pursued so extensively and intensively if the scale and significance of capital formation on small farms had been recognized.

Disregard of this capital formation resembles neglect of the extent and role of trading activity. In both cases the extent and importance of the neglected activity should have been evident from direct observation of economic activity in poor countries. Indeed, reflection on readily available statistics alone would have indicated the importance both of capital formation in agriculture and also of trading activity: statistics such as those of exports and imports and of the volume of freight handled on the railways, and also changes in these magnitudes over time, all of which are relevant and informative in this context.

The Scope and Effectiveness of Economics

I have here been criticizing features of mainstream development economics. Let me recapitulate briefly. In recent decades major shortcomings disfigured this branch or subdiscipline of economics. These have included the disregard of trading activity; the neglect of major determinants of economic performance such as cultural and political factors; the notion of the vicious circle of poverty; and the practice of price-less economics, that is, the disregard of the relationship between price and quantities supplied and demanded.

These are failures of observation or failures to apply basic economic reasoning. These defects have had serious practical consequences, some of which I have alluded to earlier in this lecture. The neglect of cultural and political factors necessarily involves disregard of the reciprocal interaction between the familiar variables of economic analysis and these determinants of economic performance and progress.

You will appreciate that I am not saying here that economists have little or nothing to contribute by way of explaining economic phenomena and processes in the Third World, and thereby assisting in the framing of economic policies. On the contrary, they have much to offer. Economic analysis is generally applicable as a major step in understanding the likely effects of a change in any of the familiar economic variables. Economists working in unfamiliar settings will, however, be more effective if, in addition, they recognize that cultural and political factors, usually taken as given, may be influenced by changes in one or other of these variables. For example, a change in the foreign trade regime, and hence in the availability of imported goods, is likely to affect the spread of new ideas and information, and thereby people's attitudes and modes of behavior.

The potentialities of economics both for explanation and policy in poor countries have been enriched by recent advances in other fields of economic enquiry, such as the economic theory of politics and bureaucracies, the economics of property rights, the analysis of the dichotomy between insiders and outsiders in the labor market, the economics of transaction costs, and the theory of effective protection.

Critical assessment of contemporary development economics therefore must not serve to obscure the relevance of economics for the understanding of economic activities and sequences in the less developed world. Many years of work in this field have reinforced my confidence in the scope and effectiveness of economics in the most diverse institutional settings.

References

Bauer, Peter. *The Development Frontier: Essays in Applied Economics*. Cambridge, Mass.: Harvard University Press, 1991.

Grassby, Richard. "English Merchant Capitalism in the Late Seventeenth Century." *Past & Present* 46 (1970): 87–107.

Hancock, William Keith. *Survey of British Commonwealth Affairs*. Westport, Conn.: Greenwood Press, 1977.

Mangat, J.S. *A History of the Asians in East Africa, 1886 to 1945*. Oxford: Clarendon Press, 1960.

Meier, Gerald M. *Emerging from Poverty: The Economics that Really Matter*. New York: Oxford University Press, 1984.

Mui, Hoh-cheung, and Mui, Lorna H. *Shops and Shopkeeping in Eighteenth Century England*. London: Routledge, 1989.

Price, Jacob M. "What Did Merchants Do? Reflections on British Overseas Trade, 1660–1790." *Journal of Economic History* 49 (1989): 267–84.

Rottenberg, Simon. "Note." *Review of Economics and Statistics* 35 (1953): 168–70.

18. Economic Development and Economic Freedom

Bryan T. Johnson and Thomas P. Sheehy

The Economic Freedom Factor

For years, efforts to promote economic development in poor countries have centered on programs to alleviate poverty. The World Bank, International Monetary Fund, and national foreign-aid agencies have spent billions of dollars on programs to feed, clothe, and educate the poor. The programs have dealt with the symptoms of poverty, not its causes, and have yielded few lasting benefits. They have ignored the means to economic development (see Bauer 1993).

The poverty afflicting so much of the world is no aberration. It is the typical condition of mankind through most of human history. What is exceptional is the wealth of modern developed countries. Unfortunately, there has been considerable misunderstanding about how the wealth was created. Instead of being celebrated as the agent of change that made it possible, classical liberalism has often been demonized. As Ludwig von Mises (1962) has written, "That there is want and misery in the world is not . . . an argument against [classical] liberalism. It is precisely want and misery that [classical] liberalism seeks to abolish, and it considers the means that it proposes the only suitable ones for the achievement of this end."

The essence of classical liberalism is economic freedom, namely, the ability of individuals to engage in economic activity largely unimpeded by the state. Our Index of Economic Freedom is a quantitative measure of economic freedom in various countries (Johnson

---

Bryan T. Johnson is a Policy Analyst in International Economic Affairs at the Heritage Foundation. Thomas P. Sheehy, a former Jay Kingham Fellow at the Heritage Foundation, is Staff Director at the House International Relations Committee's Subcommittee on Africa. They thank the Fraser Institute and the many scholars associated with the Rating Economic Freedom Project for their work on measuring economic freedom.

and Sheehy 1995, 1996). It indicates a strong correlation between economic freedom and economic development, and highlights the importance of moving away from the collectivism that has devastated so much of the world in this century.

Measuring Economic Freedom

The relation between economic freedom and economic development should be food for thought for the international bureaucrats responsible for structural adjustment programs in developing countries. The Index of Economic Freedom demonstrates that countries with the greatest degree of economic freedom enjoy the greatest economic prosperity. The Index measures economic freedom by pitting private economic actors against the state. The countries that score highest on the Index demonstrate the greatest degree of economic freedom and enjoy the greatest economic prosperity. They have the lowest taxes, fewest trade barriers, and the strongest protection of private property.

Economic freedom is not always the concern of the World Bank, IMF, and other international financial institutions, however. The international financial institutions have different norms. Whereas the Index rewards a lean government (one consuming a minimal percentage of gross domestic product) and low tax rates, international financial institutions often encourage governments to collect more taxes for the sake of balanced budgets. Moreover, other factors affecting economic freedom, such as regulation, largely escape the attention of the international financial institutions.

It is not surprising that the international financial institutions and the governments they deal with are not sensitive to economic freedom. The essence of government bureaucracy is the exercise of power. By identifying the world's most prosperous countries as those with the least economically active governments, the Index is a prescription for empowering private-sector activity over government bureaucracy. Certainly the benefit of the doubt should be given to the private sector when delineating private and public roles. This rule of thumb is not a pleasant one for bureaucrats.

Methodology

The Index of Economic Freedom gauges the freedom of private actors to engage in economic activity free of government intervention. The Index assesses the degree of economic freedom in over

100 countries. There are 10 factors in the Index: trade policy, taxation policy, government consumption of economic output, monetary policy, foreign investment, banking policy, wage and price controls, property rights, regulation, and black market activity. The Index scores each factor on a scale of 1 to 5, then calculates a composite score for each country, with 1 representing the highest degree of economic freedom and 5 representing the lowest (Johnson and Sheehy 1995, chap. 4). The Index weights the 10 factors equally in calculating the composite (average) score for each country.

Trade Policy

This factor measures government control over trade by considering the average tariff rate and nontariff barriers to trade. The lower the trade barriers, the lower the score and the greater the economic freedom.

Taxation Policy

This factor measures government confiscation of private wealth by considering national corporate and personal tax rates and other taxes, including value-added taxes, capital gains taxes, sales taxes, property taxes, and state and local taxes. The lower the level of taxation, the lower the score and the greater the economic freedom.

Government Consumption of Economic Output

This factor measures government involvement in economic activity by considering government consumption of GDP. The lower the level of government consumption, the lower the score and the greater the economic freedom.

Monetary Policy

This factor measures a country's ability to maintain the value of its currency by considering the average annual inflation rate. The lower the average annual inflation rate, the lower the score and the greater the economic freedom.

Foreign Investment

This factor measures government control over foreign investment by considering investment codes, legal protections, and the sanctity of contracts. The lower the level of government control over foreign investment, the lower the score and the greater the economic freedom.

Banking Policy

This factor measures government control over banks and other financial institutions by considering banking and securities laws. The freer the banks are of government control, the lower the score and the greater the economic freedom.

Wage and Price Controls

This factor measures government control over wages and prices by considering wage and price control laws. The lower the level of government control over wages and prices, the lower the score and the greater the economic freedom.

Property Rights

This factor measures government protection of private property by considering, among other things, the extent of past property expropriations. The higher the level of private property protection, the lower the score and the greater the economic freedom.

Regulation

This factor measures government control over economic activity by considering business regulations and the level of official corruption surrounding the enforcement of regulations. The lower the level of regulation, the lower the score and the greater the economic freedom.

Black-Market Activity

This factor measures the level of economic activity rendered illegal by government policy by considering the level of black-market activity as a percentage of GDP. The lower the level of black-market activity, the lower the score and the greater the economic freedom.

Some of the factors are complementary. For example, the size of the black market is a function of wage and price controls and regulation. Government consumption of economic output is largely a function of taxation. While additional factors could be considered, the 10 factors in the Index together provide a comprehensive picture of an economy and allow for a judgment of its level of economic freedom.

The Link between Economic Freedom and Economic Performance

The Index of Economic Freedom divides its scores into four categories. Countries scoring 1.00–1.99 have free economies; countries scoring 2.00–2.99 have mostly free economies; countries scoring 3.00–3.99 have mostly not free economies; and countries scoring above 4.00 have repressed economies. (The appendix gives the 1997 ratings.)

Figure 1 illustrates the link between economic freedom and economic performance. In general, countries with more economic freedom (lower Index scores) have experienced higher levels of economic growth, as measured by real per capita income between 1980 and 1993. Likewise, those countries with less economic freedom

FIGURE 1

ECONOMIC GROWTH AND ECONOMIC FREEDOM

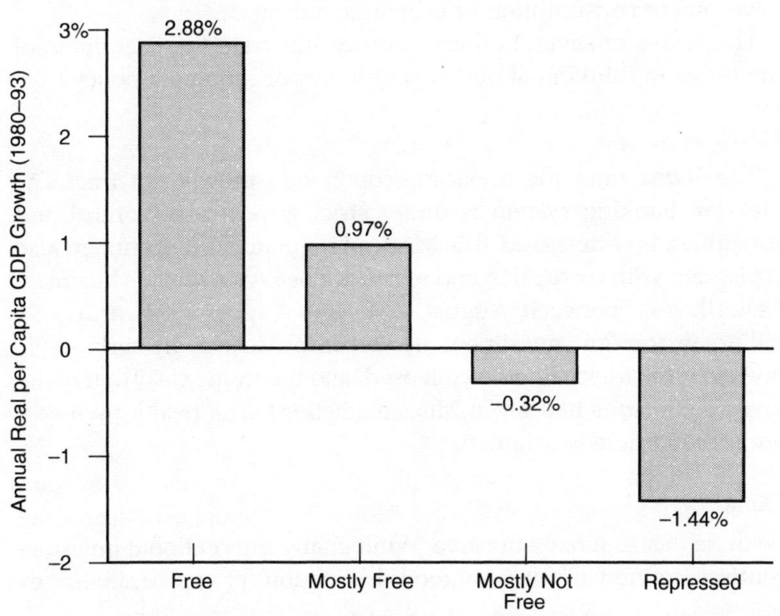

NOTE: Per capita GDP is expressed in terms of purchasing power parities.
SOURCE: Beach and Davis (1997, p. 9).

(higher Index scores) have experienced lower economic growth (Beach and Davis 1997, p. 8).

Interestingly, some developed countries have less economic freedom than some developing countries. Sweden, for example, scores 2.45, while Chile scores 2.25 (Holmes, Johnson, and Kirkpatrick 1997, p. xxix). Sweden's higher score reflects its relatively high level of taxation and the large economic role played by the Swedish government. That outcome, however, does not invalidate the positive relation between economic freedom and economic development. The Index of Economic Freedom is a snapshot, assessing the current state of economic freedom within a country. It makes no accounting for the economic history of Sweden or Chile. Sweden is wealthier than Chile, though being less economically free, in part because Sweden began industrialization long before Chile, giving it more time to develop and accumulate wealth. However, if Chile maintains its current superior rates of economic growth, it will eventually surpass Sweden in wealth. The Index suggests that this development is a certainty if Sweden continues with its high tax rates and high government consumption of economic output.

The scores of several other countries illustrate the usefulness of the Index in thinking about current issues of economic policy.[1]

Mexico

The Index rates the Mexican economy as mostly not free. The Mexican banking system is under strict government control and corruption is widespread. The Mexican regulatory environment also is plagued with corruption and imposes a heavy burden on business. Nevertheless, between August 1993 and August 1994, nearly $9 billion in foreign investment flowed into Mexico. In early 1995, however, the Mexican peso collapsed, and it became clear that many investment firms had given Mexico a better bill of health than economic conditions warranted.

China

China is also mostly not free. While many international investors continue to view China as a good destination for capital, the Index

[1]All scores are taken from the 1997 Index found in Holmes, Johnson, and Kirkpatrick (1997).

indicates that the Chinese economy remains under tight government control. It is no coincidence that the bulk of foreign investment is concentrated in experimental pockets of economic freedom, primarily in Guangdong and Fujian Provinces. Expanded foreign investment throughout China and general economic prosperity remain unlikely until China embraces economic freedom on a national level.

The Czech Republic

With the fall of the Iron Curtain in 1989, many analysts looked to Hungary and Poland to be in the vanguard of economic liberalization. Instead, those countries have been backsliding with their economic transitions, while the Czech Republic has advanced the furthest with reform among the former East bloc states. In fact, over 80 percent of the Czech economy is now in private hands. The Czech economy is also prospering, having received a surge of foreign investment. The Czech Republic's Index score is lower than the scores of Hungary and Poland, reflecting its superior economic conditions.

An important factor in the successful economic liberalization of the Czech Republic has been its irreverent attitude toward the World Bank and the IMF. Czech Prime Minister Václav Klaus (1993) publicly recognized the danger of development aid: It delays economic reforms. He also complained about the statist orientation of the international financial institutions (Tammen 1993). That insight encouraged Klaus to avoid the "foreign aid trap" and to accelerate economic liberalization in order to enhance economic freedom in the Czech Republic.

Japan and the United States

American policymakers frequently argue that the Japanese market is one of the most protected in the world and that businesses operating in Japan are strangled by government regulation. Indeed, this has become a mantra in Washington. Yet the Index finds the United States and Japan have approximately equal levels of regulation. While Japan has especially tough safety standards, it does not have such onerous regulations as the Americans with Disabilities Act and civil rights laws that encourage litigation. Japanese regulation is less burdensome than regulation in most of the world, Washington rhetoric notwithstanding.

The Relation between Economic Freedom and Political Freedom

Among the countries with the top 10 scores on the Index of Economic Freedom, Freedom House (1994, p. 39) classifies four as partially free or not free politically. The four are Hong Kong, Singapore, Bahrain, and Taiwan. Of course, the hope is that they and other countries that have free economies will gradually develop free political systems. This is happening in Taiwan, as it happened in South Korea.

Indeed, to the extent that an Asian model of development exists, it appears to be one of economic freedom being a precursor to political freedom rather than political repression being a permanent condition. Nevertheless, there has been considerable discussion of Asia charting its own, decidedly non-Western course into the next century. The belligerence shown by Singapore, Indonesia, and other Asian countries in recent human-rights spats with the West have been used as evidence. Yet South Korea, the Philippines, and Taiwan show no signs of shunning the general Western conception of individual political liberty. The real battle is not likely to be over maintaining democratic gains in Asia, but between the Indonesian or similarly repressive regimes and the forces of political liberalization within their own societies.

The donor community seems to endorse the Asian model for Africa. No African country except Botswana is enjoying great success in economic development; nevertheless, the countries that at least have positive real economic growth are those with the most economic freedom. Some are far from politically free. Uganda, for example, scored a 2.90 on the Index. Its economy is vibrant by African standards, but President Yoweri Museveni has not encouraged political liberalization. After dallying with the legalization of political parties, Museveni renounced multiparty politics. This has not stopped Uganda from becoming the star pupil of the international financial institutions. Museveni's commitment to economic liberalization has been enough, and Uganda has been rewarded with generous development aid. Even the United States, the donor nation most sensitive to democratic values, has largely overlooked Uganda's lack of political freedom.

Some countries are attempting substantial economic and political liberalization simultaneously. Boris Yeltsin is waging this struggle in Russia. Unfortunately, actual economic liberalization in Russia has been less than impressive. Zambia is another country in the same predicament. President Frederick Chiluba, who came to power in 1991 as Zambia's first democratically elected president, has had little success liberalizing Zambia's statist economy. As with Yeltsin, Chiluba's efforts have threatened his government and the cause of democracy in Zambia. In both countries, economic liberalization would probably be easier under a less democratic regime.

Milton Friedman (1962) long ago stated vividly how economic freedom is an indispensable means of achieving political freedom. More recently, James Pinkerton (1994) noted that many countries with a high degree of economic freedom are not politically free. According to Pinkerton, "Capitalism without the saving graces of non-economic liberty and tolerance for diversity loses much of its moral stature." The two perspectives are compatible. Friedman and Pinkerton surely would agree on the foolishness of providing development aid to a country such as Ethiopia (Index score: 3.60), which is struggling toward democracy without moving aggressively to shed its Marxist past. Without economic freedom, Ethiopia remains a fallow field for democracy.

Conclusion

That a correlation exists between economic freedom and economic development is indisputable. Countries with the most economic freedom enjoy the most economic prosperity.[2] The implication for policymakers is that developing countries wishing to escape poverty must unleash and reward the economic energies of their citizens.

Appendix: Index of Economic Freedom, 1997 Rankings

The following table ranks countries from most economically free to least economically free. In case of a tie, countries were ranked alphabetically.

[2]Other studies have reached the same conclusion (e.g., Gwartney, Lawson, and Block 1996). For a comparison of the various economic freedom surveys, see Hanke and Walters (1997). Also, see Easton and Walker (1992) for early work on rating economic freedom.

APPENDIX TABLE 1
INDEX OF ECONOMIC FREEDOM (1997 RANKINGS)

Rank	Country
Free	
1	Hong Kong
2	Singapore
3	Bahrain
4	New Zealand
5	Switzerland
	United States
7	United Kingdom
	Taiwan
Mostly Free	
9	Bahamas
	Netherlands
11	Czech Republic
	Denmark
	Japan
	Luxembourg
15	Canada
	Belgium
	United Arab Emirates
18	Australia
	Austria
20	Ireland
	Germany
22	Chile
23	Finland
	Thailand
25	Estonia
26	Kuwait
27	Norway
	South Korea
	Sri Lanka
	Sweden
31	France
	Iceland
	Panama
34	El Salvador
	Trinidad & Tobago
36	Cyprus
	Italy
	Jamaica
	Malaysia
	Portugal
	Spain
42	Argentina
43	Belize
	Jordan
	Uruguay
46	Paraguay
	Morocco
	Oman
	Tunisia
50	Costa Rica
	Barbados
	Guatemala
	Israel
	Philippines
	Saudi Arabia
	Swaziland
	Turkey
	Western Samoa
59	Bolivia
	Botswana
	Greece
	Indonesia
	Zambia
64	Hungary
	Peru
	Uganda
67	Benin
	Gabon
	Latvia
	Lebanon
	Malta
	Namibia
Mostly Unfree	
73	Djibouti
	South Africa
75	Ecuador
	Kenya
	Slovak Rep.
78	Colombia
	Ghana
	Lithuania
	Mali
	Pakistan
	Papua New Guinea
	Slovenia
85	Honduras
	Poland
87	Fiji
	Nigeria
89	Algeria
	Madagascar
	Senegal
	Tanzania
93	Mongolia
94	Brazil
	Ivory Coast
	Mexico
	Moldova
98	Romania
99	Cape Verde
100	Armenia
	Dom. Rep.
	Guinea
	Egypt
104	Burkina Faso
	Guyana
106	Cambodia
	Malawi
108	Bulgaria
	Cameroon
	Ethiopia
	Gambia
	Nepal
	Nicaragua
	Venezuela
115	Albania
	Lesotho
	Russia
118	Bangladesh
	Croatia
	India
	Niger
	Zimbabwe
123	Congo
	Ukraine
125	Burundi
	Chad
	China
	Mauritania
129	Belarus
	Georgia
	Sierra-Leone
132	Yemen
Repressed	
133	Haiti
	Mozambique
	Suriname
136	Rwanda
	Sudan
	Syria
	Zaire
140	Burma
141	Angola
142	Azerbaijan
143	Iran
	Libya
	Somalia
	Vietnam
147	Iraq
148	Cuba
	Laos
	North Korea

SOURCE: Holmes and Kirkpatrick (1996).

References

Bauer, Peter. "Development Aid: End It or Mend It?" San Francisco: International Center for Economic Growth, 1993.

Beach, William W., and Davis, Gareth. "The Index of Economic Freedom and Economic Growth." In Holmes, Johnson, and Kirkpatrick (1996, chap. 1).

Easton, Stephen T., and Walker, Michael A. *Rating Global Economic Freedom.* Vancouver: Fraser Institute, 1992.

Freedom House. *Freedom Review* 25 (January–February 1994).

Friedman, Milton. *Capitalism and Freedom.* Chicago: University of Chicago Press, 1962.

Gwartney, James; Lawson, Robert; and Block, Walter. *Economic Freedom of the World: 1975–1995.* Vancouver, B.C., Canada: The Fraser Institute, 1996.

Hanke, Steve H., and Walters, Stephen J.K. *Liberty, Equality, Prosperity.* A Report to the Senate Joint Economic Committee. Washington, D.C.: Government Printing Office, July 1997.

Holmes, Kim R.; Johnson, Bryan T.; and Kirkpatrick, Melanie. *1997 Index of Economic Freedom.* Washington, D.C., and New York: The Heritage Foundation and Dow Jones & Co., Inc., 1997.

Johnson, Bryan T., and Sheehy, Thomas P. *The Index of Economic Freedom.* Washington, D.C.: Heritage Foundation, 1995.

Johnson, Bryan T., and Sheehy, Thomas. *1996 Index of Economic Freedom.* Washington, D.C.: Heritage Foundation, 1996.

Holmes, Kim R., and Kirkpatrick, Melanie. "Freedom and Growth." *Wall Street Journal,* 16 December 1996, p. A16.

Klaus, Václav. "Interplay of Political and Economic Reform Measures in the Transformation of Postcommunist Countries." Heritage Foundation Lectures 470. Washington, D.C.: Heritage Foundation, 1993.

Mises, Ludwig von. "The Free and Prosperous Commonwealth: An Exposition of the Ideas of Classical Liberalism." Indianapolis: Institute for Humane Studies, 1962.

Pinkerton, James P. "The New Asian Offering: Capitalism without Freedom." *Newsday* (15 December 1994): op-ed.

Tammen, Melanie S. "Time to Retire the World Bank and the International Monetary Fund." In *Market Liberalism,* pp. 311–23. Edited by David Boaz and Edward H. Crane. Washington, D.C.: Cato Institute, 1993.

19. Economic Inequality and the Quest for Social Justice

Karl Brunner

The problem of economic inequality has attracted much attention in recent years. International income differentials were the central concern of the Brandt Report on the so-called North-South Dialogue. The report conveyed a conviction that such differentials are unacceptable and immoral. Responsibility for this condition, moreover, is assigned to wealthy nations. One of Washington's major intellectuals, Sam Donaldson of ABC, also said on David Brinkley's show that the existing income distribution in the United States "is obscene."

Donaldson's attitude and the Brandt Report's evaluation dominate the intelligentsia and the views found in the public arena. We should not, however, be swayed too quickly by such social consensus. We need to ponder the underlying reasons, the problems associated with institutional efforts to establish a more egalitarian society and the consequences of such arrangements. We also may usefully consider whether an egalitarian view of social justice offers the only feasible intellectual position.

Two Views of Justice

Two alternative notions of justice need to be considered: the "end-state," or outcome pattern, concept of justice and its alternative, the "process" concept of justice. We should not draw too firm a line between the two. Some overlapping is possible, which can be elaborated and justified to some extent. Nevertheless, the distinction between them is broad enough to be relevant here. The end-state

---

Karl Brunner was Fred H. Gowen Professor of Economics and Director of the Center for Research in Government Policy and Business at the Graduate School of Management at the University of Rochester. This chapter is reprinted from the late author's article in the Spring/Summer 1987 *Cato Journal* (Brunner 1987).

concept basically characterizes social justice in terms of the outcome of the social process. John Rawls's theory of justice belongs to this category and so too does the widely held egalitarian position. Rawls (1971) defines justice as fairness in terms of an admissible class of income distributions. The comparative fate of the lowest income group forms the criterion of admissibility. However, Rawls's discussion seems much too subtle and sophisticated for the public arena. One would look in vain for any discussion of these issues in the pastoral letter of the U.S. Catholic Bishops or in pronouncements offered by other groups on the issue. The basic idea continuously conveyed deplores income inequality. It is evil per se and every decline of inequality moves us closer to social justice.

It is very unclear, however, whether ultimately one really wants to achieve an egalitarian position. The rhetoric seems to be somehow geared to measure the prevailing degree of injustice against this egalitarian scale. Arthur Okun was quite explicit on this point in some of his work, presenting an egalitarian position as the only rational and adequate view of the requirements for justice (see especially Okun 1975). However, he says some tradeoffs in favor of efficiency are unavoidable.

We should also note the views offered by some theologians. Their arguments, however, are generally quite thin and remarkably irrelevant, showing little perception of the relevant issues (see Brunner, et al. 1986). One reads, for example, that justice, as a matter of linguistic logic, can only mean an egalitarian state of income distribution. This rhetoric merely covers theology's inability to cope seriously with the problem of justice. So, we also read that as we all participate equally in Jesus' love, therefore there should be an equal distribution of income. Such assertions remind me of the medieval philosopher who argued that there are seven planets, not eight, not six, not nine, and not five, because there are seven openings in the human head. These arguments share the same level of irrelevance. They contribute nothing to a useful examination of a serious intellectual and social problem of our time.

The "process" concept offers an alternative approach to the problem of justice. Justice is defined not in terms of a specific outcome pattern but as general characteristics of a social process. Outcomes are just to the extent they result from a process that satisfies these broad characteristics representing justice. The process view may be somewhat modified with some redistributive constraints. Such constraints would be designed to protect the lowest income groups in society and "buy" their participation in a social and political consensus.

The Manna Syndrome

Advocates of an outcome pattern view of justice, typically presenting an egalitarian position, regularly suffer from a peculiar "manna syndrome." We encounter this syndrome in the pastoral letter published by the U.S. Catholic Bishops, and in statements made by the World Council of Churches. The syndrome has also surfaced in the United Nation's advocacy of an international agency to control exploitation of minerals at the bottom of the seas. The manna syndrome is expressed by the view that wealth appears as manna, a gift from God. It follows therefore that all the Earth's resources, as gifts of God, belong to mankind. They must therefore be fairly distributed among all men and women.

The manna syndrome essentially means that its victims deny any feedback from the distribution of wealth to the creation of wealth. The creation of wealth appears thus as an exogenous process showering wealth on society, irrespective of institutional conditions and the resulting behavior of men. It follows naturally that wealth seems arbitrarily redistributable without ill effects on the welfare of society. Once one denies any feedback connection from distribution to creation, any pattern of redistribution may be safely proposed. The wealth creation process, however, depends crucially on the fact that agents can reasonably expect to capture the fruits of their endeavors. Once this connection is broken, the wealth creation process will be seriously impaired.

The Sociological Model of Man

Failure to recognize this problem is closely associated with the prevalent perception of man represented by the sociological model. Arthur Okun's book *Equality and Efficiency* (1975) relies to a large extent on this perception. Man reflects commercial values when operating in the context of private property and market transactions. In the context of nonmarket institutions, man will be guided by higher values that go beyond the dollar and other mean things pursued in commercial transactions. Self-interested behavior can ultimately be overcome by suitable social engineering and by placing man within a proper institutional context. The sociological model thus offers a useful rationale and intellectual support for the end-state vision of justice.

Unfortunately, much confusion about the concept of self-interest prevails in the debate over justice. Such behavior is expressed by the fact that people generally prefer to make their own decisions concerning their affairs. This behavior is quite consistent with altruism. But concern for other people reflects the assessment and evaluation of the concerned. Even concern for the public's welfare is filtered by the underlying biologically conditioned self-interest. I elaborated this difference in the perception of man a decade ago in an article tracing its consequences for the conception of political institutions (Brunner and Meckling 1977). It also plays a subtle and pervasive role in the assessment of the issues considered here. The sociological model emphasizes the cultural relativity of self-interested behavior and denies a persistent biological component common to all men expressed by general self-interested behavior independent of the institutional context. This context, however, exerts an effect on the specific details or forms in which it will be expressed. Self-interested behavior prevails under market-oriented institutions in some form, and also under nonmarket institutions, but with very different forms of expressions. It will be particularly expressed by competition for power and the manipulation of power mechanisms that operate under nonmarket institutions.

Implications of the Egalitarian Vision

We recognize, therefore, that behind the prevalent view of justice defined in terms of a specific outcome pattern and, in particular, represented by an egalitarian position, lurk two fundamental empirical hypotheses about man and social processes. Wealth is created exogenously, independently of human intentions and volitions guided by institutional incentives. Moreover, the sociological model of man supports and justifies this view. Both positions seem difficult to reconcile with the historical experiences of thousands of years. What now are some of the major implications that follow from all this?

Creation of an Institutional Vacuum

One implication, which I have observed time and again in discussions of social justice, particularly with philosophers, is the presence of a peculiar institutional vacuum. This neglect of any institutional context follows from the two points stated above. If wealth is exogenous and a sociological model of man is used, then the specific implementation of redistributional *activities* really does not matter very much. It has simply no feedback and therefore is not worth discussing.

Rawls's book on justice, *A Theory of Justice* (1971), excellent and interesting as it is in many ways, reflects the institutional vacuum so prevalent in many discussions of our subject. We rarely encounter any attempt to examine the detailed nature of the institutional implementation of any particular end-state criterion. Neither do we find a searching examination of the consequences to be expected from such implementation. Economic analysis tells us that we should expect serious consequences. Every institutional arrangement influences the opportunity set confronting individuals, and therefore affects the behavior of those individuals. Any *change* in institutional arrangements also changes opportunity sets and modifies individual behavior. The implementation of any particular criterion of outcome pattern would really amount to a sequence of continuous reimplementations with new institutional efforts directed to force society into the procrustean bed so ardently advocated. The dream of an egalitarian society will never be realized, and attempts to impose it produce only poverty, stagnation, and oppression.

Disregard of the Production-Distribution Nexus

The egalitarian view is occasionally justified with the observation that there exists no systematic connection between economic growth and income inequality. This observation seems to suggest to some that there is no feedback from distribution to productive efforts and ingenuity. However, economic inequality is not a sufficient condition of economic growth. Economic inequality and stagnation or poverty are frequently the joint result of policies that obstruct economic development. The policies of many Third World countries foster stagnation and, simultaneously, a redistribution of wealth to the ruling oligarchy and its clientele. Economic inequality will often result from institutional arrangements that obstruct economic growth. The observation that economic growth and income inequality are uncorrelated thus offers no support for the thesis asserting the possibility of an egalitarian society without any effect on general welfare.

The Loss of an Open Society

A society guided by an egalitarian vision is committed to choose institutions that establish pervasive instruments of political repression together with conditions of poverty and stagnation. Our search for justice needs certainly to look elsewhere for humane solutions. The process concept of justice deserves substantially more serious attention than it has been granted in the public arena. This conception of justice addresses a fundamental question bearing on the nature of social and political institutions that offer members of society the best opportunity to shape their lives and improve their lot. Such arrangements unavoidably allow a persistent inequality in the distribution of income. This does not mean, however, that specific social groups are permanently locked into particular positions of the income distribution. An open society produces substantial social circulation within the income distribution pattern over successive generations. We need also to emphasize once more that a society guided by the egalitarian principle will necessarily develop institutions of control and management that ultimately maintain substantial inequality of economic status and political power.

References

Brunner, Karl. "Economic Inequality and the Quest for Social Justice." *Cato Journal* 7 (Spring/Summer 1987): 153–58.

Brunner, Karl, and Meckling, William. "The Perception of Man and the Conception of Government." *Journal of Money, Credit, and Banking* 4 (1977): 70–85.

Brunner, Karl, et al. *Economics, Theology, and the Social Order*. Center Symposia Series No. CS-18. Rochester, N.Y.: Center for Research in Government Policy and Business, University of Rochester, 1986.

Okun, Arthur. *Equality and Efficiency: The Big Tradeoff*. Washington, D.C.: Brookings Institution. 1975.

Rawls, John. *A Theory of Justice*. Cambridge: Harvard University Press, 1971.

20. Taxation, Economic Growth, and Liberty

Alvin Rabushka

The Third World, often called the less developed countries (LDCs), consists of over 100 nations in Africa, Asia, the Middle East, the Western Hemisphere, and the Mediterranean. Most of these countries are former British, French, or Dutch colonies that received independence after World War II. Although Central and South American countries were long independent, their failure to sustain economic growth consigns them to the category of Third World economies. A few oil-exporting nations enjoy higher per capita incomes than the majority of non-oil exporting countries, but even these select nations recently fell on hard times as world oil prices declined.

Although the British and French bequeathed constitutional democracy to their former colonies, representative institutions proved to be fragile in the Third World. With some exceptions, such as India, Sri Lanka, Malaysia, Costa Rica, and some island mini-states in the Caribbean, many LDCs succumbed to military dictatorships, one-party states, lifetime presidents, extended states of emergency rule or martial law, and totalitarian regimes of the left or the right (though democracy made a strong comeback in Latin America in the mid-1980s). Some authoritarian rulers permitted, indeed encouraged, the development of private enterprise-based market economies; most relied on state planning and control. Few allowed a free press, freedom of speech, and other civil liberties that are constitutionally guaranteed and that flourish in Western democracies.

Development specialists paid considerably less attention to taxation than such other aspects of development policy as international

---

Alvin Rabushka is a Senior Fellow of the Hoover Institution at Stanford University. This chapter is an abridged version of his Spring/Summer 1987 *Cato Journal* article (Rabushka 1987).

transfers, central planning, import-substitution schemes, the role of multi-national corporations, and raising expenditure levels. The relationship between taxation and liberty for more than three billion inhabitants of the Third World remains virgin territory.

Taxation and Development: Changing Views

In the early postwar years, Peter Bauer and Basil Yamey (1957) were nearly alone when they warned that taxation could adversely affect economic development:

> It is therefore likely that in many under-developed countries taxation falling on activity in the money sector will reduce the supply of effort to that sector below what it would be otherwise. This reallocation of resources affects adversely total real income. The lower national income and the retardation of the spread of the exchange economy in turn impede long-term growth [p. 199].
>
> The proceeds of compulsory savings are not a simple addition to total saving. It is not even certain that total saving will be increased in the process. Even when savings are increased in the short run, the repercussions of the taxation may reduce the flow of savings in the long run by retarding the spread of the exchange economy and the growth of specialization [pp. 199–200].

Bauer and Yamey also warned that restricting private saving would dampen the supply and effectiveness of local entrepreneurship because state control over savings would be diverted to expand public undertakings.

In contrast, mainstream development economists and such international institutions as the World Bank and the International Monetary Fund generally pushed tax increases, both as an overall share of national income and specifically to "soak" the rich through punitive tariffs on luxury imports, steeply graduated rates of personal income taxation, wealth taxes, and strengthened enforcement. Richard Bird and Oliver Oldman (1975) compiled a representative cross-section of readings on taxation in developing countries. In their introduction to part one, "Fiscal Policy and Economic Development," they refer to an "orthodox" position among development economists: "[M]ost developing countries tax little, and should tax more, particularly through progressive taxes and land taxes."

A cross-section of citations from this literature demonstrates the prevailing intellectual background against which tax planners in LDCs worked:

- A personal income tax with a narrow base but high rates on large incomes, buttressed by administrative efforts concentrated on this area, may be a suitable instrument for achieving some of the ends of economic policy and distributive justice [Heller 1975, p. 27].
- The shortfall in revenue is thus largely a reflection of failure to tax the wealthier sectors of the community effectively. Though progressive income taxes and inheritance taxes exist on paper in most of the underdeveloped or semideveloped countries—sometimes imposed at high nominal rates, mounting to 80 percent or more on the highest incomes—there are few cases in which such taxes are effective in practice [Kaldor 1975, p. 31].
- Most economists have advocated a development strategy aimed at raising the level of domestic savings through budgetary policy—i.e., reducing personal consumption by increasing taxation. . . . Yet most economists argue for still more taxes. . . . The World Bank attaches importance to increase in tax revenues from country development plans [Please 1975, pp. 39–40].
- Taxation not only can help to bridge the gap between savings and investment but can also be used as one of the instruments for resource allocation, income redistribution, and economic stabilization [United Nations Secretariat 1975, p. 58].
- In taxing foreign income and the income of foreigners, one might latch on to the principle of equality: tax the foreigner the same as the national is taxed; a second starting point might be the principle of charging as tax whatever the traffic will bear: soak the foreigner as much as he will pay without his ceasing to engage in activities the LDC wants him to engage in [Oldman 1975, p. 203].
- The Declaration of Punta del Este, which set up the Alliance for Progress, established as one of its goals: To reform tax laws, demanding more from those who have most . . . to satisfy concerns of equity and meet pressure for more revenues to finance added government responsibilities [Tanzi 1975, p. 233].
- An important economic function of the capital gains tax is to curb speculation. . .and to encourage investments that are economically productive [Amagong 1975, p. 246].

- A net wealth tax, if well designed and effectively administered, can supplement a personal income tax and achieve greater equity in personal taxation [Tanabe 1975, p. 269].
- Owing to the heavy responsibilities that governments are assuming, not only for capital formation, but also for the provision of current services, the underdeveloped countries cannot promote saving merely by maintaining low taxes. Most underdeveloped countries need to raise more revenue, many of them, much more [Goode 1975, p. 273].

The impact of tax rates—especially marginal tax rates—was largely ignored or at least underemphasized, in the traditional development literature. Why? In a paper prepared for a 1985 Conference on Taxation and Development sponsored by the U.S. Agency for International Development, Vito Tanzi of the International Monetary Fund answered:

> First, there has been the traditional view that, in developing countries, high incomes do not originate from work effort or entrepreneurship; they are assumed to reflect mostly inherited wealth. Thus, they are more in the nature of rents than of genuine incomes. As a consequence, they could be taxed away with little negative effects. Second, that high incomes inevitably result in high consumption and / or capital flight. Third, that in any case the government can generate a high rate of saving for the country by raising taxes while holding down its own consumption. In this way, whatever negative effect high marginal tax rates might have on the individuals' propensity to save could be more than compensated by higher government saving. Fourth, because of lack of knowhow and entrepreneurship in the private sector, the government had to take the initiative in carrying out investment. The government was seen as the engine of growth in the economy. Fifth, the negative effect on labor supply could be ignored because of the overabundance of labor. Some influential studies assumed that the supply of labor schedule was perfectly elastic at a subsistence level of wages. Sixth, that private investment in desirable sectors could be stimulated through the use of specific tax incentives, so that low tax rates on corporate income were not necessary. Seventh, that in any case there was little *solid* evidence that marginal tax rates were important in determining the propensity to save, invest, or to supply greater effort [pp. 1–2].

Although all development economists did not share these assumptions, Tanzi notes that many of the assumptions were prevalent throughout much of the literature on economic development and taxation until recent years. How did they prove to be faulty? According to Tanzi (1985, pp. 2–4):

> First, in developing countries, large incomes are often more the result of . . . implicit taxes, than of property ownership. In many developing societies today it is more important to have access to subsidized credit, to scarce foreign exchange at official exchange rates, to import licenses, or to be able to produce behind a protective wall than to own property. . . . Rents based on government policies have replaced rents based on property ownership.
>
> Second, the assumption that high income inevitably results in high consumption has been challenged in various theories of the consumption function. Some of these challenges are as relevant for developing countries as they are for industrial countries.
>
> Third, . . . in many countries the increase in the tax burden that took place over the years did not result in higher public saving, as had been anticipated, but in higher public consumption. Furthermore, whatever public investment did take place, it was often misallocated resulting in very low or negative rates of return.
>
> Fourth, . . . the government does not have a monopoly over knowhow or entrepreneurship. A country without entrepreneurs in the private sector is not going to produce them in the public sector.
>
> Fifth, it has been recognized that even though the overall labor supply may be abundant . . . it is rarely abundant for particular skills.
>
> Sixth, the argument on whether one can stimulate more investment by low corporate tax rates or by investment incentives is still a debatable one.
>
> Finally, while in the past it was often argued that there was no evidence that high marginal tax rates had any effects on the propensity to save, invest, and work harder, in recent years more and more studies using sophisticated techniques have shown that taxation may in fact have some negative effects.

This changed worldview is reflected in publications by Keith Marsden and Chad Leechor of the Industry Department of the World

Bank. Marsden (1983) argued that on the basis of a sample of 21 countries in the Americas, Asia, Africa, and Europe, countries that imposed a lower effective tax burden on their populations achieved substantially higher real growth than did their more highly taxed counterparts. Marsden (1985) later specifically examined 17 LDCs in Asia and Africa and concluded that low tax rates stimulated economic incentives and economic growth in the high and medium growth economies.

Leechor (1986) contended that tax policy influences private saving and capital formation and that tax increases often shrink the tax base or foster tax evasion and damage the private sector. Instead, tax policy should aim at improving incentives. Based on a comparative study of Colombia, Korea, Mexico, and Thailand, Leechor recommended reducing marginal tax rates, broadening the tax base, exempting savings from the tax base, indexing the tax system against inflation, restructuring corporate taxes by permitting expensing of investment costs in the first year, and granting exporters full tax rebates and duty drawbacks on purchased inputs.

Despite the recent transformation in thinking that Tanzi summarized and that Marsden and Leechor illustrate, the old views have not yet been fully rejected by both scholars and policymakers in LDCs. It is still common to find countries with marginal income tax rates of 70, 80, or 90 percent that take effect at relatively low incomes (by industrialized nation standards). Even though these top marginal tax rate thresholds represent several multiples of per capita gross domestic product (GDP) in LDCs, multiples of per capita GDP do not determine incentives to work, save, or invest. Individuals with entrepreneurial talent, specialized skills, or capital are generally aware of the better opportunities that exist in other countries; and it is critical for developing nations to retain these talented people. The loss of this minority of potential entrepreneurs, scientists, engineers, professionals, and skilled laborers could grind the entire process of development to a screeching halt. High marginal tax rates that affect a small minority of the population and supply less than one-tenth of total revenue in many LDCs could have severe repercussions on economic growth. People and human capital are no less internationally tradeable and transferable than are commodities and capital.

Some development analysts believe that the emphasis marginal tax rates receive in current thinking about fiscal policy and incentives for growth is misplaced. Even if marginal tax rates are important in the development process, these analysts contend that income taxes are insignificant compared with the wide range of other government policies that discourage growth. These forms of "implicit taxes" also deny people a rate of return on work, saving, or investment that is effectively equivalent to a tax levied on a market rate of return. In some LDCs, implicit taxes overwhelm the impact of the statutory tax system on levels of economic activity.

The statutory tax system, however, serves as something of a proxy for a range of government policies. For purposes of analysis, it is easier to obtain quantitative data on taxation than on such other governmental interferences with the market as overvalued exchange rates, farmgate prices, and minimum wages. There are almost no data on many of these important factors—at least none that are available to researchers. But a variety of government agencies and commercial firms publish data on statutory tax systems, and the IMF publishes substantial figures on aggregate levels of taxation.

Principles of Taxation for Developing Countries

An ideal tax system should meet five practical requirements that foster a climate of growth. First, sufficient revenue should be generated to finance a major part of overall public expenditure—to pay for the limited, legitimate activities of government—and maintain fiscal reserves at a satisfactory level.

Second, the tax system should remain neutral toward the internal cost/price structure, the supply of human effort, and private investment decisions. This means, in effect, that the emphasis should be on proportionality apart from a modest degree of progressivity on personal taxation to leave the poorest classes untouched by direct taxation.

Third, the laws governing the tax system should be revised from time to time to make them consistent with changing commercial practices.

Fourth, each and every levy—direct or indirect—should be simple and easy (and, therefore, inexpensive) to administer and not encourage evasion.

Fifth, the tax system should be only exceptionally used to achieve nonfiscal objectives. Such policy objectives should be pursued directly through public expenditure programs and by appropriate legislative measures, not indirectly by adjustments to tax rates and amendments to tax laws. Once a government starts to use the tax system to pursue economic and social policies, the consequences are unpredictable and usually irreversible and the costs are unquantifiable.

Taxation, Growth, and Liberty

Analysts of American and European taxation enjoy access to a wealth of generally reliable data on national income accounts, tax systems, and other aggregate economic indicators. Analysts of LDCs are less advantaged; they have to patch together often incomplete, unreliable, or downright inaccurate data from a variety of private and public international sources. The most helpful and most frequently consulted sources are "World Development Indicators," published annually by the World Bank, and "Government Finance Statistics" and "International Financial Statistics," published monthly and annually by the International Monetary Fund. The IMF also publishes an annual "Supplement on Economic Indicators." But mixing and matching these sources into a unified data file is not an entirely straightforward process. The IMF roster of developing countries numbers 104, but World Bank indicators are available for only 98. The gap of six is compounded by some non-overlapping; the British Crown Colony of Hong Kong, for example, is not a member of the IMF and its financial statistics are not published in IMF bulletins, whereas Hong Kong's development indicators appear in World Bank publications. Only a few basic indicators appear in World Bank tables for small countries with populations under one million.

This picture overdramatizes the availability of data on LDCs. Among the 104 LDCs for which the IMF publishes financial statistics, complete national income accounts exist for only 57. Partial GDP information is published in the "Supplement on Economic Indicators" for 95 LDCs, but the accuracy of many of these numbers are suspect.[1] The percentage of public receipts collected in the different

[1]Kuwait, Oman, and the United Arab Emirates were eliminated from the data file because all receipts are derived from oil exports and their various high-score development indicators are due solely to the interplay of high oil receipts and small populations. These three cases constituted serious outlyers and were removed to eliminate unnecessary distortion in the analysis.

forms of taxation is available for 104 LDCs. The timing of IMF financial statistics ranges from as recent as 1984 to as far back as 1978 or 1979 for some countries. Many African nations have been slow to get their financial statistical houses in order.

Neither the World Bank nor the IMF release detailed information on the structures of their member countries' tax systems. Details on the rates of direct and indirect taxation, what is and is not taxed, along with exemptions, deductions, credits, special incentives, and other features of taxation, must be culled from other sources. For information dating from 1975, the most readily accessible data appear in the publications of two commercial international tax service organizations. Beginning in 1975, Price Waterhouse has published the structure of tax rates and tax brackets for individual income taxes in those countries, numbering 94 in 1985, in which it maintains offices. Since 1982, Coopers and Lybrand has published a competitive volume. When colonies and dependent territories are excluded from the two firms' joint listing of 104 separate taxing entities, only 77 countries remain, some of which are mini-states of little consequence. Several of the 77 are oil-exporting nations that rely solely on oil proceeds for revenue.

The best source of tax data before 1975 is an annual series published between 1958 and 1973 by Great Britain's Inland Revenue Department. The series contains annual tax specifics for approximately 40 countries between 1958 and 1973. The early volumes were titled *Income Taxes in the Commonwealth* and *Income Taxes Outside the Commonwealth* (1958–66); the successor series combined both into one annual volume titled *Income Taxes Outside the United Kingdom* (1966–73). Comparable data on overseas French and Dutch territories are not readily available, nor are data on Latin American nations before 1975. To assemble these data requires the scrutiny of legislation on a country-by-country basis, which no clearinghouse has yet assembled on a historical basis. The International Bureau of Fiscal Documentation in Amsterdam publishes current information on explicit taxes for all regions of the world and maintains an extensive library, but its historical collections are sporadic and incomplete. As a result, attempts to link indicators of economic performance to long-run changes in effective marginal tax rates on individuals and effective tax rates on businesses, industries, and economic sectors cannot encompass the entire developing world and are severely restricted by the paucity of longitudinal data.

More data are available for economically important and heavily populated countries than for extremely poor, economically unimportant, lightly populated LDCs. Neither Price Waterhouse nor Coopers and Lybrand maintain an overseas office or local correspondent in those developing countries with the least attractive business opportunities.

Few scholars have attempted to link tax policies and other indicators of economic performance with measures of political and civil rights. If sustained economic growth has no effect on the evolution of democratic institutions or civil liberties or if overly rapid growth engenders totalitarian regimes that repress individual freedom, then stressing growth policies would require serious reconsideration. On the other hand, if a necessary condition of democracy and improving individual liberties was high growth, policies that fostered prosperity would also nurture free institutions and individual rights.

Data on political freedoms, civil rights, and democratic institutions are routinely published in the annual January/February issue of *Freedom House,* which allows us to assess the relationship between economic performance and several measures of political and economic liberties. *Freedom House* ranks virtually all nations by civil liberties and political rights on a seven-point scale from "most free" (a score of 1) to "partly free" (3–5) to "not free" (a score of 7). Political rights range from the presence of a fully competitive electoral process to a limited role for opposition parties within a predominantly one-party state to the complete absence of free elections where despots rule unconstrained by public opinion or popular tradition. Civil liberties encompass freedom of the press, court protection of the individual, free expression of personal opinion, and free choice in occupation, education, religion, residence, and so on, to the other extreme of pervading fear, little independent expression even in private, and swift imprisonment and execution by a police-state.

A complete analysis of developing countries, therefore, should encompass both economic and political dimensions. Economic development takes place within a sovereign political entity that maintains specific institutions of government that permit or suppress political freedoms and civil liberties. It is important to know whether growth, the chief indicator of development, is correlated with the spread of democratic institutions and individual freedoms.

A fully specified model linking important economic and political variables with growth cannot be tested because extant data exclude potentially important factors. Available data include such standard measures as tax shares of gross national product; the composition of taxes; top marginal rates and thresholds of the individual income tax; long-term annual average changes in exports, imports, investment, public and private consumption, industrial and agricultural output, public and external debt, and several political indicators. Data on implicit taxes that affect growth and development, however, are even more difficult to obtain than evidence on changing tax rates over time. Precise, statistical information on farmgate prices is available only on a sporadic, case-by-case basis. Another crucial implicit tax on exporters (and subsidy for importers) is exchange-rate overvaluation, for which quantitative estimates may be available only in the confidential files of the IMF. The World Bank's preliminary study of exchange rate distortions for 31 countries shows only 12 with medium or high distortions, which limits the ability to include these data in analyses encompassing between 50 and 100 developing countries.

There are two other potentially important variables: (1) the extent to which the tax laws are enforced (compliance) and (2) the extent to which the presence of an underground economy vitiates the disincentive effects of statutory systems of taxation. Data on these variables are virtually nonexistent. Indeed, the overriding difficulty in analyzing taxation and development is the lack of data by which hypotheses can be tested. An important aspect of future work must be the extent to which one counterproductive dimension in a tax code is a proxy for an entire system of explicit and implicit taxation that retards growth.

Findings

Analysis reveals that *rates of taxation are more important than overall tax burdens in affecting growth in LDCs.* For 49 LDCs, countries with higher incomes have somewhat higher levels of aggregate taxation; the simple correlation of taxation as a share of GNP with the prior 22 years of average annual economic growth rate (on a per capita basis) is a relatively modest .274 (significance = .028). High growth countries, which became prosperous, have relatively larger aggregate tax burdens than slow growth countries; their economies are based more on industry than on agriculture. As these countries prospered, their governments took away a higher percentage of national income in taxes, which is what happened in Western industrial democracies. But larger aggregate tax burdens in LDCs do not necessarily reflect higher rates of tax on individuals, corporations, and commodities. For example, Hong Kong's aggregate tax burden is higher than that found in many LDCs, even though its tax *rates* are the lowest.

The overall level of taxation in 49 LDCs is not significantly linked with high or low rankings on political or civil liberties.

When the analysis is shifted from aggregate tax levels to the composition of taxes, the universe of LDCs expands to over 100, reflecting more abundant data. Greater dependence on direct taxes (individual income taxes, corporate taxes, social insurance contributions, and property taxes) is positively related to overall economic growth, the growth of private consumption, per capita income, and the level of public spending. Rich, high-growth countries collect a higher share of receipts in the form of direct taxes than do poor countries. They have developed an urbanized, industrial, commercial economy on which direct taxes can be imposed (though, as shown later, tax rates matter significantly).

As dependence on indirect taxes rises, countries fare less well in their annual growth rates of imports, investment, industry, overall economic growth, and, consequently, private consumption and per capita income. Most of this adverse effect is due to the application of international trade taxes, not domestic excises or sales taxes. Most LDCs depend heavily on exports and imports; the correlation between per capita income and international trade taxes, for example, is −.415. Over-reliance on indirect taxes may retard export-led growth from either the industrial or agricultural sector.

To the extent that the system of taxation and the structures of tax rates influence economic growth, taxation indirectly affects the prospects for individual liberty in LDCs. The relationship between annual average rates of economic growth over 22 years and the scale score for political rights and civil liberties shows that countries with negative growth have very poor scores on individual rights. But once economic growth exceeds 3 percent, political and civil rights scores significantly improve. In particular, I found that for 93 LDCs on which both growth and freedom measures exist, countries with sustained low growth show negative ratings on political rights and civil liberties; high-growth countries show a more encouraging distribution. High growth may not be a sufficient condition of individual liberties, but it appears to be a necessary condition for the gradual emergence of political and civil rights.

Furthermore, countries with low per capita incomes, the result of decades of no growth to slow growth (not necessarily low starting points, since even the high-growth Pacific Rim economies began their postwar ascent with per capita incomes of below $200), fare badly on political rights and civil liberties. Twenty-five countries had per capita GNP figures below US$400 at the end of 1982. Of these, only six received a score of 1–4 on political rights and four received a score of 1–4 on civil liberties. Fewer still earned scores of 1–3. In contrast, 19 of 25 received dreadful ratings on political rights and 16 received equally dismal ratings on civil liberties. The leaders of the economic basket cases of the world inflict the greatest political deprivations on their subjects.[2]

Tax Rates and Economic Growth

The link between tax rates and development is revealed in Table 1, which groups countries by top marginal rates and the brackets at which the top rate applies in that country. I have subdivided countries into nine working classifications, based on a high, medium, or low top marginal rate, and whether the top rate applies at high, medium, or low thresholds of income. Only one country, Hong Kong, maintained a low top marginal tax rate. Hong Kong also enjoyed the highest growth rate in per capita income. In general, countries with high thresholds turned in consistently higher growth than those with low thresholds. For medium tax rate, high threshold countries, the average was 4.5 percent; for high tax rate, high threshold countries, the average was 3.9 percent. Even the high rate, medium threshold countries averaged 3.1 percent.

This point is worth belaboring. So long as high top marginal rates do not bite at low levels of income, they do not inhibit human endeavor on a wide scale. No individual is deterred from moving out of the subsistence sector into the cash economy by the disincentive of

[2]Tables showing the long-run relationship between economic growth and civil and political liberties, as well as the relationship between per capita income and freedom, for selected LDCs, are available from the author upon request.

TABLE 1
MARGINAL TAX RATES AND AVERAGE ANNUAL ECONOMIC GROWTH IN LDCs, 1960–82

Country by Tax Rates and Thresholds	Marginal Tax Rates (%)	Tax Thresholds ($)	Economic Growth Rate (%)	Mean Growth per Tax Group (%)
Low Tax Rates—All Thresholds	0–24	All		7.0
Hong Kong			7.0	
Medium Tax Rates—Low & Medium Thresholds	25–49	0–50,000		2.1
Argentina			1.6	
Bolivia			1.7	
Ivory Coast			2.1	
Paraguay			3.7	
Solomon Islands			1.3	
Medium Tax Rates—High Thresholds	25–49	50,001 +		4.5
Indonesia			4.2	
Singapore			7.4	
Venezuela			1.9	
High Tax Rates—Medium Thresholds	50 +	20,001–50,000		3.1
Belize			3.4	
Botswana			6.8	
Brazil			4.8	
Cyprus			5.9	
Dominica			−0.8	

Malaysia			4.3	
Morocco			2.6	
Nigeria			3.3	
Philippines			2.8	
Senegal			0.0	
South Africa			2.1	
Trinidad & Tobago			3.1	
Zimbabwe			1.5	
High Tax Rates—High Thresholds	50 +	50,001 +		3.9
Dominican Republic			3.2	
Ecuador			4.8	
Egypt			3.6	
Korea			6.6	
Liberia			0.9	
Mexico			3.7	
Nicaragua			0.2	
Panama			3.4	
Taiwan			7.0	
Thailand			4.5	
Tunisia			4.7	
High Tax Rates—Low Thresholds	50 +	0–20,000		1.9
Bangladesh			0.3	
Barbados			4.5	
Chile			0.6	

(continued)

TABLE 1
MARGINAL TAX RATES AND AVERAGE ANNUAL ECONOMIC GROWTH IN LDCs, 1960–82 *(continued)*

Country by Tax Rates and Thresholds	Marginal Tax Rates (%)	Tax Thresholds ($)	Economic Growth Rate (%)	Mean Growth per Tax Group (%)
High Tax Rates—Low Thresholds				
Costa Rica			2.8	
Fiji			3.2	
Ghana			−1.3	
India			1.3	
Jamaica			0.7	
Kenya			2.8	
Malawi			2.6	
Malta			8.0	
Pakistan			2.8	
St. Lucia			3.4	
St. Vincent			0.6	
Sudan			−0.4	
Swaziland			4.2	
Tanzania			1.9	
Turkey			3.4	
Uganda			−1.1	
Zaire			−0.3	
Zambia			−0.1	

high marginal rates of tax on low cash incomes. The effective marginal tax rate remains low for the overwhelming majority of the economically active population. Even at the medium threshold, between $20,000 and $50,000, most taxpayers face effective low rates. It is the low threshold countries, where the top marginal rates take hold at very low incomes for professional, skilled, mobile, middle- and upper-middle-class populations, that show the worst performance. Even if only a small proportion of a country's population is caught in the income tax net, that small fraction is the human engine that drives growth through decisions to invest, work, save, or shift money and human capital abroad and substitute leisure for effort.

Like commodities and capital, people can be viewed as internationally tradeable or transferable. Individuals export their talents as well as their capital. For those residents of developing countries who possess highly valued skills that are in demand in other countries, they may be tempted to migrate to earn higher after-tax returns on their human capital. Therefore, to view the earnings of this small, but important, minority who provides entrepreneurial, technical, professional, and other skills and services as a multiple of per capita income in their own countries is potentially misleading as an indicator of this group's economic well-being and incentives. Even if a Pakistani, Indian, Jamaican, Briton, or other foreign resident enjoys a relatively high income in his own country, he may still migrate to another country in which the application of his skills or talent provides a sharply higher after-tax real income and, equally important, a lower top marginal rate on incremental units of output.

Bangladesh, Ghana, Jamaica, and several East African nations show especially dismal economic performances. The high rate, low threshold average for 21 countries is 1.9 percent, and this grouping includes many of the economic basket cases of the world. *Even moderate top marginal rates that bite at relatively low incomes cripple growth.*

It is possible to refine each of these categories. When the last category is recalculated to include only those countries with thresholds below $10,000, or whose marginal tax rates exceed 70 percent when the threshold falls between $10,000 and $20,000, the average growth rate of this subgroup of 14 nations was only 0.8 percent. Of the 14, 4 had negative growth and only 3 displayed average annual growth rates of over 2 percent.

Overall, per capita income for 63 developing countries is negatively correlated with high marginal tax rates ($r = -.443$; significance = .000). (This relationship is much stronger than that reported earlier for aggregate tax burdens and growth.) The poorest countries of the world consistently maintain systems of individual income taxes with the highest marginal rates. A similar pattern holds for per capita income and tax thresholds for the top rate: lower thresholds go hand-in-hand with smaller per capita incomes ($r = .26$; significance = .026).

Finally, higher top marginal tax rates correlate negatively with the size of the budget surplus/deficit as a percentage of gross national product. To be specific, countries with lower rates tend toward balanced budgets or modest deficits; countries with higher rates tend to run the largest deficits. High tax rates do not foster balanced budgets, and raising tax rates to further reduce deficits seems counterproductive.

A cursory examination of corporate tax rates shows a large measure of uniformity throughout the developing world. I could find no statistically significant patterns relating corporate tax rates with per capita income, economic growth, macroeconomic trends, or political variables. A more complete analysis of the effect of corporate taxes on development would have to take into account depreciation schedules, investment credits, provisions for special deductions against foreign exchange losses, bad debts, and so forth. Given the widespread variability of these factors affecting actual corporate tax liabilities, it is somewhat surprising that statutory rates are so uniform.

Apart from the overall rate of economic growth, other indicators of macroeconomic performance did not emerge as significantly correlated with political rights or civil liberties. High-growth, high-income nations are more likely to evolve competitive party, democratic systems of government. Democracies, of course, are more respectful of political freedoms and civil liberties. Growth, which leads to rising prosperity, is a necessary but not sufficient condition of democratic institutions and individual freedoms. *Stagnation, which breeds poverty, is almost a sufficient condition for authoritarian governments, political repression, and the denial of civil liberties.* A humanist view of the developing world dictates the application of low-tax-rate, growth-oriented economic policies.

References

Amagong, Juanita D. "Taxation of Capital Gains in Developing Countries." In Bird and Oldman (1975, pp. 246–55).

Bauer, Peter T., and Yamey, Basil S. *The Economics of Underdeveloped Countries.* Chicago: University of Chicago Press, 1957.

Bird, Richard M., and Oldman, Oliver. *Readings on Taxation in Developing Countries,* 3d ed. Baltimore and London: Johns Hopkins University Press, 1975.

Goode, Richard. "Taxation of Savings and Consumption in Under-Developed Countries." In Bird and Oldman (1975, pp. 273–93).

Heller, Walter W. "Fiscal Policies for Underdeveloped Countries." In Bird and Oldman (1975, pp. 5–28).

Kaldor, Nicholas. "Will Underdeveloped Countries Learn to Tax?" In Bird and Oldman (1975, pp. 29–37).

Leechor, Chad. *Tax Policy and Tax Reform in Semi-Industrial Countries.* Industry and Finance Series Volume 13. Washington, D.C.: World Bank, January 1986.

Marsden, Keith. "Links Between Taxes and Economic Growth: Some Empirical Evidence." World Bank Staff Working Papers, No. 604. Washington, D.C.: World Bank, August 1983.

Marsden, Keith. "Private Enterprise Boosts Growth." Mimeo, 1985.

Oldman, Oliver. "Taxation of Foreign Income and Income of Foreigners." In Bird and Oldman (1975, pp. 201–8).

Please, Stanley. "Saving Through Taxation—Reality or Mirage?" In Bird and Oldman (1975, pp. 38–47).

Rabushka, Alvin. "Taxation, Economic Growth, and Liberty." *Cato Journal* 7 (Spring/Summer 1987): 121–48.

Tanabe, Noboru. "The Taxation of Net Wealth." In Bird and Oldman (1975, pp. 256–70).

Tanzi, Vito. "Personal Income Taxation in Latin America." In Bird and Oldman (1975, pp. 233–39).

Tanzi, Vito. "Comments on Tax Policy and Economic Growth in Developing Nations." Paper prepared for a conference on Taxation and Development sponsored by the U.S. Agency for International Development, Washington, D.C., 2–3 October 1985.

United Nations Secretariat. "Tax Reform Planning." In Bird and Oldman (1975, pp. 58–64).

Index

About the Editors

James A. Dorn is Vice President for Academic Affairs at the Cato Institute and Editor of the *Cato Journal*. He also directs Cato's annual Monetary Conference. He has lectured at the Central European University in Prague and Fudan University in Shanghai, and currently is a Professor of Economics at Towson University in Maryland. Dorn has written widely on public policy issues and has edited nine books including: *The Future of Money in the Information Age; From Plan to Market: The Future of Post-Communist Republics; Economic Reform in China: Problems and Prospects; Economic Liberties and the Judiciary; The Search for Stable Money*; and *Money and Markets in the Americas*. His articles have appeared in the *Financial Times*, the *Asian Wall Street Journal, El Economista, Forbes Digital Tool*, the *Journal of Commerce*, and in scholarly journals. From 1984–90, he served on the White House Commission on Presidential Scholars. Dorn is a member of the Mont Pèlerin Society. He holds an M.A. and a Ph.D. in economics from the University of Virginia.

Steve H. Hanke is Professor of Applied Economics at The Johns Hopkins University in Baltimore. He is also Chairman of Friedberg Mercantile Group, Inc., President of Toronto Trust-Argentina, and President of FCMI NZ Financial Corporation, Ltd. In addition, Hanke is a regular columnist at *Forbes* magazine. During 1981–82, he served as a Senior Economist on President Reagan's Council of Economic Advisers. He has served as economic advisor to Yugoslavia's Vice President, Zivko Pregl (1990–June 1991), and to Argentina's Minister of Economy, Domingo Cavallo (1995–96). From 1994–96, he served as State Counselor to the Republic of Lithuania. Currently, he is an advisor to the President of Bulgaria, Petar Stoyanov. Hanke is a Member of the Steering Committee of The G-7 Council in Washington, D.C., and a Fellow at The World Economic Forum in Geneva. His books include: *Currency Boards: The Financing of Stabilization; Alternative Monetary Regimes for Jamaica; Currency Boards for Developing Countries; Russian Currency and Finance; Capital*

Markets and Development; Prospects for Privatization; and *Privatization and Development*. Hanke holds a Ph.D. in economics from the University of Colorado.

Sir Alan Walters is Vice Chairman and Director of AIG Trading Group, Inc. He has been Chief Economic Advisor to Mrs. (now Lady) Margaret Thatcher, and an advisor to the World Bank, various governments, central banks, and financial institutions. He has held a number of academic positions in Great Britain and the United States, including professorships at The Johns Hopkins University, the University of Birmingham, and the London School of Economics, where he was the Sir Ernest Cassel Professor of Economics. He has held visiting professorships at Northwestern University, the University of Virginia, the Massachusetts Institute of Technology, and Monash University. He is a widely published author whose 13 books include: *Growth without Development; The Economics of Road User Charges; Money in Boom and Slump; Microeconomic Theory* (with Richard Layard); *Britain's Economic Renaissance;* and most recently *Sterling in Danger: The Economic Consequences of Pegged Exchange Rates.* Sir Alan was knighted by Queen Elizabeth II in June 1983. He holds degrees in economics from University College, Leicester and Nuffield College, Oxford.

Cato Institute

Founded in 1977, the Cato Institute is a public policy research foundation dedicated to broadening the parameters of policy debate to allow consideration of more options that are consistent with the traditional American principles of limited government, individual liberty, and peace. To that end, the Institute strives to achieve greater involvement of the intelligent, concerned lay public in questions of policy and the proper role of government.

The Institute is named for *Cato's Letters,* libertarian pamphlets that were widely read in the American Colonies in the early 18th century and played a major role in laying the philosophical foundation for the American Revolution.

Despite the achievement of the nation's Founders, today virtually no aspect of life is free from government encroachment. A pervasive intolerance for individual rights is shown by government's arbitrary intrusions into private economic transactions and its disregard for civil liberties.

To counter that trend, the Cato Institute undertakes an extensive publications program that addresses the complete spectrum of policy issues. Books, monographs, and shorter studies are commissioned to examine the federal budget, Social Security, regulation, military spending, international trade, and myriad other issues. Major policy conferences are held throughout the year, from which papers are published thrice yearly in the *Cato Journal.* The Institute also publishes the quarterly magazine *Regulation.*

In order to maintain its independence, the Cato Institute accepts no government funding. Contributions are received from foundations, corporations, and individuals, and other revenue is generated from the sale of publications. The Institute is a nonprofit, tax-exempt, educational foundation under Section 501(c)3 of the Internal Revenue Code.

CATO INSTITUTE
1000 Massachusetts Ave., N.W.
Washington, D.C. 20001